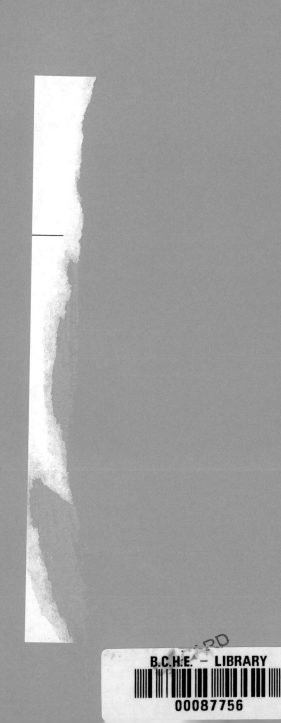

Early Islam

Collected articles

EARLY ISLAM

Collected articles

W. Montgomery Watt

Edinburgh University Press

Edinburgh University Press
22 George Square, Edinburgh

Set in Linotronic Times Roman
by Koinonia Limited, Bury, and
printed in Great Britain by
The Alden Press Ltd., Oxford

British Library Cataloguing
in Publication Data
Watt, W. Montgomery (William Montgomery) 1909–
Early Islam
1. Islam, history
I. Title
297.09

ISBN 0 7486 0170 8

Contents

Contents

Introduction

The articles selected for reproduction here are those which contain material not found, or at least not found in such detail in my books. The selection has been restricted to my main fields of research, namely, Muḥammad, the Qur'ān and the early history of the Islamic sects.

'The condemnation of the Jews of Banū Qurayẓa' (A.1) was a first attempt to justify the assumptions underlying my use of the sources in my books on the life of Muḥammad. I felt this to be desirable, especially because of the publication of Joseph Schacht's *Origins of Muhammadan Jurisprudence* (Oxford, Clarendon Press, 1950). In this he seemed to be questioning the authenticity of all anecdotal material about Muḥammad. I believe I was correct in distinguishing 'historical Traditions' from the legal ones with which Schacht was mainly concerned, and I now go so far as to maintain that for Muslim scholars the historical material and the legal and dogmatic material constituted two separate disciplines, namely, Sīra and Ḥadīth, with little overlapping. Earlier European scholars had tended to assume that because the Traditions or Ḥadīth dealt with the sayings and doings of Muḥammad they were a source for his biography, but this is clearly not the case, as I have pointed out in the second article (§6). It follows that the criticisms of Ḥadīth made by Schacht and others do not apply directly to the material used for describing Muḥammad's career. I have not pursued further the study of *isnāds*, but in view of the large amount of early historical work now known to exist, some interesting results could probably be obtained from such a study.

The second article, on 'The Reliability of Ibn Isḥāq's Sources' (A.2), was by way of defending the general authenticity of Sīra-material against more recent attacks. It followed the lines of an earlier article, 'The Materials used by Ibn Isḥāq', which was a paper read at a conference on Islamic historiography held in London in 1958 and was published in the report of the conference – *Historians of the Middle East*, edited by Bernard Lewis and P. M. Holt (London, Oxford University Press, 1962), pp. 23-34. In the original paper I used illustrative material from the account of the battle of Badr, but replaced this in the later version with material from the battle of Uḥud.

As a pupil of Richard Bell I like to emphasize the importance of the work which he did on the Qur'ān. The article on 'The Dating of the Qur'ān' (A.3) isolates the points relevant to this topic and perhaps expresses them more clearly than was done in my revisal of his *Introduction to the Qur'ān*. For this reason it seemed worth while including it here.

The article on 'Conversion in Islam' (A.4) is based on a paper given to a conference in London in 1972 on conversion to Islam, and repeated at Toronto in a revised form in 1978. It underlines a difficulty to be faced in Muslim-Christian dialogue, namely, the fact that most Muslims have little factual knowledge about other religions.

The article entitled 'His Name is Aḥmad' (A.5) is of considerable importance. Since its publication in 1953 no evidence has been produced to invalidate its main contention that until about 125 A.H. Aḥmad was not regarded as an alternative form of the name Muḥammad and was not given to any Muslim boy. In the article I attempted to explain this fact by suggesting that it was linked with the interpretation of the Qur'ānic phrase (61.6) *ismu-hu aḥmadu* and arguing that for long the word *aḥmadu* here was taken as an adjective and not as a name. This explanation may be queried, but the fact remains a fact and demands some explanation. The fact was accepted by Joseph Schacht in the article 'Aḥmad' in the *Encyclopaedia of Islam*, new edition. Geoffrey Parrinder *(Jesus in the Qur*'ān, London, Faber, 1965, 97) makes the additional point that neither Ibn Isḥāq (d. 767) nor his editor Ibn Hishām (d. 833) seemed to be aware that *aḥmadu* in this phrase could be taken as a proper name.

'The Camel and the Needle's Eye' (A.6) is perhaps chiefly a curiosity; but it calls attention to the fact that Islam came in part from the same cultural milieu as Christianity. This is something which is further illustrated by 'Two Interesting Christian-Arabic Usages' (A.11).

'The Men of the Ukhdūd' (A.7) argues, on the basis of recently available material, against the eschatological interpretation of Sūra 85 favoured by various Western scholars, and suggests that it contains a historical reminiscence. This is a point which could be of importance in future Muslim-Christian dialogue.

'God's Caliph' (A.8) is firstly a study of the use in the Qur'ān of *Khalīfa* and other forms of the same root, but this leads to a discussion of the Umayyad dynasty's justification of its rule. It thus contributes to a reassessment of the place of the Umayyads in Islamic history, since the traditional accounts are based on the anti-Umayyad propaganda of the 'Abbāsids.

'Reflections on some Verses of Sūrat al-Ḍuḥā' (A.9) indicates how the earlier part of the Qur'ān was not just the proclamation of a new religion, but was also a support for Muḥammad in his own spiritual life.

'The Christianity criticized in the Qur'ān' (A.10) is of some importance for future Muslim-Christian dialogue. There were people in Mecca who had some knowledge of Christianity, but it was limited and inaccurate. This was presumably due to the inadequate understanding of their faith by the Christians with whom the pagan Meccans came in contact. It would follow that mistaken statements about Christianity in the Qur'ān should not be taken as indications of ignorance among the Meccans but rather of inadequacies among the Christians with whom they came in contact.

'The Early Development of the Muslim Attitude to the Bible' (B.1) is probably the most important article here reproduced. Its contention, which I believe to be fully justified, is that the doctrine of the complete corruption *(taḥrīf)* of the scriptures of the Peoples of the Book was not explicitly stated in the Qur'ān, and probably not even implied there, but was elaboratd by Muslim scholars in the first Islamic century. The scholars claimed that the doctrine is found in the Qur'ān, but their arguments do not stand up to examination.

The formulation of this doctrine is the first important example of what became a normal practice among Muslim scholars, namely, the exaltation of theological dogma above historical fact and the requirement that history should conform with dogma. The doctrine was presumably worked out in order to protect ordinary Muslims from Christian criticisms of the Qur'ān, and this it did effectively, since Muslims could reject any argument based on a Biblical text. It has, however, bedevilled subsequent Muslim-Christian relations, and perhaps even weakened Islam itself. Christians clearly cannot accept the view that the text of the Bible is corrupt on the basis of dubious arguments from a few verses of the Qur'ān, and without any attempt to prove it from existing texts of the Bible. The modern discipline of literary criticism has led the more educated Christians to sophisticated views of how the Bible has reached its present form; and it is important for Muslim-Christian dialogue that Muslims should abandon their blanket rejection of the Bible and pay attention to modern Christian views.

'Some Muslim Discussions of Anthropomorphism' (B.2) raises the question of how religious language is related to the realities to which it refers. This is a subject which requires much fuller discussion at the present time by both Christians and Muslims within their own religions; and it will also be found important for inter-religious dialogue. In later writings I have suggested 'amodal' and 'amodality' as translations for *bi-lā kayf* and *balkafiyya*, but of course these terms still need to be explained.

A closely related topic is dealt with in 'Created in His Image' (B.3). Muḥammad was reported on one occasion to have used the Biblical phrase 'God created Adam in his image', but because of the strong objections of Muslim thinkers to anthropomorphism the majority refused to accept the Biblical interpretation, that this meant in God's image. One cannot but admire the ingenuity shown in finding alternatives.

'The logical Basis of Early Kalām' (B.4) is a translation with comments of part of the first chapter *(aṣl)* of al-Baghdādī's *Uṣūl al-dīn*. In making the translation I was hoping both to bring the material to the attention of scholars and also to suggest standard translations for technical terms, such as 'widely transmitted' for *mutawātir*. Some of the remarks about the sects in my comments need to be revised to bring them into line with my later views. Although there are some interesting points in the remainder of the chapter, it was never translated, partly through pressure of other work and partly because much of it is concerned more with legal matters than with Kalām.

'The Origin of the Islamic Doctrine of Acquisition' (B.5) was my first scholarly article, and arose out of work on my Ph.D. thesis – *Free Will and Predestination in Early Islam* (London, Luzac, 1949). It called in question the assumption current at that time that the doctrine of 'acquisition' *(kasb)* had been originated and developed by al-Ashʿarī and his followers, and it suggested instead that the doctrine had probably been invented by Ḍirār. This was the first time attention had been called to the possible importance of Ḍirār, for until then he had not been mentioned in writings about the early sects. The importance of the role of Ḍirār has been confirmed by Josef van Ess in recent work, such as his article on Dirār in the *Encyclopaedia of Islam*, Supplement.

The treatment of the Jahmiyya in the article must now be regarded as unsatisfactory, since I have come to realize that the Jahmiyya was not strictly a sect but rather a term of abuse used by Ḥanbalites and others for groups of which they disapproved. (See 'The Great Community and the Sects', below p. 173 and my *Formative Period*, 143-8, 'The Alleged Sect of the Jahmiyya'.) It is perhaps worth remarking that until about 1950 scholarly knowledge of the Islamic sects was based mainly on al-Shahrastānī's *Milal* and to a lesser extent on al-Baghdādī's *Farq bayn al-firaq*. It is to be noted too that these authors spoke of sects rather than individuals, even when the teaching of a supposed sect, such as the Thumāmiyya or the Jāḥiẓiyya, was merely that of the man after whom it was named. This is probably because conservative Muslim scholars objected to the repetition of heretical views, and al-Baghdādī and al-Shahrastānī had to justify what they were doing by claiming that they were expounding a *ḥadīth* which stated that there were seventy-three sects in Islam.

As more of the early sources have been studied by Western scholars it has become clear that the later standard accounts of some of the sects, such as the Muʿtazilites and the Imāmites, are not in accordance with the earlier material. It has also become clear that some of the names of sects were originally nicknames and were used differently by different people. This question of sect-names is discussed in 'The Great Community and the Sects' (B.11). The articles on the Khārijites and the

Shīʿites contain further illustrative material on the points mentioned.

'The Significance of Khārijism under the ʿAbbāsids' (B.7) is intended to show how what had originally been a reforming and revolutionary movement for the whole of Islam was transformed into the distinctive creed of a small community, serving to mark it off from others and to increase its internal cohesion. Some evidence for this transformation is contained in 'Was Wāṣil a Khārijite?' (B.6), but the main purpose of that article was to argue against the hypothesis that Wāṣil was a propagandist for the ʿAbbāsids. It also shows that the beginnings of Muʿtazilism were rather different from what the later accounts suggest.

The three articles on Shīʿism are similarly concerned with the relation between early sources and the later standard accounts. Thus 'The Reappraisal of ʿAbbāsid Shīʿism' (B.8) examines in detail relevant material in al-Nawbakhtī's *Firaq al-Shīʿa*, and shows that from 750 to 874 the imams later recognized by the Imāmites cannot have been explicitly claiming to rule the whole Islamic world. 'Sidelights on Early Imāmite Doctrine' (B.9) made use of material found in Shaykh Ṭūsī's List of Shīʿite Books. This originated in a paper read at a conference in honour of Shaykh Ṭūsī, and an almost identical version was published in *Publications of the School of Theology of the Mashhad University,* no. 6, 7 (1352/1973), 1-18, under the title 'Materials from Shaykh Ṭūsī's Fihrist for the Early History of Imāmite Doctrine'.

'The Significance of the Early Stages of Imāmite Doctrine' (B.10) is important in that it discusses in greater detail than does *The Formative Period* the distinction between the lesser occultation and the greater occultation, especially in respect of their political implications.

Finally, 'The Beginnings of the Islamic Theological Schools' (B.12) brings together material illustrative of the early stages of theological teaching in Islam.

Part A

Muḥammad and the Qur'ān

A1. The Condemnation of the Jews of Banū Qurayẓa A Study of the Sources of the *Sīra*

1. *Material.* One of the well-known incidents in the life of Muḥammad is the judgement pronounced on the Jews of the tribe of Qurayẓa after their unconditional surrender to the Muslims in A.H.5. The men of military age were condemned to death, and the women and children to enslavement. According to the standard account the sentence was pronounced not by Muḥammad himself but by the leading man among the Arab confederates of the Qurayẓa, Saʿd b. Muʿādh. This account, however, has been questioned by one of the foremost writers on these matters.

'By this version the tradition has tried to remove from Muḥammad the direct responsibility for the inhuman massacre of about 900 innocent persons; the artifice of the traditionists is so transparent that it is hardly necessary to set it in relief. The sentence of Saʿd was in any case dictated and inspired by the Prophet, who certainly made him understand what was the decision required of him. The responsibility for the slaughter falls entirely on the Prophet' (Caetani, *Annali dell' Islam,* I, p. 632).

In the present article the sources for this incident are examined in detail, partly in order to refute this suggestion of Caetani's about their unreliability, but more particularly for the light thrown on the sources for the life of Muḥammad in general. The question of the morality of the sentence is a separate one which may be left aside here. It will be convenient to start by tabulating the material. (The biographical notes added to the names in the *isnād* or chain of authorities are mostly taken from *Tahdhīb al-Tahdhīb* by Ibn Ḥajar al-ʿAsqalānī.)

IBN SAʿD (d. 230), *Ṭabaqāt,* III, 2, pp. 3ff., article on Saʿd b. Muʿādh.

A. (pp. 3f.)

c. Yazīd b. Hārūn: d. 206; lived in Wāsiṭ; mawlā.

b. Muḥammad b. ʿAmr b. ʿAlqama: d. 144-5; in Medina; connected with B. Zuhra.

b? ʿAmr b. ʿAlqama: in Medina.

a. ʿAlqama (b. Waqqās al-Laythī): d. c. 70; in Medina.

a. ʿĀ'isha: d. 58; in Medina.

(Part of a long story.) On being wounded during the siege of Medina by the Meccans Sa'd b. Mu'ādh prayed that God would not bring his life to an end until he had seen vengeance on the Banū Qurayẓa. Subsequently, when the Jewish tribe was hard pressed by the Muslim besiegers, they asked for Sa'd and surrendered only when it was agreed that he should decide their fate. When Sa'd came to Muḥammad, the latter told those present to stand in honour of their *sayyid* or chief; 'Umar said, Our *sayyid* is God; at that Muḥammad only said, Help him down. Sa'd then gave his judgement: their fighting men were to be put to death, their women and children enslaved, and their property divided. Muḥammad remarked, You have judged their case with the judgement of God and of His Messenger (*la-qad ḥakamta fī-him bi-ḥukm Allāh wa-ḥukm rasūlihi*). Sa'd prayed.

B. (p. 5, 5)

c. Wakī' b. al-Jarrāḥ: d. 196; in Kūfa; Ru'āsī.
c. Isrā'īl (b. Yūnus): d. 160-2; in Kūfa; Sabī'ī; Hamdānī.
b. Abū Isḥāq ('Amr b. 'Abdallāh): d. 126-9; Kūfa; Sabī'ī.
a. Abū Maysara: d. 63; Kūfa; Hamdānī.

(Similar to A but much shorter.) Sa'd prayed for vengeance but there is no mention of the B. Qurayẓa asking that he should pronounce their sentence. When Muḥammad asked him to judge, he said he was afraid he might not hit upon God's judgement about them; Muḥammad simply replied, Judge. Sa'd gave the first two parts of the sentence as in A, and Muḥammad remarked, You have indeed hit upon God's judgement in respect of them. (No mention of *sayyid*.)

C. (p. 5, 12)

c. 'Ubaydallāh b. Mūsā: d. 213-4; Kūfa; Shī'ī.
c. Isrā'īl: d. 160-2; Kūfa.
b. Jābir (al-Ju'fī): d. 127-32; Kūfa; Shī'ī.
b. 'Amīr (al-Sha'bī): d. 103-10; Kūfa.
a. 'Abdallāh b. Yazīd al-Anṣārī: d. c. 70?; Kūfa; Khaṭmī (of Aws); for 'Alī at Camel, later for Ibn al-Zubayr.

(Even shorter than B.) Similar to B, except that in sending for Sa'd Muḥammad says to men of his clan, Call your *sayyid*.

D. (p. 5, 16)

c. Yaḥyā b. 'Abbād: d. 198; Baṣra; of B. Ḍubay'a of Aws.
c. 'Affān b. Muslim: d. 219-20; Baṣra; held Qur'ān uncreated.
c. Abu 'l-Walīd al-Ṭayālisī: d. 227; Baṣra. All from
c. Shu'ba: d. 160; Baṣra.
b. Sa'd b. Ibrāhīm: d. 125-8; Wāsiṭ, etc.; of B. Zuhra of Quraysh; anti-Umayyad.
a. Abū Umāma b. Sahl b. Hunayf: d. 100; of B. Aws; father fought

for ʿAlī at Ṣiffīn.
a. Abū Saʿīd al-Khudrī: d. 74; of B. Khazraj.

Only the story of the judgement. When Saʿd arrived, Muḥammad said, Stand for your *sayyid* or the best of you. His final remark is, You have judged their case with the judgement of the angel (v.l, king) (*malak, malik*). ʿAffān said *malik*, but Yaḥyā and Abu'l-Walīd said *malak*. Ibn Saʿd thinks the former more correct.

E. (p. 5, 24)
c. Yaḥyā b. ʿAbbād: d. 198; Baṣra.
c. Sulaymān b. Ḥarb: d. 224; Baṣra; said to report according to the sense, not the letter.
c. Ḥammād b. Salama: d. 168; Baṣra.
b. Muḥammad b. Ziyād: d. ?; Medina, later Baṣra; of B. Jumaḥ of Quraysh;
a. ʿAbd al-Raḥmān b. ʿAmr: grandson of Saʿd b. Muʿādh.

Muḥammad asked Saʿd for advice. Saʿd replied, I know God has given you a command about them, and you will fulfil it. Muḥammad said, Yet counsel me. Saʿd said, If I were in charge of their case, I would put to death, etc. Muḥammad said, You have counselled me to do what God commanded.

F. (p. 6, 12)
c. ʿAbdallāh b. Numayr: d. 169; Kūfa.
b. Hishām b. ʿUrwa; d. 145-7; of B. Asad of Quraysh.
b. ʿUrwa: d. 91-4; Medina; brother of ʿAbdallāh b. al-Zubayr.

(ʿUrwa had previous part of story from ʿĀ'isha, but not this.) It was (apparently) Muḥammad's own decision to give the responsibility to Saʿd. No mention of *sayyid*. The final remark is given as a separate item (F*) introduced by the words of ʿUrwa, I was informed that Muḥammad . . . said, You have judged their case with the judgement of God.

G. (p. 6, 17)
c. Khālid b. Makhlad al-Bajalī: d. 213-4; Kūfa; Shīʿī.
c. Muḥammad b. Ṣāliḥ al-Tammār: d. 168; Medina; mawla of Anṣār.
b. Saʿd b. Ibrāhīm b. ʿAbd al-Raḥmān: d. 125-8; (see D).
a. ʿĀmir b. Saʿd: of B. Zuhra of Quraysh; son of following.
a. Saʿd b. Abī Waqqāṣ: d. 50 or 55; 'brother' of Saʿd b. Muʿādh.

Very brief. Instead of 'fighting men' Saʿd says 'those on whom the razors have gone', and Muḥammad's remark runs: He has judged their case with the judgement of God which He gave above seven heavens.

AL-WĀQIDI (d. 207), tr. Wellhausen, 215f.

H.

c. Khārija b. ʿAbdallāh: d. 165; Medina: of B. Najjār of Khazraj; had Zubayrid sympathies.
b. Dā'ūd b. al-Ḥuṣayn: d. 135; Medina; Khārijī.
a. Abū Sufyān: d. ? 90; friend of B. ʿAbd al-Ashhal of Aws.
a. Muḥammad b. Maslama: d. 46; Ashhalī; neutral in civil wars.

Similar to G in both Saʿd's judgement and Muḥammad's, Muḥammad appointed Saʿd judge at the request of Aws. The source is uncertain whether Muḥammad told all or only the Medinans to rise in honour of Saʿd.

IBN HISHĀM (d. 218 or 213), Sīra, based on Ibn Isḥāq (d. 151).

I. (688f)
c. Ibn Isḥāq
b. Al-Zuhrī: d. 123-5; of B. Zuhra of Quraysh; friend of ʿUrwa. (general source for story of B. Qurayẓa – p. 684).

Muḥammad entrusts judgement to Saʿd because Aws claim equal treatment with Khazraj. The words 'Stand for your *sayyid*' are said by the Muhājirūn to mean the Anṣār, but the latter say they referred to all Muslims. (Ibn Hishām mentions as a variant that it was the Jews who asked for Saʿd.)

I*.(689)
c. Ibn Isḥāq.
b. ʿĀṣim b. ʿUmar b. Qatāda: d. 120-29; Medina; of B. Ẓafar of Aws.
b. ʿAbd al-Raḥmān b. ʿAmr: grandson of Saʿd b. Muʿādh.
a. ʿAlqama b. Waqqāṣ: d. c. 70.

Muḥammad said, You have judged their case with the judgement of God from above seven heavens.

AL-ṬABARĪ (d. 310), *Annales*, I, 1492f.
Repeats Ibn Isḥāq's account with the addition:

J.
c. Ibn Wakīʿ: d. 247; Kūfa.
c. Muḥammad b. Bishr: d. 203; Kūfa.
b. Muḥammad b. ʿAmr: d. 144-5; (see A).
b? ʿAmr:
a. ʿAlqama: d. c. 70;
a. Abū Saʿīd al-Khudrī: d. 74; (see D).

Muḥammad said, Stand for your *sayyid* (or 'for the best of you'). No comment on this. The sentence and Muḥammad's remark are as in A.
K. With the same *isnād* as J, except that Abū Saʿīd is replaced by ʿĀ'isha, al-Ṭabarī (1486, 15-1487, 12) gives an abbreviated version of A.

2. *The Contents of the Traditions*. The variants in the story can be

explained as modifications of a basic account from political and theological motives. The basic account would run somewhat as follows: The Jews surrendered unconditionally to Muḥammad. The Aws, or some of them, pleaded for their Jewish confederates (or at least were discontented at their probable fate); Muḥammad therefore appointed Saʿd judge of the case, and when he came made a remark applying the words 'your *sayyid*' to Saʿd. After Saʿd had passed judgement, Muḥammad said, You have judged their case with the judgement of God.

The reason for the appointment of Saʿd must have been the interest of the Aws in the case. Some of the Aws probably felt that they had to support their confederates, the B. Qurayẓa, right or wrong, against Muḥammad, who was by no means the unquestioned ruler of Medina at this period, but primarily the chief of the 'tribe' of Muhājirūn from Mecca. Whether the Aws fully expressed their feelings to Muḥammad or not, his motive would be the same, to avoid dissension between the Meccan Muslims and the Aws.

The suggestion that the request for Saʿd came from the Jews (A, K) may simply be to make a good story; they hoped for a more lenient judgement but did not get it. Alternatively, the true account of the mysterious incident of Abū Lubāba (which cannot be discussed fully here) may be that he undertook to use the influence of the Aws to secure lenient terms for the B. Qurayẓa. In the latter case the variant in A and K is not contrary to the other account but complementary.

The variant in E, that Muḥammad merely asked Saʿd for advice, is doubtless a later modification intended to magnify the position of the Prophet and his successors. The point was to give full responsibility to a man who was a confederate of those to be punished.

The phrase 'Stand in honour of your *sayyid*' had uncomfortable implications, for the Anṣār could and did take it to mean that one of them was worthy and capable of having authority over Quraysh. Muḥammad probably did use it; it would help to impress recalcitrants among the Aws that Saʿd's judgement had to be accepted. Later especially in the period between Muḥammad's death and the murder of ʿUthmān, those of the Anṣār who objected to a caliph from Quraysh would remember it and exaggerate its importance. The versions in H and I record the disputes about the interpretation. The remark of ʿUmar in A is lofty in sentiment, but certainly a pure invention. The alternative phrase given in D and J is much less objectionable and removes the sting. The form in C is ingenious, for there, while the word *sayyid* is kept, the remark is so changed that it would normally be addressed only to men of Saʿd's clan, and thereby it becomes harmless. This form might conceivably be a genuine historical reminiscence; but the saying is so trivial that it would not have been recorded unless the standard version had been already in circulation. This would not be until at least six years after the event (and might have been much longer), and it is improbable that anyone would remember the precise form of a trivial remark for that length of time. The form in C is therefore almost certainly an invention.

The alteration of 'God' to 'angel' or 'king' in D is doubtless due to the desire to avoid the appearance of attributing to Saʿd something akin to prophethood. The same desire is responsible for the addition in B and C of a remark by Saʿd, which has the effect of making Saʿd responsible for the phrasing of Muḥammad's comment (which is also less objectionable theologically). The form in D read with 'king' is the only one of all the versions which does not imply that Muḥammad approved of Saʿd's judgement.

The use of a picturesque phrase instead of 'fighters' in G and H, and of an unusual word for 'heavens' in I*, maybe taken as an indication that these are the original forms of the sayings. But it is possible that, as people became aware that traditions were being forged, the more subtle forgers introduced archaic expressions to conceal their forgeries. It seems unlikely, however, that this has happened here.

This examination could be continued through other variations from the basic account, but these are the main ones, at least in the present connection. The basic account must have become quite firmly established, for this examination of the variants has made it clear that the *sayyid* incident and the final comment, despite the difficulties they caused, could neither be entirely ignored nor directly denied. Further discussion of the basic account may be deferred until the *isnāds* have been examined.

3. *The Authorities for the Traditions*. The various scraps of material, or 'traditions', are all provided with an *isnād*, that is, a chain of authorities, each of whom heard the anecdote personally from the person whose name follows. The practice of giving such *isnāds*, however, was probably not common until the beginning of the second century.[1] Indeed, Ibn Isḥāq (d. 151) sometimes gives no authority, and frequently names only his immediate informant (as in I); in not a few cases, on the other hand, he has a complete chain going back to an eye-witness of the event. Al-Wāqidī (d. 207) is similar, for in the case of events like the battle of Uḥud he names several general authorities without specifying the precise contribution of each. His percentage of complete *isnāds* is perhaps slightly higher than that of Ibn Isḥāq. In Ibn Saʿd (d. 230), on the contrary, it is the rule to find complete *isnāds*. This greater attention to sources is in keeping with general intellectual changes, but it may be specially connected with the insistence of al-Shāfiʿī (d. 204) that the basis of law ought to be traditions going back to Muḥammad with an unbroken *isnād*.[2]

The corollary of this desire for a complete chain of authorities is that the *isnād*, as it were, grew backward. The generation whose date of death falls between A.H. 100 and 150 handed on its anecdotes, we may suppose, with only slight indications of their sources in many cases – sometimes perhaps none at all. It was therefore left to later scholars to complete the *isnād*. This does not necessarily mean that the earlier part of the *isnād* is sheer invention, though the most recent student of legal traditions, Dr. Schacht, assigns a large role to such invention. In the more purely historical sphere *isnāds* may rather be said to have grown by a process of 'hypothetical reconstruction'. In other words the later scholars set down the sources from which they supposed – perhaps not altogether without justification – that their informant had got his material. Even if the persons named were not the real sources, such hypothetical *isnāds* may still give an indication of the sort of milieu from which the information came. One of the differences between legal doctrine and historical material of the types under consideration is that, while the former may have originated in the second century, the latter if genuine must have come from someone in contact with the actual events.

Another line of thought also points to the importance of the generation which died between 100 and 150. During the first century there were current romanticized tales of the *maghāzī* or expeditions of Muḥammad; we may also assume that individuals, families and other groups treasured and handed on isolated memories of the Prophet. It was not till toward the end of the first century that we find the first scholarly attempts to produce an orderly and tolerably complete account of the *Maghāzī,* those of ʿUrwa b. al-Zubayr (d. 91-4) and Wahb b. Munabbih (d. 110-16). Following on these two was a series of men learned in the biography of the Prophet. Since *isnāds* were only coming into fashion, these men were presumably more interested in the historical facts than in the sources of their knowledge of the facts, though they doubtless mentioned their authorities sporadically. In respect of this relative unconcern for authorities the first 'collectors' of the life and expeditions of Muḥammad may be called unscientific. Ibn Isḥāq may be regarded as the first of the succeeding group of 'scientific' transmitters of biographical material; and therefore the first or unscientific collectors come to an end with those, whose death-date is 150. It may further be noticed that the study of the biographies of the transmitters commenced about 150; Shuʿba (d. 160) was one of the first noted for this study (Ibn Ḥajar, *Tahdhīb*, IV, no. 580; cf., Goldziher, *M. S.*, II, index).

The scientific biographers may be further divided. The first section – from Ibn Isḥāq to al-Wāqidī – consists of those who generally give authorities for their statements but do not merely repeat the exact words they have heard and do not always give a complete chain of authorities back to the Prophet. With Ibn Saʿd commences the second section, those who attempt to give complete chains for all statements. This latter subdivision, however, is not important for the special question under discussion, and it will be sufficient to classify the persons mentioned in the *isnāds* under three heads:

a. informal transmitters	d. up to 100.
b. Early or unscientific collectors	d. 100-150.
c. Scientific scholars	d. 150 on.

The names in the material in §1 have been marked with the appropriate letter. The divisions, of course, are not hard and fast, for the classes merge into one another, but the classification is a useful working guide as we turn from general considerations to an examination of the special material.

In confirmation of some of the above remarks it may be noticed that the shortest and most incomplete *isnād* is found in the earliest writer, namely in I where Ibn Isḥāq refers only to al-Zuhrī. This incomplete character of many of the chains in Ibn Isḥāq, together with the similarity of the *isnāds* in the two independent recensions of Ibn Hishām and al-Ṭabarī, justifies us in thinking that the editors have generally left the *isnāds* in the form given to them by Ibn Isḥāq himself. It is also noteworthy that 'Urwa, the earliest of the unscientific biographers, in some cases at least apparently gave no references (F and F*).

The first collectors and transmitters of material, those of class B, are tolerably definite figures about whom we have some biographical details, and of whose tendencies we can learn something by studying the traditions they handed on. Thus Jābir al-Ju'fī (d. 127-32) is known to have been an ardent partisan of the Shī'a,[3] and is also reported by Wakī' to have been the first to disseminate traditions in Kūfa.[4] Sa'd b. Ibrāhīm, a grandson of 'Abd al-Raḥmān b. 'Awf, one of the earliest Muslims, held the doctrine of Qadar (or free will) and had friends among the sect of Khawārij; these facts show that he was inclined to be an opponent of the Umayyads. One of these Khārijī friends was Dā'ūd b. al-Ḥuṣayn (in H). He appears to have given some information about his sources, at least most of the scanty biographical details about Abū Sufyān in Ibn Sa'd[5] come by way of Dā'ūd. The similarity of the earlier part of the *isnāds* in A and K suggests that the early collector there, Muḥammad b. 'Amr, must himself have stated his sources in full; this is quite in keeping with the fact that his death-date is only about half a dozen years before that of Ibn Isḥāq.

From these early collectors the material was handed on by a succession of scholars, and, apart from deliberate forgeries, the *isnād* is a record of this process of handing on. Prior to the early collectors, however, the *isnād* has a different character; it is a statement of how second-century scholars imagined the material came to the early collectors, and was probably added to the material in the middle and later part of that century. Thus in E the *isnād* ends with 'Abd al-Raḥmān b. 'Amr, whereas in I* it is taken beyond him to 'Alqama. 'Abd al-Raḥmān, indeed, like others of the later first-century figures such as ʿAmr b. ʿAlqama and Abū Sufyān, is very shadowy and does not receive an article in Ibn Ḥajar's *Tahdhīb*.[6] The earlier first-century authorities, on the other hand , are often well-known worthies, like Abū Saʿīd al-Khudrī, but their connection with specific traditions may well be doubted. By contrasting A and F we get some light on the use made of the name of ʿĀ'isha. In A the whole long story is ascribed to her, but in F a clear break is made just before the part we are specially concerned with, and Saʿd's appointment and judgement are given on ʿUrwa's authority alone, and Muḥammad's final comment on the authority of an unnamed informant of ʿUrwa. These distinctions may be due to the careful scholarship of Ibn Hishām or – perhaps more likely – to that of ʿAbdallāh b. Numayr who may have noticed that ʿĀ'isha could not have been an eye-witness of the last part of the story and may therefore have deleted her name. A comparison of A with I* and J, in all of which the name of ʿAlqama appears, further suggests that the name of ʿĀ'isha may have been added to an *isnād* which previously ended with ʿAlqama, and similarly in J that of Abū Saʿīd. Before the biographical study of the authorities was far advanced it seems to have been believed that ʿAlqama was a primary witness of events about this period. Ibn Ḥajar quotes at second hand a report from Yazīd b. Hārūn from Muḥammad b. ʿAmr from ʿAmr – the same chain as in A – that ʿAlqama said he had been at the siege of Medina just before the attack on the B. Qurayẓa; this is probably a later attempt to vindicate the soundness of *isnāds* which stop at ʿAlqama; but the more reliable biographers tended to hold that, though born during the Prophet's lifetime, he had not been a Companion capable of reporting his sayings.[7]

If despite these indications of later fabrication we suppose that the *isnāds* give hints of the sort of milieu in which the informal transmission took place, the material before us gives examples of at least two types, the family or clan group and the political group. Thus we have ʿAlqama with his son and grandson (A, J, K); Abū Isḥāq hands on from a fellow tribesman of Hamdān (and at the scientific stage is reported by his grandson, Isrā'īl) (B); in B, Saʿd got his information from members of his own clan of Zuhra, while the early part of the *isnād* of H suggests that H represents the clan tradition of the B. ʿAbd al-Ashhal. The best example of a political group is in C, where al-Shaʿbī was secretary to ʿAbdallāh b. Yazīd, governor of Kūfa for Ibn al-Zubayr. In the sphere of legal traditions Dr. Schacht considers transmission within a family generally suspect.[8] But the fact that forgers chose this method of trying to secure an appearance of authenticity seems to presuppose that there were genuine traditions with authentication of this type. Indeed among the more purely historical traditions included in the biography of Muḥammad there is a very large number which are handed down in a family or clan and which have every appearance of being genuine. It is only natural that the clan should remember those of its members who were honourably connected with the great events at the beginning of Islam. It is of course also natural that there should be some exaggeration of ancestral exploits, but allowance can be made for that. The main work of the first biographers of Muḥammad was the collection of such family memories from members of the families concerned. Family traditions were probably also the most reliable, since traditions handed down in a political group would tend to have a political twist given to them.

The political affinities of the later scholars, especially those of group C, are matters of great interest, but too far-reaching to be dealt with here. The most that can be done is to see whether anything can be said about the origin of the chief variants from the basic account.

In D and G the name of Saʿd b. Ibrāhīm occurs, and, as it is improbable that a scholar of Saʿd's period would hand on two divergent accounts, there is a strong presumption that Shuʿba is responsible for the *malak* variation in D; *malik* is almost certainly a conjectural emendation of *malak* by ʿAffān or by some unnamed person between Shuʿba and him. On the other hand, Isrā'īl, the common transmitter in B and C, is a little later, and might have handed on two variants. Actually the difference of the two versions is slight; B alone has the prayer for vengeance, and C alone the *sayyid* incident. We seem to have a choice between (a) holding that Isrā'īl handed on the *sayyid* incident from Jābir and that Wakīʿ omitted it, and (b) holding that ʿUbaydallāh was the author of this transformed version of the *sayyid* incident and ascribed the whole to a man of similar political views known to have been in contact with Isrā'īl. The latter possibly seems more likely.

In view of the similarity of part of the *isnād* in A and K it is practically certain that Yazīd b. Hārūn (or someone unnamed between him and Muḥammad b. ʿAmr) introduced the remark of ʿUmar about God being their *sayyid* which occurs only in A. In D and E one of Ibn Saʿd's informants is the same, Yaḥyā b. ʿAbbād, and he must therefore have handed on two versions; thus the variants must have originated not later than Shuʿba and Ḥammād. A separate line of thought has already led us to suspect Shuʿba in D. In E suspicion tends to fall, therefore, on Ḥammād, though his immediate source is a possible alternative. Thus in most cases the variations seem to have come into being during the second century.

4. *Conclusions*. For the Western scholar the results of the examination of *isnāds* are more conjectural and less satisfying than those of the examination of contents, yet the former study is a necessary complement of the latter. If we come back to the basic account that we assumed, the *isnāds* (especially F and F*) seem to show that Muḥammad's final word of praise was originally handed down separately from the rest of the story. The omission of the *sayyid* incident in some accounts suggests that

it may also have been separate, though added to the story at an earlier time than the final comment.

Several of the facts we have been considering point to the conclusion that the final comment was circulated by ʿAlqama, or perhaps even by a member of Saʿd's family in the name of ʿAlqama. That would be in the second half of the first century. The most plausible motive for so doing would be the desire to defend Saʿd from a charge of inhumanity. It is impossible to know whether there is any historical basis for the anecdote. The most likely time for the *sayyid* incident to have been put into circulation is soon after 11 and certainly before 36. It does not appear in our material without some addition or modification which reduces the objectionable character of its implications.

It is further worthy of note that the alleged first-century authorities mostly belong to the clan of Saʿd b. Muʿādh, the B. ʿAbd al-Ashhal, to the clan of his 'brother' in Islam, Saʿd b. Abī Waqqāṣ, the B. Zuhra, or to the family of al-Zubayr with which the B. Zuhra were on good terms, or else had some special connection with one of these. The *isnāds* of B and C are Kufan throughout, those of H and I (with I*) are Medinan; those of D and E begin in Medina and finish up in Baṣra; and so on.

It should be quite clear by this time that Caetani's suggestion that the judgement was attributed to Saʿd in order to avoid making Muḥammad directly responsible for the 'inhuman massacre' is completely baseless. In the earliest period his family and their friends remembered his appointment as judge as an honour and glory, and it appears to have been they who later made Muḥammad a bulwark for Saʿd, not Saʿd a scapegoat for Muḥammad. Caetani's alternative suggestion that Saʿd pursued not the course that he thought best but that dictated to him by Muḥammad is more difficult to dispose of. The prayer of Saʿd for vengeance might have been introduced to defend him from a charge of subservience. On the whole, however, it seems unlikely that a man who had been one of the foremost supporters of Muḥammad from the time of his earliest contacts with the Anṣār should not have been in general agreement with Muḥammad's policy, of which this was an integral part. Allegiance to Islam involved readiness to sacrifice or disavow old clan attachments where these were contrary to the good of the *umma* or Islamic community.

Finally, let us try to see this discussion in true perspective. The matters which cause difficulty to the Muslim scholars, notably the *sayyid* incident and the closing comment, are in a sense secondary matters. About the primary matters, the broad outlines of events, there is practically no doubt. The B. Qurayẓa were besieged and eventually surrendered; their fate was decided by Saʿd; nearly all the men were executed; Muḥammad did not disapprove. About all that, there is, *pace* Caetani, no controversy. The Western scholar of *sīra* must therefore beware of paying so much attention to the debates to be traced in his sources that he forgets the solid core of undisputed fact. This solid core is probably more extensive than is usually realized: in the special material examined in this article the percentage of solid core, so to speak, seems to be below average. The presence of this core of fact is the distinctive feature of the historical element in the traditions about Muḥammad, as contrasted, for example, with the legal element. Any theory, therefore, about the sources for the biography of the Prophet must account somehow or other for the transmission of this solid core of undisputed material. This study in detail of the sources for a single incident is an attempt to make a contribution towards such a theory.

A2. The Reliability of Ibn Isḥāq's Sources

Some twenty years ago I published a brief study on 'The Materials used by Ibn Isḥāq'.[9] While I have found no reason to modify in any important respect the views I there expressed, recent attacks on the credibility of the whole corpus of sources for the early history of Islam[10] make some reexamination of the sources appropriate.

For much of the first half of this century many Western scholars approved of the somewhat sceptical views held by Henri Lammens and Carl Heinrich Becker. The essence of these views was that the *Sīra* of Ibn Isḥāq consisted primarily of 'the already existing dogmatic and juristic *ḥadīth*. . . collected and chronologically arranged', and that to this had been added expanded versions of historical allusions in the Qur'ān.[11]This view has two weaknesses: firstly, it does not explain where the chronology came from, since the *ḥadīth* were not dated; and secondly, it wrongly assumes that all the statements about Muḥammad in the *Sīra* fall within the category of 'dogmatic and juristic *ḥadīth*'. Muslim scholars always regarded *sīra* as a separate discipline from *ḥadīth,* and the probability is that it was the earlier to be established. The corollary of the Lammens-Becker view was that the only reliable source for the biography of Muḥammad was the Qur'ān itself, and this point was well expressed by Régis Blachère.[12] Since the Qur'ān in isolation from the *Sīra* yields hardly any historical information, the conclusion was that hardly anything can be known about the life of Muḥammad.

Scepticism was taken a stage further by John Wansbrough when he adopted the view that the text of the Qur'ān did not take its present shape until a century and a half after Muḥammad; and two of Wansbrough's disciples went on to reject all the Muslim sources for the early history of Islam and to postulate an alternative first phase of that religion which they renamed 'Hagarism'. Though scholarly opinion in general has not accepted the main conclusions or the assumptions of these writers, the argument against their assumptions has not yet been stated as fully as possible, and some consideration of reliability is therefore relevant to any discussion of the sources used by Ibn Isḥāq. Before examining these in detail, however, it is worth reminding ourselves of a general principle of all historical research, namely, that the ostensible sources for any series of events are always to be accepted unless some grounds can be shown for their rejection or partial rejection. In the particular case of early Islamic history, including the career of Muḥammad, grounds had indeed been shown for doubting the reliability of 'dogmatic and juristic Ḥadīth', but the Lammens-Becker view failed to take account of other types of material to which the objections did not apply and which have not subsequently been criticized on other grounds.

Let us now therefore try to list the various types of material used by Ibn Isḥāq. It is important to realize, however, that probably all of this material had already been worked over by several generations of scholars. Fuat Sezgin names nineteen earlier scholars who had dealt with the biography of the Prophet.[13] Ibn Isḥāq's immediate teacher was the well-known al-Zuhrī (d. 742).

1: The Main Events of the Maghāzī or the Basic Framework. First and foremost among the materials used by Ibn Isḥāq must be mentioned the basic framework of the Sīra, which I formerly called 'the *maghāzī*-material'. This is to be taken as comprising the list of *maghāzī* or expeditions, the group against whom each was directed, the leader and the number of participants and in some cases their names, the results, and the approximate date and relative chronological position. In the case of major events like the battle of Badr this material also includes an outline of the battle or other event. Ibn Isḥāq's arrangement of his *Sīra* presupposes this *maghāzī*-material, since it provides his underlying chronological framework. The further information in it he usually gives without an *isnād*, as does also al-Wāqidī. Into the framework he inserts the anecdotes about the various expeditions; but these are distinct from the *maghāzī*-material, usually deal with minor details of the event and have some *isnād,* even if not a complete one.

Virtually none of this basic framework or *maghāzī*-material can be derived from the Qur'ān. It would appear to be impossible to discover from the Qur'ān the chronological order of the main events: Badr, Uḥud, Khandaq, al-Ḥudaybiya, conquest of Mecca, Ḥunayn, Tābūk; and the minor expeditions are not even mentioned. Nor can the basic framework be derived from the collections of Ḥadīth. Only in the *Ṣaḥīḥ* of al-Bukhārī among the major extant collections is there a section (64) on *Maghāzī*. This occupies 140 pages in the European edition and follows the usual chronological order of the expeditions, which is not surprising since al-Bukhārī lived nearly a century after Ibn Isḥāq. It does not mention all the expeditions, however, and the material presented has not been critically pruned. Thus in the first paragraph of the section he quotes a Companion as saying that the first expedition in which Muḥammad himself took part was to al-'Ushayra and also quotes a later scholar as confirming this, and then adds that Ibn Isḥāq mentions two other expeditions of Muḥammad as occurring before al-'Ushayra. In other words, al-Bukhārī, despite his later date, shows the kind of material from which Ibn Isḥāq and his predecessors distilled the basic framework of the Sīra.

The esteem in which Ibn Isḥāq is held is doubtless due to the fact that there is nothing in his *Sīra* which could not be accepted by the community as a whole. There were several expeditions to which he felt unable to assign a date, and these he placed together at the end. There were also some minor chronological details on which al-Wāqidī corrected him, presumably on the basis of further information not accessible to Ibn Isḥāq; and in several cases Ibn Hishām adds the name of the man left in charge in Medina while Muḥammad was away on an expedition. These points show that the scholarly process of working out the chronological framework of the Sīra continued for some time after Ibn Isḥāq. A careful study of the section on *Maghāzī* in al-Bukhārī might yield some valuable insights into the procedures of the scholars both before and after Ibn Isḥāq.

In order to assess the reliability of this basic framework or *maghāzī*-material we must look for evidence of possible bias (a) in the historical scholars themselves and (b) in those from whom they obtained the materials with which they worked. With regard to (a) something will be said towards the end of the article about traces of bias in Ibn Isḥāq himself; and it will be suggested that these do not give any grounds for thinking that there has been any serious distortion of the basic framework. With regard to (b) we are on somewhat hypothetical ground, and can at best look at the possible motives of those who preserved memories of the expeditions. One such motive would probably be pride in the achievements of the Islamic community, and for many Arabs this feeling would merge with the pride their pre-Islamic ancestors had felt in the achievements of the tribe. Presumably Ibn Isḥāq and the other historians were also moved by such a pride. Another possible motive would be the desire to maintain the honour of one's family or tribe; and some of the *maghāzī*-material seems to have been preserved because it included an incident which redounded to the honour of a particular family or tribe. In such cases the importance of the incident would often be exaggerated, but the implied information about the main event would usually be correct. Scholars like Ibn Isḥāq could have been aware of these exaggerations and made allowance for them.

One cannot insist sufficiently on the overriding importance of this *maghāzī*-material, which includes the chronological order of the expeditions and some basic information about them, together with the detailed outline of what happened on the main ones. This material was not noticed as a distinct category by Lammens and Becker, and it is not open to the objections they and others raised against dogmatic and juristic Ḥadīth, although it is fact presupposed by Becker when he speaks of arranging Ḥadīth chronologically. It has also to be presupposed before the Qur'ān can be used as a historical source in line with Blachère's suggestion (and neglecting the speculations of Wansbrough).

The Crone-Cook rejection of the Muslim sources for the early history of Islam thus appears to be contrary to sound historical methodology. When one further considers the vast amount of material involved – many thousands of interlocking items – it is incredible that some person or group about the eighth century could have invented all these details and got them universally accepted. It is also incredible that some one at that date should have been so sophisticated as to realize that invented material tends to be wholly consistent and then to introduce discrepancies and corrections in order to put 20th-century investigators off the scent! Most incredible of all is that no traces have been left of the process of invention. On the other hand, when the basic framework is accepted as in the main reliable, it is possible to give a coherent account of the career of Muḥammad and the subsequent history of Islam. Into this account the various passages of the Qur'ān fit in a credible way, and allowance can also be made for much 'tendentious shaping' and distortion of the anecdotes about Muḥammad and other Muslims.

2. *Documentary Material.* The main document used by Ibn Isḥāq is that commonly referred to as the Constitution of Medina. This is generally accepted as a genuine document, though there are difficulties about its precise interpretation. It appears to be a conflation of two or more versions of the original agreement between Muḥammad and the inhabitants of Medina together with some later modifications. The list of Muslims present at Badr may also have come from a document, since this was a matter which affected the payment of stipends by the Islamic state; but it is also possible that this and other lists were compiled by the scholars who collected historical material. Other documents, apparently authentic but not used by Ibn Isḥāq, are to be found in the *Ṭabaqāt* of Ibn Saʿd (i/2). Whatever Ibn Isḥāq bases on documents has clearly a *prima facie* reliability.

3 *Arab Genealogies and pre-Islamic Events.* Ibn Isḥāq's *Sīra* in the edition by Ibn Hishām begins with a genealogy of Muḥammad going back to Adam. In this the Arabian genealogies have been grafted on to Biblical genealogies from the book of *Genesis,* but the whole is presented as a single entity and there is no mention of any source. It is well-known that the Arabs attached great importance to genealogies, and that in each generation several men were known for their expertise in this field. One such was the first caliph Abū Bakr, and his knowledge doubtless helped Muḥammad politically when he had to deal with rivalries between tribes and within a tribe, since genealogists usually had also a good knowledge of the 'days' of the Arabs, that is, their battles. Genealogies also served to give a kind of chronological structure to accounts of pre-Islamic events.

Genealogies are mentioned here because they are a distinct type of material not derived from Qur'ān or Ḥadīth. Following Ignaz Goldziher[15] scholars are inclined to think that the genealogical schemes were modified during the Umayyad period to reflect contemporary groupings of tribes, and this means that the earlier parts must be used with great caution. Nevertheless a historian of Muḥammad's career would be justified in regarding the genealogies of individuals as mainly correct from about the time of Muḥammad's birth.

4. Poetry. For the historian of Muḥammad the chief value of the poetry quoted by Ibn Isḥāq is that it sometimes throws light on the relations of friendship or enmity between tribes. From this point of view the value may be retained even when the passage is not by the person to whom it is ascribed. The reason is that there is a high likelihood that any forger would belong to the same tribe and give a similar picture of tribal relationships. Where the poetry is authentic it may give confirmation and additional information about points otherwise known. Its contribution to our knowledge of Muḥammad, however, is at best a very minor one.

5. The Qur'ān and the Expansions of it. The Lammens-Becker view holds that a section of the Sīra consists of 'exegetical elaborations of Qur'ānic allusions'. This point deserves a thorough examination, especially in the light of Blachère's claim that the Qur'ān itself is the main historical source.

The Qur'ān itself, apart from elaborations and expansions, is certainly a historical source, but it is very difficult to elicit precise historical information from it. As an example of this difficulty one may refer to the passage about the change of Qibla (2.142-50). It does not give a clear account of what actually happened, though it seems to imply that there was a period of hesitation. Even this, however, is sufficient to cast doubt on two versions of how the change came about, namely, the late story that Muḥammad received the command to change while engaged in leading the *ṣalāt* and that he and his followers at once made an about-turn, and the more plausible story that 2.144 was revealed by night and communicated to the Muslims on the following day.[16] It is noteworthy that Ibn Isḥāq has no more than a tentative statement about the date of the change of Qibla (introduced by *qīla*), and has no reference to the Qur'ān. It will be seen presently, however, that he was well aware of the historical value of the Qur'ān and, where he knew the outline of events from other sources, used it to give confirmation of this and sometimes to yield additional information.

The expansions and elaborations of the Qur'ān are of different types. Firstly, there were the detailed versions given by popular preachers of the Biblical and other stories to which there were only brief allusions in the Qur'ān. Sometimes the accounts might be based on the Bible, sometimes old folk-beliefs might be incorporated, and sometimes there

to each; (c) minor anecdotes, for which an *isnād* is given, though this is not always complete. The first type is roughly what was described as the basic framework, and the second type might be called extensions of that. The third type, on the other hand, consists mostly of accounts of minor incidents of the sort which men involved in the events would have liked to tell their descendants. These have been collected from many sources and 'chronologically arranged' within the material of the first two types. Not all mention Muḥammad, and sometimes, even when he is mentioned, he is not the central figure in the story. As an example one might give the story of a man called Qatāda, who picked up Muḥammad's broken bow at Uḥud and kept it, and who also had a bad eye-wound which was tended by Muḥammad.[18] The story is told by his grandson 'Āṣim, a writer on the Sīra, who adds that Qatāda later maintained that this eye was better than the other.

The reasons given above for accepting the reliability of the basic framework apply also to most of the extensions. The anecdotes of the third type are not in general open to the objections raised against Ḥadīths (in the strict sense), though they may be liable to some forms of exaggeration. Each story, too, must be examined for possibilities of distortion. Thus it may well be that Ibn Isḥāq included the story about Qatāda because he thought that it suggested that Muḥammad had some power of healing, although he does not say this in so many words. Despite this possibility the story may be true in essentials; that is, Qatāda did have an eye-wound, even if not as bad as stated, and Muḥammad did tend it; and Qatāda may well have said later that he saw better with this eye. This is precisely the kind of thing one would expect to be handed down in a family.

In his book on *The Origins of Muhammadan Jurisprudence* (170) Joseph Schacht speaks of Ḥadīths handed down in a single family and condemns them all as spurious, regarding the 'family *isnād*' as a device to give an appearance of authenticity. While this may be so in the legal field, the use of such a device presupposes that there had been genuine 'family *isnāds*', presumably in the historical field. Curiously enough, it happens that I personally, despite the fact of being a European living in 1980, know of an event which happened about 200 years ago but is not recorded in any book or document, and base my knowledge on a 'family *isnād*'. My maternal grandfather as a small boy was told by his great-grandmother (called Mrs Burns, but no relative) that she had once entertained to tea the poet Robert Burns in her house in Kilmarnock, and she added that at this period 'he was not much thought of'. He died in 1796. If this can happen in the non-oral culture of nineteenth- and twentieth- century Europe – and I have no reason to doubt the truth of the story – one might reasonably expect that in the predominantly oral culture of seventh-century Arabia families would preserve tolerably reliable reports of encounters between their ancestors and Muḥammad; and it appears that some reports were written down within about a century of the events.

Such considerations tend to confirm the view expressed above that the basic framework and its extensions are on the whole reliable. They also suggest that anecdotes of the third type may contain genuine reminiscences and should not be rejected without examination.

THE PROCEDURES OF THE HISTORIANS

The materials collected by those first interested in the biography of the Prophet were presumably family memories. It is perhaps significant that many of the first collectors and historians themselves came from the families of men who had played an important part under Muḥammad. Thus of the first ten writers mentioned by Sezgin, no. 1 is the son of Sa'd ibn 'Ubāda, the leader of the Khazraj, no. 4 is a son of the poet Ka'b ibn Mālik, no. 7 is 'Urwa the son of al-Zubayr, no. 8 is a son of no. 1, no. 9 is a grandson of the caliph Abū Bakr, and no. 10 the grandson of Qatāda already mentioned; no. 6 may be the son of the caliph 'Uthman, but there is some confusion about him.[19] The number of scholars who left written material about the *maghāzī* or other aspects of the Sīra, such as the lists of names, shows that there must have been a great amount of activity in this field.

The nature of this activity and its vast extent, together with its early date, serves to explain the absence of the *isnād*. Thus when Shuraḥbīl (no. 8) drew up lists of the Emigrants to Medina and of the men at Badr the important thing was the list and not how he arrived at it, except perhaps in one or two doubtful cases; the presence of most of the names on the lists would be matters of general knowledge, capable of being known from dozens of sources, or in technical language *mutawātir*. The fact that two Companions (as recorded by al-Bukhārī) said that the expedition to al-'Ushayra was the earliest in which Muḥammad himself took part became irrelevant after Ibn Isḥāq and al-Wāqidī had established that there were two or three earlier ones. The historians must quickly have realized that some of the family memories communicated to them were inaccurate, not through deliberate misrepresentation but because of ignorance or some oversight. Since there was no point in handing on inaccurate memories, the practice of the historians came to include the rejection of some of the material collected. This may be part of the reason why Sīra developed as a discipline completely distinct from Ḥadīth-study. The early students of Sīra must have devoted a great deal of scholarly labour to the sifting of memories and other evidence, and what they handed on was only the assured results of this process as they saw them. The use of the *isnād* was known at least from the time of al-Zuhrī (d. 742), who was both a Ḥadīth-student and the outstanding historian of his generation, but it was not *de rigueur* as it later became. When Ibn Isḥāq quotes al-Zuhrī, he sometimes gives his sources and sometimes not. Presumably the information which Ibn Isḥāq gives without any source is what was generally regarded by students of the Sīra as 'assured results', known by *tawātur*.

All these considerations justify a general confidence in the historical methodology of Ibn Isḥāq and his predecessors. The essential work seems to have been done in the first Islamic century, perhaps in the first half of it; and this established the chronological order of the main events and many of the minor events – the basic framework which Ibn Isḥāq gives without *isnād*. After the appearance of the first written works the chief effort of subsequent scholars such as Ibn Isḥāq was to obtain from these as much information as possible. The high esteem in which the *Sīra* of Ibn Isḥāq is held is probably due to his relative completeness and accuracy, together with the type of picture he gives of the Prophet. Al-Wāqidī corrects Ibn Isḥāq's chronology on some minor points and has also some additional information, but he does not seem to have been so popular.

Some special features of the *Sīra* of Ibn Isḥāq may be mentioned briefly. Firstly, he was accused of Shī'ite and Qadarite sympathies; but the evidence for this is slight. Certainly he states that 'Alī was the first male Muslim and neglects the reports that it was Abū Bakr or Zayd ibn Ḥāritha; but on the other hand he omits specifically Shī'ite material like the Ḥadīth about Khumm. Again, his inclusion of two anecdotes from the Qadarite 'Amr ibn 'Ubayd hardly justifies an accusation of Qadarism. Secondly he was criticized for taking material from Jews and Christians. This appears to have been mainly in the first part of his *Sīra*, the *Mubtada'* or *Mabda'*, which is omitted in the edition of Ibn Hishām. The criticism is little more than a reflection of later attitudes. Thirdly, he tends to exalt the figure of Muḥammad above the merely human, as in the suggestion that his touch healed Qatāda's eye. Another example is in the story of the death of Quzmān who, after being badly wounded at Uḥud, hastened his own death by cutting a vein. Al-Wāqidī has here a more primitive version, in which Muḥammad in effect says that suicide leads to Hell; but Ibn Isḥāq reports that Muḥammad had been in the habit of saying 'He belongs to the people of Hell', and thus makes it an example of Muḥammad's supernatural foreknowledge. In other cases, however, al-Wāqidī has stories not found in Ibn Isḥāq which illustrate Muḥammad's supernatural powers.

Sufficient has been said here to show that it would be possible to write a complete book about the early writers on the career of Muḥammad. What it is important to emphasize at the present juncture is that in this examination of materials for the Sīra nothing has been found to justify the complete rejection of Ibn Isḥāq, al-Wāqidī and their predecessors;

and that on the other hand reasons have been given for accepting virtually the whole of the basic framework and its extensions and, with a due exercise of caution, much of the other types of material also.

A3. The Dating of the Qur'ān: a Review of Richard Bell's Theories

The appearance of Richard Bell's *Introduction to the Qur'ān*[20] is a suitable occasion for considering the general principles underlying the detailed dating of the Qur'ān in his translation. This leads on to the question of the extent to which even approximate dates can be assigned to the various sections, and also to an estimate of advances to be expected in this branch of Qur'ānic studies. Bell's work further raises questions of interpretation, but these are not discussed here except in so far as they bear on the dating.

Underlying Bell's system of dating are two general principles. Since these are a convenient focus for discussion, it will be well to begin with a formulation of them. They are:

(1) *The normal unit of revelation is the short passage.*

(2) *The text was 'revised' by Muḥammad himself.*

These principles are fundamental to all the chronological side of his work. Indeed, if they are sound, and if it is possible to apply them in detail to an appreciable extent, they must be fundamental to all future work on the dating of the Qur'ān.

A third principle has greatly influenced the external appearance of Bell's translation, namely:

(3) *The passages were, at least sometimes, committed to writing.*

This is held by Bell to be necessary to explain the *order* of various passages; but it is seldom, if ever, directly relevant to the dating.

About the first of these principles there is, in a sense, wide agreement among both Muslim and non-Muslim scholars. Traditional Muslim accounts of the 'occasions of revelation' often refer to short passages containing only a verse or two, and this is reflected in the headings of the sūras in the official Egyptian edition, where sūra 9, for example, is described as 'Medinan, except the last two verses which are Meccan'. Nöldeke likewise recognized that some sūras contained passages belonging to different dates, and most non-Muslim scholars, without considering the matter in detail, have accepted this point of view. Régis Blachère, in his chronological arrangement of the sūras in his translation, goes so far as to split up some of the sūras and to date the sections separately.

So, it would be generally agreed that the Qur'ānic revelations frequently consisted of short passages. There would be room for discussion, however, whether the whole, or nearly the whole, of the Qur'ān was made up of short passages, or whether the unit of revelation was not sometimes a nearly complete sūra. There are some sūras that possess a formal unity, and look as if they had each been revealed as a piece. This formal unity is exemplified in one way by the story of Joseph in sūra 12, and in another way by the parallel stories of former prophets, with similarities of wording, which are found in a number of sūras, such as 11 and 54. It seems clear, then, that not all the Qur'ān consists of short passages, but that sometimes long passages constituted a single revelation.

The existence of long passages seems to be admitted by Bell. Yet, taking as his basis the principle that the short passage was the normal unit of revelation, he has gone much further than any other student of the Qur'ān in attempting to identify and date the original units of revelation. In the course of this attempt he has been led to propound some additional theories about the original form of the revelations, and the way in which they assumed their present shape. His second main principle, namely, that 'revision' took place, is relevant here, but it may be left aside meantime. Apart from that Bell's suggestions may be divided into two groups.

(a) Firstly, he held that the short passages of the original revelation consisted of several different types.[21] One important type in the earliest days was the 'sign-passage', that is, a short passage citing various natural phenomena as evidence of God's power and goodness; and this type continued to appear in later days also. Another type is the punishment-story, that is, an account of the punishment of a tribe or community which rejected the message of the prophet sent to them. Yet another type is what Bell calls the 'slogan'. By this he means a short statement usually introduced by the word 'Say', and he thinks these 'slogans' were designed to be repeated by Muḥammad's followers. Then there was a type of passage reminiscent of the Arab *Kāhin* or soothsayer, which contained a number of oaths forming a jingle, but without much sense. From this Bell distinguishes asseverative passages, where the oaths had a bearing on what was to be asserted. He also speaks of '"when" passages' containing descriptions of the Last Judgement, of dramatic scenes, of narratives and parables (pp. 74-8).

In addition to all these types Bell gives a description of what is not so much a separate type of passage as a general form of paragraph which might be found in more than one type. He gives 49.13 as an example and then remarks:

> 'Here, following the address, we have an indication of the subject that has called for treatment, then comes a declaration regarding it, and finally the passage is closed by a sententious maxim. This form is found not only in passages with direct address, but in a

multitude of others. They begin by stating their occasion; a question has been asked, the unbelievers have said or done something, something has happened, or some situation has arisen. The matter is dealt with shortly, in usually not more than three or four verses; at the end comes a general statement, often about Allah, which rounds off the passage.'

These short pieces of various kinds Bell supposes to have circulated independently. In his propaganda, he thinks, Muḥammad from the earliest times made use of slogans (p. 75). Similarly, 'sign' passages were one of the means that he adopted at all stages of his career in order to appeal to men, while punishment stories, which seem to have had a separate existence (p. 121), were used to inspire men with fear and thereby soften their hearts to accept the message.

In all this conception of types of short passages there is little that could not be generally accepted. The novelty in Bell's view is the thought, implicit rather than explicit, that the different types had different functions. Some were for persuading possible converts, some for repetition by Muslims facing opponents, some for use in worship, and so on. This is an attractive idea and would bear further study.

(b) The second group of suggestions made by Bell as he works out his first basic principle (that the normal unit of revelation is the short piece) has as its centre the view that Muḥammad himself put together short pieces to make a longer composition. From the standpoint taken by both Muslim and non-Muslim scholars this is much more of an innovation. Yet reflection tends to justify it. The traditional standpoint seems to rest on assumptions that have not been carefully scrutinized. Though it has commonly been admitted that short passages were often revealed separately, the implications of this admission have not been worked out; and it has been supposed that in many cases whole sūras, or large parts of sūras, were revealed at once, and that the fitting together of separate passages could be ascribed to those who 'collected' the Qur'ān after Muḥammad's death.

If, however, the short passages are the general rule and the long passages are the exceptions, then it would be strange that the 'collectors' should group together what Muḥammad left as separate items. It would have been more natural to treat each separate passage as a separate sūra. Even if the 'collectors' are responsible for only a little grouping of passages, they doubtless had some precedent for it. It is difficult to avoid the conclusion that Muḥammad himself was responsible for combining separate revelations into sūras. The challenge in 11.13/16 to produce ten sūras would seem to imply that more than ten sūras were then extant. These might conceivably have been sūras consisting of single short passages, like some of the sūras at the end of the Qur'ān as we have it. Since nearly all the sūras in the present Qur'ān are composite sūras, however, it seems more likely that the reference is to sūras of this kind, and that therefore separate revelations had been combined into sūras by Muḥammad himself.

The tendency to ascribe all combinations of separate revelations to 'collectors' and not to Muḥammad is perhaps connected with the desire of orthodox Islam to safeguard the miraculous nature of the Qur'ān by insisting that Muḥammad could neither read nor write. Yet, even on the view that Muḥammad was illiterate in this sense, he may still be credited with combining separate passages. He could either have relied solely on memory, since to remember a group of passages together would be no more difficult than to remember separate passages; or he may have employed amanuenses to write down the composite sūras.

It ought to be assumed that, if Muḥammad combined separate revelations in this way, he did so because he believed it was in accordance with the command of God. With the exception of one passage to be discussed presently, there is no explicit command to this effect. The Qur'ān seems to imply, however, that the revelations constituted a unity, though they 'came down' separately; and thus the work of combining them would be simply the restoration of the original unity (cf. 17.106/107).

The one passage that might be taken to be a command to combine separate revelations is the opening of sūra 73, especially the words *rattili'l-qur'ān^{a} tartīl^{an}*. The usual Muslim interpretation of this is that it prescribes leisurely cantillation or chanting in measure. The basic application of *ratila*, however, seems to be to front teeth, and it means that they are even in growth and well set together. The word is also used metaphorically of a thing that is well arrranged or disposed, and this metaphorical use predominates in the second stem. For *rattala'l-kalām* Lane gives the meaning 'he put together and arranged well the component parts of the speech, or saying, and made it distinct'. It would therefore seem that 73.4 may originally have been taken to refer to the combining of separate fragments of revelation. The only other instance of the word in the Qur'ān (25.32/34), where God says *rattalnā-hu tartīl^{an}* has been much discussed by commentators; it is noteworthy that the Muslim Pickthall translates 'We have arranged it in right order'.

Bell gives sūra 80 as an example of a composite sūra which has been put together, he thinks, by Muḥammad. It consists of five distinct passages, but they 'are so arranged that we can follow a line of thought binding them together', and thus 'form more or less of a unity'.[22]

In Muḥammad's work of combining short pieces into larger units, Bell thinks he was guided by certain ideas, and that these changed from time to time. Apart from an early period before Muḥammad began to combine separate pieces, there are two main periods in his activity, the Qur'ān period and the Book period. In the Qur'ān period Muḥammad's aim was to produce passages suitable for recitation in the course of the *ṣalāt* or worship. This period therefore begins 'about the same time as the institution of the *ṣalāt*, at any rate after Muḥammad had gained some adherents'.[23] Not all the separate passages already existing, however, were immediately incorporated into the Qur'ān. In 15.87 we read: 'We have bestowed upon thee seven of the *mathānī* and the mighty Qur'ān.' Especially if the *mathānī* are identified with the punishment stories, as Bell, following Sprenger and others, has argued, this verse will imply that parts of the present Qur'ān were not included in it when that verse was revealed. This would be in keeping with the distinct functions of the various types of short passages. For these longer compositions consisting of several short passages the term sūras was introduced, in Bell's view, some time during the Qur'ān period. He is further inclined to think 'that the Qur'ān was definitely closed about the time of the battle of Badr' (p. 132), but realizes that the evidence for this is slender.

It is clear, however, that the idea of the Qur'ān as a collection of passages for recitation in public or private worship was superseded in Muḥammad's mind by the idea of a Book, that is, of written Scriptures comparable to those of the Jews and Christians. There are numerous references to the Book in the Qur'ān. The aim was doubtless to include in the Book all the revealed material extant, whether it had hitherto been used for recitation in worship or not. The Book was thus more extensive than the Qur'ān, as the latter term was first used, but in course of time the two came to be regarded as identical. The principles on which separate pieces were combined to form sūras were doubtless the same for the Qur'ān and the Book, except that greater length might perhaps be allowed in the Book.

These, then, are the lines on which Bell works out his first main principle.

The second main principle is more revolutionary and likely to provoke opposition. It is that Muḥammad himself, in the course of combining separate pieces into sūras – and possibly also at other times – did some editing or 'revising'. This is contrary to the common idea that he merely recorded those contents of his consciousness which, somehow or other, he recognized as revelations. Yet the idea of a 'revision' of the Qur'ān by way of additions – and perhaps also of deletions, though there is no direct evidence of these – is not necessarily contrary to orthodox Muslim beliefs. Orthodoxy accepts the fact of 'abrogation', that is, the cancelling of certain prescriptions and their replacement by others. Thus 73.20 is usually taken as abrogating the obligation to spend part of the night in prayer which is laid down at the beginning of the sūra. The basis of the abrogation is presumably that what was good and edifying for the Muslim community at one period is not necessarily so at another. Now the same could hold of additions to the text. Thus – to take an example which Bell does not indicate as a revision – 5.51/56 might originally have run: 'O ye who have believed, do not choose Jews as friends; they are friends to each other; whoever makes friends is one of them.' This would be perfectly appropriate in the period between Badr and Uḥud when the verse is said to have been revealed. The words 'and Christians', which occur after 'Jews' in the present text would at that period have been inappropriate, since the Muslims in Medina had practically no contacts with Christians, while some of Muḥammad's early followers were on good terms with the Negus of Abyssinia. It was only in the closing years of Muḥammad's life when he was trying to detach Ghassān and their neighbours from the Byzantine allegiance that the words 'and Christians' would have a point. If abrogation took place, then there would seem to be no reason why 'revision' of this type should not take place, since it involved no change of principle, but merely the extension of an existing principle to new circumstances. Indeed, something very like 'revision' of this kind is implied by 16.101/103: 'When We substitute one verse for another – God knoweth best what He revealeth – they say, Thou art simply an inventor.' The possiblity of the deletion of verses or parts of verses seems to be implied by references to Muḥammad's being caused to forget by God (87.7; cf. 2.106/100). It may be concluded, then, that from the standpoint of Muslim orthodoxy there are no insuperable objections to Bell's conception of 'revision', though an attitude of conservative distrust would be only natural. The psychologically-minded modern scholar may like to suppose that Muḥammad had some method of 'listening for guidance' where he thought a passage required revision. If we accept his sincerity, he cannot be regarded as 'revising' passages except in so far as he believed he had divine authority for doing so. It is almost certain that no one other than Muḥammad would have presumed to make such 'revisions'.

Bell considers that there are a number of formal characteristics – 'roughnesses' of style – that enable us to recognize revisions and alterations (83 ff.). Sometimes it is possible to remove the rhyme-phrases of a passage and to leave a series of verses with a different rhyme. In such cases Bell argues that the secondary rhyme-phrases have been added to adapt the passage to its place in the sūra. Further signs of revision are abrupt changes of rhyme, repetition of a rhyme-word in adjoining verses, breaks in grammatical construction, abrupt changes in the length of verses, sudden changes of the dramatic situation with changes of pronoun, the appearance of seemingly contradictory statements side by side, the juxtaposition of passages of different dates, and the occurrence of late phrases in earlier passages. He also considers that in many cases explanations of a word or phrase, and reservations introduced by *illā*, 'except', are later additions. Where a subject is treated in a somewhat different way in neighbouring verses, revision is to be suspected. It can sometimes be made to seem probable, too, that a passage has had alternative continuations, and that these simply follow one another in the present text. Many examples of all these features will be found in Bell's translation.

Another sign of revision is connected with Bell's third principle, the existence of written documents. It frequently happens that an extraneous subject is found in a passage that is apparently meant to be homogeneous. This phenomenon, Bell suggests, is to be explained by supposing that the extraneous material stood on a scrap of writing material, that the addition was written on the back of this, and that, when the addition was copied out in its proper place, the extraneous material on the other side was copied out also and made to follow.

This, then, is the theoretical basis of Bell's work on the dating of the passages of the Qur'ān. It is at once obvious that it completely changes the nature of the problem of dating the Qur'ān. It is no longer a question of trying to determine the order in which the sūras were revealed, and then assigning dates to a few short passages that are clearly different in date from their context. It has now become a question of dating separately each passage of a few verses. In the case of revisions, a single word even may have a different date from the rest of the verse. The problem of dating the Qur'ān has thus been made much more complex.

In these changed circumstances, it is necessary to reconsider Nöldeke's criterion of date, namely, the length of the verses. In this respect the view that the 'short pieces' belong to different types is relevant, since it would be only natural for the style to vary with the type of utterance and the function it was intended to perform. As Bell puts it, 'style may be deliberately adopted to suit varying ends in view', and 'there are, in fact, passages in the Qur'ān which seem to suggest that different styles were used at the same time for different kinds of utterances' (p. 103). This does not mean that the criterion of style is valueless. The criterion of style, however, is insufficient to date a passage accurately, it gives no more than a rough approximation. Bell is therefore inclined to attach more weight to phraseology. When the introduction of a phrase can be linked with a definite event in Muḥammad's life, it becomes an indication of date.

In the last resort, therefore, the main criterion of date in the Qur'ān is the content of the separate passages. A careful study must be made of the ideas and implications of each passage, and of their relevance to the various phases of Muḥammad's career. In the Meccan period nothing more than the barest outline is possible, but in the Medinan period there are a number of outstanding events, whose date is known, which provide a framework into which original revelations and revisions can be fitted with a fair degree of accuracy. Even in the Medinan period, however, the work of dating is far from simple. Similar passages throughout the Qur'ān have to be laboriously compared with one another in the attempt to detect the growth of conceptions. In the end there will be many points about which the scholar can only say *wa-'llāhu aʿlam*.

Up to this point this article has consisted in a sympathetic but partly independent presentation of Richard Bell's theories. It remains to make a critical appraisal of them and of his whole attempt at dating the Qur'ān.

With regard to his first basic principle it would seem that there could be little dispute. At most there might be some divergences in detail. In a sūra like 54, where there are four punishment stories resembling one another in phraseology, they must have constituted a single whole from the first and cannot have circulated independently of one another. Similarly most of the story of Joseph in sūra 12 must have existed as a unity from the first. Bell may sometimes seem to have gone too far in breaking up passages into their component parts. For example, in making a division (albeit with hesitation) after 19.36/37, he seems to have failed to notice that verses almost identical with this verse and the next one occur together at 43.64 f. Nevertheless, as a pioneer in the analysis of sūras into their original elements he was justified in looking for as many breaks as possible and leaving it to others to correct any exaggerations. However much scholars may differ from Bell's detailed conclusions, it is no longer possible for serious scholars to do other than accept his first basic principle that the normal unit of revelation was the short piece, and its corollary that Muḥammad was responsible for at least the first stage of combining these pieces into sūras.

Much the same may be said about his second basic principle. His particular conclusions are often disputable, but in view of the great mass of detailed evidence for 'revision' which is contained in his translation, it must now be accepted that Muḥammad 'revised' the revelations to a great extent. These two principles and the subordinate theories are the basis underlying the whole of the dating, and it is difficult to see how any future work on the dating of the Qur'ān can avoid beginning from these principles.

With regard to Bell's third principle of the existence of written documents, some on the back of others, a little scepticism is justified – perhaps not so much with the principle itself as with the contemporary scholar's ability to apply it in detail. Some of Bell's applications of it are convincing, and provide a neat explanation for the appearance of extraneous passages in otherwise homogeneous contexts. Nevertheless to apply the hypothesis as widely as he has done would seem to require a more thorough theoretical justification than can readily be given. Where there are grounds for suspecting revision, Bell tends to look for two passages of equal length, and then to suppose that one was written on the back of the other. But scraps of writing material need not have been exactly filled on one side; some space may have been left on the first side, or the passage may have spilled over to the second side; the writing need not always have been of the same size; and so on. Thus in the application of Bell's third principle there cannot be the same degree of certainty that there is about his first two. In a few cases we may be fairly certain that a certain passage was written on the back of a certain other passage. In most cases, however, even if we suspect that the present order of the text is due to the use of the two sides of the writing material, we cannot with any degree of certainty say what was on the back of what.

It is unfortunate that this hypothesis has had so great an influence on the physical appearance of Bell's translation, since that gives the impression that this document-hypothesis is the central part of Bell's theories about the Qur'ān. One sees that he was justified in trying to work out the hypothesis in the fullest possible detail. Yet one also regrets the prominence it receives, since that obscures the other much more valuable parts of Bell's work. In the long run it will probably be found that his greatest contribution to the study of the Qur'ān, apart from his insistence on the two basic principles, has been his detailed dating of the fragments into which he analyses the sūras. This is especially important in the Medinan period, where the dates of many important events are known, so that the revelations can be dated in relation to them.

Along the lines thus pioneered by Bell there is good hope of further advances towards an agreed dating of the Qur'ān. Such advances, however, require a minute examination of the text of the Qur'ān and a laborious comparison of passage with passage. There is over three-quarters of a century between the first edition of Theodor Nöldeke's history and the appearance of Richard Bell's translation, and it may well be as long again before the latter's work is superseded.

BIBLIOGRAPHICAL NOTE

The following articles by Dr. Richard Bell are relevant to the subject of this article:

'Muhammad's Pilgrimage Proclamation,' *Journal of the Royal Asiatic Society* (1937), 233 ff.

'Who were the Ḥanīfs?', *Moslem World,* xx (1930), 120 ff.

'A duplicate in the Koran; the composition of Surah xxiii', *MW.*, xviii (1928), 227-33.

'The Men on the A'rāf' (vii, 44), *MW.*, xxii (1932).

'The Origin of the 'īd al-aḍḥā', *MW.*, xxiii (1933), 117 ff.

'Muhammad's Call', *MW.*, xxiv (1934), 13 ff.

'Muhammad's Visions', *MW.*, xxiv (1934), 145 ff.

'Muhammad and the previous Messengers', *MW.*, xxiv (1934), 330-40.

'Muhammad and Divorce in the Qur'an', *MW.*, (1939), 55-62.

'Sūrat al-Ḥashr' (lix), *MW.*, xxxviii (1948).

'The Beginnings of Muhammad's Religious Activity', *Transactions of the*

Glasgow University Oriental Society, vii, 16-24.
'The Sacrifice of Ishmael', *TGUOS.*, x, 29-31.
'The Style of the Qur'ān', *TGUOS.*, xi, 9 ff.
'Muhammad's Knowledge of the Old Testament', *Studia Semitica et Orientalia,* ii, Glasgow, 1945.

A4. Conversion in Islam at the Time of the Prophet

A study of conversion in Islam during Muḥammad's lifetime immediately runs into a serious difficulty. The idea of conversion in the strict sense does not occur in Islam. Of course, changes of religious allegiance occur. Christians, atheists and pagans become Muslims, and occasionally Muslims become Christians; but no single Arabic word covers all these cases. Islamic thought makes an absolute distinction between what we would call conversion to Islam and conversion from Islam. The former is described as *islām* (surrender to God) and *ihtidā'* (following guidance), whereas the latter is *irtidād* (apostasy). The two are not even regarded as two species of the genus 'change of religion'. The simplest way of studying the topic will therefore be, firstly, to consider how the Qur'ān conceives what happens when, as we say, a man becomes Muḥammad's follower or attaches himself to Muḥammad's religion; and secondly, to consider further material from the Sīra or biography of Muḥammad.

In the earliest passages of the Qur'ān there is no thought of a man changing from one religious community to another. The relevant question is whether he is going to respond or fail to respond to God's message as delivered by Muḥammad, whether he is going to count it true or count it false. Thus in Sūrat Quraysh (106) the citizens of Mecca, in thanksgiving for their prosperity, are called upon to 'worship the Lord of this House' (*fa-l-ya'budu rabba hādhā l-bayt*). It is worth looking at this verse more closely. It is almost certainly very early, and 'the House' is universally taken to be the Ka'ba at Mecca. Since the verse is included in the Qur'ān, Muslims must have identified the Lord of the House with God (*Allāh*); yet the phrase must also have indicated to contemporaries the deity (or the principal deity) already worshippepd at the Ka'ba. There is no question of conversion here. Indeed, to call upon the people of Mecca to worship the deity whom they already worship is not, it would appear, a summons to a revolutionary change of religion. As one reflects, one rather wonders whether there is any novelty at all in this sūra. I believe that there is, and that reasons can be given for such a view.

Though our knowledge of religious conditions in Mecca at this period is meagre, it can be inferred from Arabic poetry that practice of the traditional religion – about whose gods we know a little – was now vestigial. This is not surprising since it was essentially the religion of agricultural people and had little relevance to nomads. There was just sufficient life in the old religion for Muḥammad's opponents to attempt to stir up religious feelings against him. It may further be inferred from the Qur'ān that some of Muḥammad's Meccan contemporaries were coming to regard *Allāh* as a 'high god', transcending the deities worshipped in various local shrines but somewhat remote (Watt, 1971). That many Meccans should thus believe in a 'high god' is fully in accordance with the fact that belief in a 'high god' or 'a supreme god' was at this period widespread throughout the Fertile Crescent (Teixidor). The story of the 'satanic verses' is relevant here (Watt, 1953: 101-7). This story can hardly be an invention since it appears in the *Tafsīr* of al-Ṭabarī and other commentaries of the Qur'ān as an explanation of the phrase (22.52/51) about Satan 'throwing' or 'introducing' something to meet a prophet's wish. For a time Muḥammad accepted as a genuine revelation certain verses approving prayers to local deities; presumably he regarded these as a kind of angel who might be asked to intercede with the 'high god'. Subsequently, however, he realized that these verses were incompatible with strict monotheism and had been intruded by Satan.

With these points in mind the element of novelty in Sūrat Quraysh may be discerned. While there may have been a handful of genuine monotheists in Mecca, the summons to worship is best understood as addressed to those who regarded 'the Lord of this House' as the 'high god'. The wording of the sūra implies that this 'high god' is no remote being who may be neglected with impunity in many cases, but is the source of the material prosperity of the Meccans. That God is both all-powerful and beneficent to man is one of the dominant themes of the early passages of the Qur'ān, and has consequences which are little short of revolutionary. This then is the element of novelty in Sūrat Quraysh, but it is presented as a kind of expansion of an important strand in contemporary thought, so that *prima facie* no change of religion or even of direction is involved.

It was only gradually that Muḥammad's followers came to be marked off from other members of the Meccan community. The term *muslim*, and the corresponding noun *islām* as a name for the religion, are possibly not used in the Qur'ān until about the second year after the Hijra, and certainly did not at first have the full technical meaning. The term *mu'minūn*, 'believers', is both earlier and more frequently used, occurring 179 times in the Qur'ān as against 37 occurrences of *muslimūn*. For a short period the term *ḥanīf* was employed – a point to be discussed presently.

The earliest word, however, to describe the religious and moral practices of Muḥammad's followers was the verb *tazakkā* and the verbal noun *al-tazakkī* (but the corresponding participle is not found in the Qur'ān) (Watt, 1953, 165-9). The word is difficult to translate. The common renderings 'purify', 'give alms', 'purify by almsgiving' do not fit all the instances. A commentator Ibn Zayd, quoted by al-Ṭabarī on 79.18, asserts that everywhere in the Qur'ān *tazakkī* signifies *islām*; and in the Meccan period this presumably means no more than the distinctive practices of Muḥammad's followers. An examination of the various instances of the word (20.76/78; 35.18/19; 79.18; 80.3, 7; 87.14; 92.18) suggests that there is no necessary connection with almsgiving or ritual purity but that it connotes aiming at moral purity or uprightness. The aim of Muḥammad's preaching appears to be to bring about a man's *tazakkī* (80;79); and *tazakkī* leads to prosperity in the fullest sense, and to Paradise (20). Other aspects of the practice of Muḥammad's followers at Mecca are named in 87.14, 15: 'Prospered has he who *tazakkā*, and mentions (*dhakara*) the name of his Lord and worships (*ṣallā*)'. In all this, however, there is nothing that requires anything like conversion in new adherents, though *tazakkī* may have included some definite act marking a break with the past.

Eventually the new religious movement roused oposition against Muḥammad. From a relatively early period there had been passive opposition, that is, failure to respond to Muḥammad's message; and the Qur'ān says (96.6, 7) that this is because man is presumptuous (*yaṭghā*) and prides himself on his wealth (*istaghnā*). This moves towards the denial of the truth of the messages (*takdhīb* – counting false) and unbelief (*kufr* – with a suggestion of ingratitude). The contrasted attitude is described by such words as *īmān* (faith), *taṣdīq* (counting true) and *hudā* (guidance). In accordance with this line of thought Muḥammad's function is described as that of being a 'warner' (*nadhīr*), that is, one who warns of impending punishment, whether temporal or eschatological, for conduct opposed to *tazakkī*.

Passive opposition was eventually supplemented by active opposition, that is, attempts to stop the practice of the new religion. Men were forcibly prevented from praying (96.9f.), or were incarcerated by their families. Muḥammad himself was subjected to many petty vexations, and was eventually deprived of the clan-protection without which he could not go on proclaiming his religion in Mecca. The coolness between Muḥammad and the pagan Meccans became a complete break. The 'satanic verses' were annulled, and prayers to local deities forbidden. It was insisted that there is no deity apart from *Allāh*, the 'high god', God. This break with the pagans is marked by such sūras as 109 and 112. The practices of Muḥammad and his followers are now described as his *dīn* or 'religion' (or 'way of life'); he is to say to the unbelievers, 'you have your *dīn* and I mine' (109.6).

This break with the pagans meant that Muḥammad's followers were now marked off from the rest of the community. They had to stand up to be counted; and they might be cold-shouldered by their family and friends and even made to suffer. Apart from uprightness of life and common worship we know little about their way of life. Yet it is clear that by this time adherence to Muḥammad's movement meant a great change for a man – nothing less than a break with his previous way of life. Whether the change was marked by any specific act it is difficult to say. It seems most likely that the mark of adherence was participation in the common worship. Men may also have been asked informally to indicate their acceptance of the first part of the Shahāda, namely, 'there is no deity but God'; but in the Qur'ān this formula and its variants are generally used either to instruct pagans or to encourage Muḥammad and his followers. Thus 37.35/34 runs: 'When it was said to them, "there is no deity but God", they would become arrogant and say "shall we leave our deities for a distraught poet?"'

The end result of the break with the pagans was that life in Mecca became virtually impossible for Muḥammad and his followers. When an opportunity presented itself of moving to Medina on favourable terms, he made the Hijra, and thereby found himself confronted by a community of Jews. From the first apparently Muḥammad had been led to regard the messages or revelations he received as identical in principle with the revelations to the Jews through Moses and to the Christians through Jesus. When he went to Medina he therefore expected the Jews there to accept him as a prophet and to believe the Qur'ān ; and he was surprised at their hesitation. Thus 2.40/38f. runs: 'O Israelites, remember the favour I have shown you and keep (your) covenant with me, and I shall keep (my) covenant with you . . . and believe in what I sent down confirming what (revelation) you have . . .' A later appeal to the Jews drops the request to believe in the Qur'ān and merely envisages some sort of mutual recognition: 'say "O People of the Book, come to a fair agreement between us and you, that we worship God alone, that we associate nothing with him, and that we do not take one another as Lords apart from God".'

The attempts to reach an understanding with the Jews lasted some eighteen months until just before the battle of Badr. At this point there was a series of policy changes, of which one was a complete break with the Jews, involving both the abandonment of efforts to reconcile them and the propagation of a new anti-Jewish apologetic. In this apologetic the figure of Abraham had a central part. The assertion of the Qur'ān is that he 'was neither Jew nor Christian, but a Ḥanīf, a Muslim, not one of the Polytheists' (3.67/60; cf. 1.135/129, 140/134, etc.). The main contentions were that Abraham was a prophet who had received revelations like Muḥammad, Moses and the others, and that the community of Abraham's followers had disappeared and that the Jews and Christians, though they had received basically the same revelation, had turned away from it in various points. The deviance of the Jews and

Christians was supported by various arguments; for example, since both claimed a monopoly of truth, they contradicted one another (2.111/105 – 113/107). This leaves the way open for the claim that Muḥammad and his followers are reviving the true and pure religion of Abraham (2.130/124, 135/129).

Of the two words applied to Abraham in 3.67/60 the first, Ḥanīf, is found only twelve times in the Qur'ān, and always has the general sense of 'a believer in one God', being contrasted with the *mushrikūn* or Polytheists. It is specially associated with Abraham, however, in the passages expounding the new apologetic just described, and thus has the connotation 'a believer in one God who is not a Jew or a Christian'. Though rare in the Qur'ān the word is important in Islamic history and seems for a considerable period to have been accepted as a normal way of describing Muḥammad's followers. Ibn Mas'ūd had the variant *ḥanīfiyya* for *islām* in 3.19/17, reading: 'the true religion in God's sight is the *ḥanīfiyya*'. The abandonment of the usage is probably due to Christian mockery, since the plural was virtually identical with a cognate Syriac word meaning 'pagans'. There is no record of *ḥanīf* in Arabic before the Qur'ān. Some Arabs were certainly moving towards monotheism, but there is no evidence that they applied this word to themselves (Watt, 1971: 6).

With regard to the other term, *muslim*, the verb *aslama* of which it is a participle occurs in pre-Islamic Arabic. After a careful examination of instances Helmer Ringgren (22) concluded that the usual meaning was 'to abandon something, to give something up, to let something loose entirely'. In the Qur'ān, however, it occurs only in a religious sense, gradually acquiring a technical meaning. Mostly it is used absolutely, but a few verses have the phrase *aslama wajha-hu li-llāh* (or *ilā llāh*). Here *wajha* is equivalent to *nafs*, 'self', so that the phrase means 'he gave himself up, or committed himself, entirely to God'. There is also sometimes an explicit contrast between the *muslim* and the *mushrikūn* or Polytheists (cf. 3.67/60; 6/14; etc.). A Muslim is thus someone who acknowledges God alone. Unlike the term Ḥanīf, however, Muslim implies no contrast with Judaism and Christianity. Islam is the true monotheism, and to it are regarded as belonging such persons as Solomon and the Queen of Sheba (27.44/45) and the disciples of Jesus (3.52/45; 5.111).

There has been some discussion of the date at which the terms Islam and Muslim began to be used. Karl Ahrens (112f.) and Richard Bell (108; Watt, 1970: 119) took the view that these words were used only at a relatively late period. There are weaknesses in the argument owing to the uncertainty of the date of particular verses, but some weight must be given to the general consideration that Muslim appears to have replaced Hanīf and is much less frequent in the Qur'ān than *mu'min*, 'believer'. The opponents of Ahrens and Bell quote verses which appear to be early; but it is probable that in these *aslama* was being used in a general rather than a technical sense. No more need be said here, since this controversy does not affect the points at issue, namely, (1) that at some date in the Meccan period there was a complete break with the pagans who acknowledged *Allāh* as 'high god', and (2) about the year 2 there was a break with the Jews of Medina.

The corollary of the break with the Jews was that the followers of Muḥammad had to be regarded as in some sense a distinct community – 'we have made you a middle (intermediate) community' (2.143/137). It might have been expected that this would lead to a man's adherence to Muḥammad's movement being regarded as not merely a response to God but also as joining a community; but there is no clear evidence of this, though there is some expression of concern for the unity of the community (e.g. 3.103/98 – 110/106). What we find, however, is that membership of the community is indicated by the external marks of performing the ritual worship and giving alms – 'if they repent and perform the prayer and give alms, they are your brothers in religion' (3.11, of Jews or pagans; cf. 3.5).

These general considerations from the Qur'ān about the nature of conversion or the manner in which a man expressed his adherence to Muḥammad's religion may be supplemented by a selection of the accounts of how men responded or failed to respond to the divine summons. We may begin with some of the negative responses.

Pharaoh: (God said to Moses) 'Go to Pharaoh, that presumptuous man, and say, "Have you a will for *al-tazakkī*, and that I guide you to your Lord and you fear him?" And he showed him the greatest sign; but he counted him false and disobeyed'. (79.17-21)

Noah's people: 'Noah we sent to his people, saying, "O my people, serve God, apart from whom you have no god; (otherwise) I fear for you the punishment of a great day." The council of his people said, "We see you in clear error." He said "O my people, in me is no error, but as messenger from the Lord of the worlds I bring you the messages of my Lord and counsel you, knowing from God what you do not know. Do you wonder that an admonition from your Lord comes to you by a man of your (number), that he warns you, and that to you, fearing God, mercy mayhap will be shown?" Yet they counted him false; and him and those with him we saved in the ark, but drowned those counting false our signs, a blind people they.' (7.59/57 – 64/62)

Abraham's father: '(Abraham) said to his father, "O my father, why do you serve what neither hears nor sees nor avails you aught? O my father, knowledge has come to me which has not come to you; so follow me and I shall guide you in a straight path. O my father, do not serve Satan, for Satan is disobedient to the Merciful. O my father, I fear lest punishment from the Merciful grip you, and you become close to Satan." (His father) said, "Do you turn away from my gods, Abraham? If you do not desist, I swear I shall stone you. Begone awhile."' (19.42/43-46/47)

A positive example – Jesus and his apostles: (Jesus concluded an appeal to the children of Israel with the words) '"I have come to you with a sign from your Lord; so fear God and obey me. God is my Lord and your Lord, so serve him; this is a straight path." When he perceived in them unbelief, he said, "We are God's helpers, we believe in God; testify that we are *muslimūn* (? wholly devoted to God)."' (3.50/44-52/45)

The Queen of Sheba: (On coming to Solomon and seeing a marvellous throne identical with her own – really her own brought by spirits – she was impressed) 'What she worshipped apart from God had barred (the way) to her; she was of an unbelieving people. One said to her, "Enter the palace." She thought it had a pool and uncovered her legs. (Solomon) said, "It is a palace paved with glass." She said, "O my Lord, I have wronged myself; to God the Lord of the worlds with Solomon I make submission (*aslamtu*)."' (27.43-44/45)

Turning away from Islam or ceasing to be a Muslim is, of course, seldom mentioned in the Qur'ān. Such references as there are employ non-technical phrases such as 'they will make you unbelievers after your believing' (*yaruddū-kum ba'da īmāni-kum kāfirīn*; 3.100/95; cf. 106/102). The verb *irtadda*, which occurs non-technically in the sense of 'turning back' (of physical movement), is sometimes used metaphorically of religion; e.g. 'those who turned away backwards after guidance was made clear to them' (*alladhīna rtaddū 'alā adbāri-him min ba'di mā tabayyana la-humu l-hudā*, 47.25/27); 'he from among you who turns back from his religion' (*man yartadid min-kum 'an dīni-hi*, 2.217/214; cf. 3.54/59).

The fate of apostates is grim but not hopeless. 'How shall God guide a people who disbelieved after their believing, and after they testified that the Messenger is true and there came to them the evidences; God does not guide wicked people. The recompense of these men is that upon them is the curse of God and angels and mankind together, they being eternally in (the fire), their punishment not being lightened for them nor respite granted, except for those who have repented afterwards and amended (their lives); God is forgiving, compassionate.' (3.86/80-89/93)

This material from the Qur'ān, despite occasional difficulties in interpretation, is the best evidence of how conversion to Islam was conceived during Muḥammad's lifetime. In the *Sīra* of Ibn Hishām there are stories of conversions, but these, even though true in general, may have had details modified to bring them into line with later ideas. Nevertheless many of these stories roughly confirm the picture given by the Qur'ān. A man is impressed by something or other, or is roused to action, and publicly states his adhesion to Muḥammad's religion. Ḥamza was incensed when he heard how Abū Jahl had insulted his nephew

Muḥammad, and at once went to the Ka'ba and struck Abū Jahl, saying 'you insult him, when I am of his religion and hold his views?' (185). 'Umar ibn al-Khaṭṭāb was angry to learn that his sister had become a Muslim, but greatly impressed by the verbal beauty of the Qur'ān, so that he decided to become a Muslim and went to Muḥammad with the words, 'O Messenger of God, I have come to you to believe in God, in his Messenger and in what has come from God' (227). When some pagans alleged that he had apostatized (*ṣaba'a*), 'Umar said, 'I have become a Muslim (*aslamtu*), and I bear witness that there is no deity but God, and that Muḥammad is his servant and Messenger' (229). 'Umayr ibn Wahb accepted Islam when he found that his secret plan to murder Muḥammad was known to him; he said, 'I testify that you are the Messenger of God; praise be to God who has guided me to Islam' (472f.).

In such stories we find evidence for the principle that what made a man a Muslim was repetition of the Shahāda. The case of 'Umar has just been mentioned. Another instance mentioned by al-Wāqidī (857), is Habbār, who was proscribed at the conquest of Mecca because he had been responsible for Muḥammad's daughter Zaynab having a miscarriage (and so was regarded as liable for blood); he made his way unobserved into Muḥammad's presence and, before any steps could be taken against him, said, 'I have come acknowledging Islam; I testify that there is no deity but God alone and no partner to him, and that Muḥammad is his servant and Messenger.' On at least one occasion repetition of the Fātiha (here called *umm al-kitāb*) was made the test of being a Muslim (al-Wāqidī, 558). On the other hand, a man who had died before the Hijra was claimed by his clan as a Muslim because he had praised and glorified God (Ibn Hishām, 286). Ibn Hishām (818) uses the phrase *irtadda mushrikan* for 'apostatized'.

This brings to an end the presentation of material, and it only remains to offer some general reflections by way of conclusion. There is no general idea of 'conversion' in Arabic, and therefore the plan of this paper has been to look at the developing conception of Qur'ānic religion in order to see at each stage how the act of adhesion to this religion was conceived. Throughout the material the idea of entering a community of believers or of changing from one religious community to another was secondary. The primary thought was that a man is responding to the demand of God as mediated by a prophet. It is further to be noted that this response is always described in external terms, and no attention is paid to the man's inner experiences. This is in accordance with the general outlook of the Arabs and other Semites. It has to be borne in mind, however, that, when tribes wanted to claim that some of their members had been Muslims at an early date (Watt, 1956: 80, 114), they took the slightest external signs as evidence of the inner response, thereby apparently implying that the inner response was the essential thing.

WORKS CONSULTED

Ahrens, Karl (1935) *Muhammed als Religionsstifter*. Leipzig

Bell, Richard (1953) *Introduction to the Qur'*ān. Edinburgh; Edinburgh University Press. (See also Watt, 1970)

Ibn Hishām *Sira* (ed. F. Wüstenfeld). Leipzig: Göttingen: Dieterichsche Universitäts-Buchhandlung.

Qur'ān (Verse-numbers according to the standard Egyptian edition; where Flügel's number differs it is given after a stroke)

Ringgren, Helmer (1949) 'Islam, *'aslama and muslim'*. *Horae Soederblomianae*, Uppsala: Gleerup. 2.1-34.

(al) Ṭabarī *Ṭafsīr* (various editions)

Teixidor, Javier (1977) *The Pagan God: Popular Religion in the Greco-Roman Near East*. Princeton: Princeton University Press.

(al-)Wāqidī (1966) *Kitāb al-maghāzī* (ed. Marsden Jones). London: Oxford University Press.

Watt, W. Montgomery (1953) *Muhammad at Mecca*. Oxford: Clarendon Press.

— (1956) *Muhammad at Medina*. Oxford: Clarendon Press.

— (1966) 'Ḥanīf'. *Encyclopaedia of Islam* (second edition). Leiden: Brill. Vol. 3.

— (1970) *Bell's Introduction to the Qur'*ān (revised and enlarged edition of Bell, 1953). Edinburgh: Edinburgh University Press.

— (1971) 'The "high god" in pre-Islamic Mecca.' *Journal of Semitic Studies* 16:35-40. (Also in *Actes du Ve congrès international d'arabisants et d'islamisants (Bruxelles, 1970)*, 499-505; and in the *Acta* of the 12th Congress of the International Association for the History of Religions (Stockholm, 1970) (published 1975, Leiden: Brill), 228-234.)

A5. His Name is Ahmad

A recent article in *The Muslim World*[24] makes the suggestion that the words in Sūra 61.6 *ismu-hu aḥmadu*, commonly taken to mean 'his (or whose) name is Aḥmad', were interpolated into the text of the Qur'ān some time after the death of Muḥammad. The following notes call attention to certain points which tend to confirm and extend this line of thought.

§1. THE USE OF THE NAME 'AḤMAD'

As soon as one starts to inquire into the use of the name 'Aḥmad' in the early centuries of Islam, a striking fact emerges. Muslim children were practically never called Aḥmad before about the year 125 A.H. Indeed, the point may be put even more strongly: *it is impossible to prove that any Muslim child was called Aḥmad after the Prophet before about the year 125.* On the other hand, there are many instances prior to this date of boys called Muḥammad after the Prophet; some of these had apparently received that name during the Prophet's lifetime. Some of the evidence for these statements may be briefly set out as follows.

(a) A rough indication is given by the indices of the names occurring in books written at an early date or dealing only with early events. Thus, if we look at the French translation of *Kitāb al-Kharāj* by Abū Yūsuf, which must be prior to his death in 182/798, we find that the index contains the names of 29 persons called Muḥammad, other than the Prophet, but does not mention anyone called Aḥmad. Again, in Wellhausen's version of al-Wāqidī (who died in 207/823), the index of those who transmitted material contains 36 Muḥammads but no Aḥmad. Likewise, the index to Wellhausen's *Arab Kingdom and its Fall* (Eng. tr.), a history of the Umayyad period which ended in 132/750, has 14 Muḥammads but no Aḥmad. If in the fields and periods covered by these indices there is no one at all called Aḥmad, there is a strong presumption that the same is true in all spheres.

(b) Biographical dictionaries such as the *Ṭabaqāt* of Ibn Saʿd contain many Muḥammads who died before 200 A.H. but hardly any Aḥmads. Some of the Muḥammads died in the first century, but the earliest Aḥmads are only a few years before 200. I have made a detailed examination of *Tahdhīb al-Tahdhīb* by Ibn Ḥajar al-ʿAsqalānī which contains 160 entries for Aḥmad and 888 for Muḥammad. Some of the entries are cross-references, and others concern names about which little is known; but for 103 of the Aḥmads a date of death is given. Of this hundred only one, no. 16, died before 200; and his *obiit* was 197. It is also clear that none of the undated persons could have been much earlier. In order, however, to ensure that the impression given by these facts is not a distortion of reality owing to the specialized character of the dictionary, I also examined the first 25 Muḥammads whose death-date was given (omitting those whose father was Aḥmad and who would therefore be late in date) – this covered nos. 1-27 and 39-57. Seven had died before 200, namely in the years 63, 119-21, 125-6, 151, 182, 182, 193-4 (the hyphens indicate the limits where more than one version of the figure is given). If this is a fair sample of the Muḥammads, then 28% of them died before 200, as against 1% of the Aḥmads. Moreover it is clear that, while the *Tahdhīb* deals mainly with persons who died during the third Islamic century, it has a sprinkling of names from the earlier centuries. The absence of Aḥmads during the early period thus gives rise to a strong presumption that there were none or practically none, and that the name was not in use. From death-dates a little before 200 we may assume births between 120 and 140, and may therefore argue that Muslim boys did not begin to receive the name of Aḥmad (as commemorating the Prophet) until about 125 A.H.

(c) The name Aḥmad, like Muḥammad, occurred in the Jāhiliyya. (G. A. Fischer, 'Muḥammad und Aḥmad', *Sächsische Akademie der Wissenschaften*, Leipzig, 1932 pp. 19, 25.) The solitary instance in Ibn al-Athīr's *Usd al-Ghāba* is one Aḥmad b. Ḥafṣ b. al-Mughīra al-Makhzūmī, a cousin of Khālid b. al-Walīd and Abū Jahl, whose age and family makes it impossible for him to have been called after Muḥammad. There is also the blind Abū Aḥmad b. Jaḥsh, but his *kunya*, by which he is commonly known, cannot have any reference to the Prophet, since, had there been such a reference, the fact would have been commented on in our sources. This use of Aḥmad in the Jāhiliya means that any isolated instances of Aḥmads earlier than those in Ibn Ḥajar's *Tahdhīb* would not necessarily refer to the Prophet. Thus in order to refute the point being made in these notes an opponent would not merely have to produce some Aḥmads in the first and early second century, but would have to show, or at least make it seem probable, that in each case the name was given with reference to the Prophet and was not just a continuation of pre-Islamic usage.

(d) It is now generally recognized that the name Muḥammad was in common use in the Jāhiliyya. The Prophet sometimes changed names; he would substitute 'Abdallāh, 'servant of God', for a name meaning a servant of some pagan deity. But in the case of the prominent Companion, Muḥammad b. Maslama al-Anṣārī, for instance, there is nothing to suggest any change of name. The report, that in the sixth century A.D. a number of boys were given the name Muḥammad because men had heard that there was to be a prophet of that name, need not be taken seriously.[25] Even during the Prophet's lifetime, however, some of his devoted followers called their children after him, as the pages of Ibn Saʿd show. In the first *ṭabaqa* or class of Followers in Medina there are several Muḥammads. In connection with one of them, Muḥammad b. ʿAmr b. Ḥazm al-Anṣārī, who is said to have been born in 10 A.H. and to have been given the name by express permission of the Prophet, a story is told; at some time during his caliphate ʿUmar gathered together all those called Muḥammad and told them to change their name, but they managed to prove they were entitled to use it, and the matter was dropped.[26] This indicates opposition to the use of the Prophet's name, but not necessarily at the ostensible date. Tor Andrae mentions the belief that angels pray in every house where there is an Aḥmad or a Muḥammad;[27] and it may be that the opposition to the use of the Prophet's name (and especially to the union of his name and *kunya*) is due to superstitions attached to the practice. There was a general movement, however, for the use of specifically Islamic names – names of Qur'ānic prophets, prominent Companions, and the like – and the many Muḥammads met with in history during the first and second centuries shows that the opposition was unavailing.

(e) The fact that Ibn Saʿd thinks it worth including three traditions to the effect that the Prophet's name was Aḥmad is an indication that this had not always been obvious; there are no similar traditions about his name being Muḥammad.[28] Of these traditions the second and third are as follows: 'Āminah, when pregnant with the Messenger of God, was told to call his name Aḥmad'; 'the Messenger of God said, I was called Aḥmad'. Immediately after this Ibn Saʿd places seven traditions about the 'names' of the Messenger of God, each of which has about half a dozen 'names'. There are variations of detail in the lists, but each begins with 'Muḥammad, Aḥmad, . . .' The point to notice is that, even if the traditions contain ancient material, the name Aḥmad could easily have been added at a later time.

All these points together make a strong case for holding that the name Aḥmad was not given to Muslim children as an alternative to Muḥammad until about 125 A.H. It remains to consider possible explanations of this fact.

§2. THE INTERPRETATION OF SŪRA 61.6

The article in *The Muslim World* from which these notes took their origin suggested that the words *ismu-hu aḥmadu* were a later interpolation. Such a view has its attraction, but it is also not without difficulty; for example, the more obvious interpolation would have been Muḥammad.

What the authors of the article were contending for could perhaps be secured by a simpler supposition, namely, that for the first century or so of Islam the word *aḥmadu* was regarded not as a proper name but as a simple adjective. This is quite possible. Lane discusses an Arab proverb containing the word as an adjective, and gives as possible meanings: more attributive of praise (to a thing); gaining more praise for oneself; more deserving of being praised. The clause in question can then be translated 'announcing the good tidings of a messenger who will come after me whose name is more worthy of praise'. It is just conceivable that this might be a confused reference to the words 'greater works than these shall he do' (*John*, xiv. 12). Alternatively, if *aḥmadu* is taken to mean more attributive of praise, there might be a reference to the words 'He shall glorify me' (*John,* xvi. 14).

Whether we adopt the interpolation hypothesis, or suppose *aḥmadu* to have been interpreted as a simple adjective, there are strong grounds for holding that the standard interpretation of the words *ismu-hu aḥmadu* was not commonly accepted by Muslims until after the first half of the second century. Messrs. Guthrie and Bishop found their case largely on the absence of any mention of Aḥmad in Ibn Isḥāq (d. 151/767) although he has a passage about the Paraclete in which he might have been expected to mention this had he known it. Confirmation of the point is found in the fact that al-Ṭabarī in his commentary on 61.29 though himself giving the orthodox interpretation, is unable to quote any earlier commentator as authority for it. As he is in the habit of giving strings of authorities for very slight matters, it is reasonable to suppose that he knew of no reputable exegete who had held what was in his time the standard and obvious view.

On the other hand, the passage in the *Sīra* shows that the New Testament prediction of the Paraclete had been applied to Muḥammad before the middle of the second century. Moreover, if we assume (as we ought), that Ibn Isḥāq is the author of the closing comment, then by this time the confusion of *paraklētos* with *periklutos* had taken place, for he notes that *muḥammad* is linguistically equivalent to the 'Syrian' *manḥamannā* and the Greek *baraqlīṭis*. With this must be compared, however, the first of Ibn Sa'd's traditions about the name Aḥmad, which he has from Muḥammad b. Ismā'īl b. Abī Fudayk al-Madanī (d. 199-201), who had it from Mūsā b. Ya'qūb al-Zam'ī (d.c. 153 -8), who had it from Sahl, the *mawlā* of 'Uthayma (about neither of whom have I discovered anything):

> he was a Christian of the people of Marīs and used to read the Gospel; and he mentioned that the description of the Prophet (God bless and preserve him) was in the Gospel; he was of the seed of Ishmael, his name Aḥmad.

This is an abbreviated version of a tradition [31] belonging to a group dealing with the description of Muḥammad in the Torah and the Gospel, and too much weight should not be attached to it. Yet it is by no means impossible that Mūsā b. Yaʿqūb did in fact pass on this information which he alleged he had received from a convert from Christianity. If that is so, then we may infer that the use of the name Aḥmad in connection with the Gospel predictions was known in Ibn Isḥāq's time, since Mūsā was roughly his contemporary. It is therefore conceivable that Ibn Isḥāq omitted a reference to the name of Aḥmad not because he was ignorant, but because he disapproved of this interpretation of the Qur'ānic verse. ʿAlī b. Rabbān al-Ṭabarī in *Kitāb al-Dīn wa-'l-Dawla* (232-247 A.H.) refers to certain of the passages about the Paraclete as predictions of Muḥammad, and remarks: 'the Messiah was never called Fāraqlīṭ, but Muḥammad was called by this name'.[32] Once again Aḥmad is not mentioned, but that may be because he is basing his argument on Christian sources. (The passage about the Paraclete in *The Apology of Timothy*[33] which is dated 165/781, also omits all mention of Aḥmad.)

The conclusion to which this points is that the identification of Muḥammad with the Paraclete is logically independent of any use of the name Aḥmad. The argument may run: Jesus foretold the coming of the Paraclete, and Paraclete and Muḥammad are the same in meaning. After all, Muḥammad is just as good a translation of *periklutos* as Aḥmad.

The course of events may now be reconstructed somewhat as follows. In order to meet Christian criticisms of Islam some Muslims were looking for predictions of Muḥammad in the Christian scriptures, and noticed the passages about the Paraclete in *John* xiv-xvi. One of the arguments they adduced to support the identification of Muḥammad with the Paraclete was that of the similarity of meaning (which is based on the confusion of *paraklētos* with *periklutos*. When Sūra 61.6 was read with such a view in mind, the connection between Muḥammad and Aḥmad would readily be seen, even though *aḥmadu* at this time was normally taken as an adjective. It would be specially easy for anyone familiar with the pre-Islamic name of Aḥmad to make the connection. In this way a new link would be added which would make the argument particularly convincing for Muslims, for they would naturally be much more familiar with their own Scriptures than those of any other religion. The argument, with the reference to Aḥmad included, would therefore be prominent in anti-Christian polemics directed chiefly to Muslims and designed to protect their beliefs from Christian attacks. This would account for the popularity of the name Aḥmad soon after its introduction. On the other hand, the conservatism of the exegetes would explain, for example, the absence in al-Ṭabarī's commentary of early authorities for the connection of the name Aḥmad with the Paraclete.

Since the evidence for the identification of Muḥammad with the Paraclete is prior to and independent of any reference to Aḥmad, careful scholarship is not justified in going beyond the statements of the previous paragraph. Yet it is tempting to suppose – and by no means impossible – that it was reflection on Sūra 61.6 that first set a convert from Christianity, with a slight knowledge of Greek, on the track of the argument about similarity of meaning.

APPENDIX A. OTHER NAMES FROM THE ROOT ḤMD.

Among the pre-Islamic Arabs it was common for brothers to have variants of the same name, such as ʿUtba and ʿUtayba, Munabbih and Nubayh. The name 'Maḥmūd' was known as a variant of 'Muḥammad', since Muḥammad b. Maslama had a brother called Maḥmūd, presumably because of family tradition and not with reference to the Prophet.[11] Ḥumayd also seems to have been pre-Islamic, but it was doubtless in honour of Muḥammad that ʿAbd al-Raḥmān called a son Ḥumayd.[12] There is sometimes a certain confusion between the various names from the root. The two instances of Ḥamdān and one of Ḥamdūn in Ibn Ḥajar's *Tahdhīb* are said to stand for Aḥmad and Muḥammad respectively, and the solitary man called Ḥammād in Ibn al-Athīr's *Usd al-Ghāba* is also spoken of as Muḥammad.

The following table shows the relative frequency of the various names. The gross number of entries is given in the case of the biographical dictionaries – Ibn Ḥajar's *Tahdhīb (Tah.)* and Ibn al-Athīr's *Usd al-Ghāba (Usd)*. The number of distinct persons mentioned in the index is given for the other works: Abū Yūsuf's *K. al-Kharāj* (ed. Fagnan)(=AY); Wellhausen, *Arab Kingdom and its Fall* (AKF); al-Wāqidī, ed. Wellhausen, Actors (WWA) and Transmitters (WWT), Ibn Hishām (IH); and Ibn Saʿd, index to the Matn, ix (3) (IS). Where 'Abū' is neglected in the index, it is included in the count (apart from Abū Muḥammad in IS); thus the simple occurrence of Aḥmad in Ibn Hishām is Abū Aḥmad b. Jaḥsh.

Name	AY	AKF	WWA	WWT	IH	Usd	IS	Tah
Aḥmad					1	1	8	164
Ḥāmid						1		2
Ḥammād	1					1	7	26
Ḥamdān, Ḥamdūn							3	
Ḥumayd	5	1	2	1		5	14	35
Maḥmūd	1		1	2	2	6	3	12
Muḥammad	29	14	1	36	6	73	c.100	888

When the instances in Ibn Ḥajar are further analysed, interesting results are obtained. The following table gives (a) the total number of persons whose *obiit* is explicitly stated by Ibn Ḥajar, (b) the number whose *obiit* is before 200 A.H., and (c) the actual dates of the latter group. For 'Muḥammad' the figures are those of the sample examined.

Name	Total (a)	1-200 (b)	Actual Dates (c)
Aḥmad	103	1	197
Ḥamid	2	0	–
Ḥammād	8	3	119-20, 168, 179
Ḥumayd	9	6	95-105, 130-6, 142, 142-3, 189-92 (2)
Maḥmūd	6	2	96, 99
Muḥammad	(25)	(7)	(63, 119-21, 125-6, 131, 182(2), 193-4)

These two tables, especially the second, make it quite clear that Ḥammād, Ḥumayd and Maḥmūd were in use in the first and early second century, at a time when Aḥmad was not being used. The use of Ḥumayd and Maḥmūd may owe something to pre-Islamic usage, but cannot be entirely attributed to this, as the case of ʿAbd al-Raḥmān's son shows. The use of Ḥammād is almost certainly purely Islamic; the occurrence of the name in Ibn al-Athīr is based on a tradition which seems to have been invented to justify using Ḥammād as a variant for Muḥammad. This serves to heighten the mystery surrounding the name 'Aḥmad'.

B. POSSIBLE EARLY INSTANCES OF THE USE OF 'AḤMAD'.

There is an early instance of a person apparently called Aḥmad in Ibn Saʿd, i/2. 139.7 where Abū Ṣakhr is addressed by Ibn Qusayṭ as 'Aḥmad'. It is clear, however, from Ibn Ḥajar's article on Yazīd b. ʿAbdallāh b. Qusayṭ that the proper name of the Abū Ṣakhr whom he knew was Ḥumayd b. Ziyād al-Kharrāṭ, who died 189-92. Hence we may either suppose that the text has been corrupted, or that by 160 or 170 Aḥmad had become a recognised variant of Ḥumayd. This latter would be analogous to addressing as 'Bess' a girl commonly known as 'Betty'.

In Ibn Hishām there are two instances that I have noticed of apparently contemporary references to Muḥammad as Aḥmad, viz. 799.6 from foot, and 995.10. (I have subsequently seen the much fuller list given by Omar A. Farrukh, *Das Bild des Frühislam in der arabischen Dichtung*, Leipzig, 1937, pp. 45-6; several of his examples appear to be authentic.) The former is in a poem attributed to Ḥassān b. Thābit commemorating those who fell at Mu'ta. The poem can hardly be authentic, however; Muḥammad is given an undignified position as merely one of a row of members of the house of Hāshim; and al-ʿAbbās and ʿAqīl are praised although at the date of the battle they were still in Mecca. This is therefore presumably ʿAbbāsid propaganda of the late first or early second century.

On the other hand, there are no obvious reasons for considering the other instance unauthentic. An obscure poetess speaks of a man counting false the religion of God and 'the man Aḥmad'. It looks then, as if we should have to admit an occasional reference to the Prophet as Aḥmad *in poetry*, for the sake of the metre, from his own life-time onwards. A little reflection shows that this is not inconsistent with the main thesis of the article. Aḥmad means 'more or most praised' whereas Muḥammad merely means 'praised'. There would be nothing improper in a poet calling the Prophet 'most praised', but, so long as Aḥmad was not commonly recognized as the Prophet's name outside poetry, to give an ordinary Muslim the name Aḥmad would have the appearance of setting him above the Prophet.

A6. The Camel and the Needle's Eye

It is well known that the Gospel phrase about the camel passing through the eye of the needle (*Matthew*, 19.24; *Mark* 10.25; *Luke*, 18.25) has a parallel in Qur'ān 7.40/38. This verse runs:

> For those who disbelieve our signs and disdain them the gates of heaven will not be opened nor will they enter paradise until the camel passes through the eye of the needle (*ḥattā yalija l-jamalu fī sammi l-khiyāṭi*).

It is also well known that two interpretations of the word 'camel' are to be found in the commentaries on the Gospels; it may mean either the animal or a thick rope. It is not so well known that these two interpretations are also to be found in commentaries on the Qur'ān. The purpose of the present brief article is to call attention to this curious fact and to discuss what signficance it may have.

The first point to note is that the interpretation of *kamēlos* as thick rope was known to Christian scholars long before the time of Muḥammad. There is a clear example in a book by Cyril of Alexandria (d. 444) in which he replies to the emperor Julian's attack on the Christians. In a Latin translation the passage runs:

> accipit ergo demonstrationem; foramen acus et camelus; non animal, ut opinatur Iulianus impius . . . sed potius rudens crassus qui in omni nave. Ita enim mos est nominandi iis qui docti sunt res nautarum.[34]

In a book of disputed authorship of about the same date, called *Tractatus de divitiis*, it is stated that *camelus* means *Nautica funis*. There are several other later instances. A full study of this question would indeed be interesting, but what has been said is sufficient for present purposes.

Next it may be noted that the eye of the needle was familiar to the Arabs as a metaphor for something difficult to find or to pass through. The word *khirrīt* means a skilful guide, and is said to get this meaning from the fact that such a man can slip through the eye of a needle (*khart al-ibra*).[35] This derivation of *khirrīt* is also mentioned by al-Zamakhsharī (on the verse under consideration) along with the proverb 'narrower than the eye of a needle' (*aḍyaq min khart al-ibra*). This is part of his defence of the obvious interpretation of the verse; for the needle's eye is the example *par excellence* of what is small and narrow and the camel of what is large and bulky. The opposing view, which he mentions, is that rope is more appropriate than the animal since rope and thread are things of the same sort. The metaphorical use of the needle's eye seems to have been widespread in the Middle East, for the Babylonian Talmud has the elephant passing through the needle's eye as a type of the impossible.

Against this background the long account in the *Tafsīr* of al-Tabarī may be examined. This contains thirty or thirty-one distinct 'reports', that is, statements of the view of an early commentator supported by an *isnād* or chain of transmitters. Several 'reports' may be of the view of the same commentator by different chains of transmitters. The transmitters do not necessarily agree with the views they report, for there are several instances, even in the 'reports' on this verse, of scholars transmitting contradictory views. Over half the reports here are of persons who adopt the view that the correct reading is *jamal* and that this means 'camel'. This is the view of 'Abd-Allāh ibn Mas'ūd (as transmitted by Ibrāhīm al-Nakha'ī – d. 715 – and Mujāhid), of al-Ḥasan al-Baṣrī (d. 728), of Abū'l-'Āliya (d. 711) and al-Ḍaḥḥāk (d. 723), as well as of Ibn 'Abbās, at least as reported by his son 'Alī and by the later scholar Ibn Sa'd. On the other hand, Ibn 'Abbās was reported by his pupils Mujāhid (d. 721) and 'Ikrima (d. 724) to have held that the reading was *jummal* meaning 'rope of a ship'. This is also said to have been the personal view of Mujāhid and 'Ikrima, except that in one report 'Ikrima is held to have said that it meant a rope for climbing palm trees. Another disciple of Ibn 'Abbās, Sa'īd ibn Jubayr (d. 713), read *jummal* according to one report and *jumal* according to another. It was suggested that the latter meant a collection of ropes or fibres, since the form *ajmala* can mean 'collect' or 'bring together'.

The reading *jumal* and other variants mentioned by al-Zamakhsharī and al-Bayḍāwī may be neglected, it is probable that *jumal* is produced by the desire to connect a strange word with an Arabic root. Thus the commentators may be said to be sharply divided between those who adopted 'camel' and *jamal* and those who adopted 'rope' and *jummal*.[36] Al-Ṭabarī himself comes down decisively in favour of the first view. When this is compared with the Christian interpretations of the metaphor in the Gospels, it seems clear that the Muslim commentators have not simply been imitating the Christian commentators; for if they had been imitating, it is unlikely that the one Greek word *kamēlos* would have been transformed into the two Arabic words, *jamal* and *jummal*. The word *jummal* must have existed previously, and cannot be something invented by a commentator. Lane mentions the phrase *ḥisāb al-jummal,* meaning the use of the letters of the alphabet to represent numbers, and quotes Ibn Durayd (d. 933) as doubting whether it is Arabic.

There are numerous biographical notices of the commentators

mentioned, but nothing of the material there seems relevant to the present investigation, except the fact that Mujāhid consulted Christian and Jewish scholars and tended to favour rationalistic interpretations,[31] and the fact that ʿIkrima had travelled widely in the Islamic world and had been to Egypt among other places.[38]

Can any explanation be given of this strange coincidence that both Christian and Muslim commentators are divided between 'camel' and 'rope'? Our information is fragmentary and there are many gaps. As a very provisional hypothesis the following might be suggested. There was in the polyglot nautical slang of the Eastern Mediterranean a word which became *kamēlos* in Greek and *jummal* in Arabic (presumably pronounced *gummal* in Egypt); the ultimate origin of the word is obscure, but that does not concern us here. A Christian who found the Gospel saying difficult and was familiar with the nautical word might feel that it made the saying a little less harsh. Cyril of Alexandria presumably had opportunities to learn about this word. Mujāhid might have heard from Christian scholars of the two interpretations of the Gospel saying, and because of his rationalistic bent might have been attracted by the 'rope'. He might have heard the word *jummal* in actual use somewhere or might have been told about it by another scholar. ʿIkrima might have heard the word in Alexandria, but he seems to prefer ʿIrāqī non-nautical usage. The phrase *ḥisāb al-jummal* is one that might well occur in connection with sea-borne trade, while Ibn Durayd would really be correct in holding that *jummal* was not Arabic. Finally, it would follow that the interpretation of *kamēlos* as 'rope' was not a sheer invention but had an authentic linguistic justification.

A7. The Men of the Ukhdūḍ (Sūra 85)

It was argued by Hubert Grimme (*Mohammed*, ii, 1895, 77) and by Josef Horovitz (*Koranische Untersuchungen*, 1926, 12, 92f.) that the Qur'ānic passage 85.4–7 was to be understood not of a historical event, such as a persecution of Christians in Najrān, but eschatologically of punishment in Hell referring to the opponents who were persecuting Muḥammad's followers in Mecca. This interpretation was followed by Richard Bell (*Translation*, 1939, *ad loc.*). With this interpretation the first eight verses of the Sūra might be translated roughly as follows (along the lines of Paret's German):

1 By the sky with its constellations,
2 by the day (of Judgement) promised (to men).
3 by him who (then) bears witness and by what is witnessed –
4 cursed be the Men of the Trench,
5 the fire (of Hell) with its (unlimited) fuel;
6 beside (the fire-trench) they are sitting.
7 and bearing witness (compulsorily) to how they have (during life) treated the believers;
8 they tortured them only because they believed in God. . .

The arguments for this interpretation advanced by Horovitz and others may be summarized as follows:

(1) The word *qutila* is to be taken as a curse as in 51.10; 74.19, 20; 80.17/16.

(2) Oaths such as that in 85.1–3 are never elsewhere found preceding an account of a past event. It is argued further that the oaths in 89.1ff. and 91 are not exceptions to this statement.

(3) The passage has none of the usual formulas for introducing the account of a historical event.

(4) It is unlikely that the Qur'ān would have spoken of the persecution of believers without also mentioning the punishment of the persecutors.

(5) There is no mention of a trench filled with fire in the stories told by the commentators.

The points raised by these arguments may now be looked at more fully.

(1) The interpretation of *qutila* as a curse may be accepted, but it would seem that it is inappropriate for men who are not merely destined for Hell, but are spoken of as already in hell. The additional point may be

made here that verse 6 – 'beside it (or 'over it') they are sitting' – is also inappropriate for men who are being punished in Hell. If it is suggested that this describes the moment when they bear witness against themselves before they are flung into the Fire, then more emphasis is placed on bearing witness than on the punishment; and this is unlikely.

(2) It is apparently true that there is no other instance in the Qur'ān of an oath followed by material such as that in verses 4ff. On the other hand, while in most cases the oath emphasizes the statement of a religious principle (called in Arabic *jawāb al-qasam*), in a few cases the oath does not appear to emphasize a following statement; e. g. 38.1; 50.1. Sura 89.1ff. may be looked at in this connection; 'By the dawn / and the ten nights / and even and odd / and the night as it passes / is there in that an oath for the reasonable? / Did you not see how your Lord dealt with 'Ād? . . . On them your Lord poured a share of punishment. / Your Lord is at the watch-post.' The verse 'is there in that an oath for the reasonable?' (as Bell; or with Paret 'is that not for a man of understanding an effective oath?') is not a principle to be emphasized, but is best regarded with Bell as a kind of parenthesis. Either, then, there is no proper *jawāb*, or the *jawāb* is 'Did you not see how your Lord dealt with 'Ād? . . .' Al-Zamakhshari says that the *jawāb – al-muqsam 'alay-hi* – is omitted and is in fact 'he will indeed punish' (*la-yu'adhdhibanna*, or perhaps the passive); he holds that this is implied by the following verses 'Did you not see. . .' Horovitz's point about the change of assonance at 'Did you not see. . .' is unsound in view of 52.1-8. It may be concluded that the oath in 85.1-3 is no reason for rejecting a historical reference in verses 4ff.

(3) On any interpretation the passage has unusual features, and so the absence of any common historical formula cannot be pressed as an objection to the historical interpretation.

(4) The punishment of the persecutors is implied in *qutila*, and perhaps also in verses 2 and 3. *Qutila* is best understood as 'cursed', since the indicative, 'killed', is less adequate as a punishment.

(5) The word *ukhdūd* is difficult on any interpretation. It is not appropriate to Hell, nor to the Christians of Najrān, nor to the fiery furnace of Daniel's companions (as Régis Blachère and others have preferred). I am inclined to think that the word is somehow corrupt. It is possible that there has been confusion with the pre-Islamic story of men burnt in an *ukhdūd* recorded in *Aghāni,* 19. 129-), but in this case one would have expected more traces in the commentators.

There are certain additional points which may now be made.

(6) The verb *shahida 'alā* may mean either 'bear witness to' or 'witness, observe'. If *shuhūd* in verse 7 means 'bearing witness to', we should expect it to be followed by a perfect (as Paret himself notes). The meaning can hardly be that they '*will* bear witness to what they are now doing',

especially in view of the perfect 'tortured' in verse 8.

(7) The phrase in verse 5 *al-nār dhāt al-wuqūd* fits in well with material recently published by Irfan Shahid in *The Martyrs of Najrān: New Documents* (1971), 46f., where we read:

> And the Jews thus brought all their (bones) together into the church and heaped them in the centre of the church; and they brought in the presbyters, the deacons, . . . and the laity, both men and women, . . . and they filled the whole church from one side to the other (with the Christians), all of whom came to about two thousand, as those who came from Najrān have said. And they brought wood and surrounded the church from the outside and threw fire into it and burnt it together with all that was found in it.

(8) The oath of verses 1-3 can be understood in a way that is appropriate to the Najrān interpretation of the following verses. The 'constellations' of verse 1 suggest the passing of the years which will bring a reversal of fortune. The 'day (2) is that of resurrection and judgement when the martyrs will be vindicated and the persecutors punished. Of the various possible ways of understanding the 'witness' (3) the most likely is that it is either God or a recording angel (cf. 10.61/62; 21.78), who observed the crime and reports on it at the judgement. The 'witnessed' will then be the crime itself.

All these considerations seem to rule out the eschatological interpretation and to support a historical one, more particularly the reference to the martyrs of Najrān. A reference to the companions of Daniel is not impossible, but the Arabian incident is more likely to have been known, even if only in a garbled version, to some people in Mecca in the early seventh century. It is worth remarking, however, that the point emphasized by the passage – the eventual punishment of those who persecute believers – remains valid whether there is a precise historical reference or not. The first hearers of the passage presumably thought that it referred to a particular event, but their tradition-based understanding of this event may have been inaccurate. In conclusion a translation may be given of the passage with a mimimum of interpretation:

> 1 By the sky with its constellations,
> 2 by the day promised,
> 3 by the witness and the witnessed –
> 4 cursed be the Men of the Trench,
> 5 of the fire with its fuel;
> 6 over it they are sitting
> 7 as they witness how they are treating the believers;
> 8 they tortured them only because they believed in God.

A8 God's Caliph
Qur'ānic Interpretations and Umayyad Claims

I. THE MEANING OF *KHALĪFA* IN THE QUR'ĀN

The semantic development of the Arabic root KH.L.F is fascinating in its width.[39] The basic meaning is presumably 'behind' (in place), but this easily passes into 'behind' (in time) or 'after'. The phrase *khalafa-hu* may mean 'he came after him', 'he seized him from behind' or 'he spoke (evil) of him behind his back' and so 'he deceived him'. Intransitively used the word can mean 'to fall behind', literally or metaphorically; thus *khalafa ʿan khuluq abī-hi* is 'he was altered (for the worse) from the natural disposition of his father'. The last is not far from the meaning of 'differed' which is prominent in the eighth stem. In such a phrase as *ikhtilāf al-layl wa-l-nahār* 'the alternation of night and day', the eighth stem means 'following reciprocally', and this leads both to 'going to and fro' or 'frequenting' and 'being different'. Similarly the third stem may mean 'to oppose', as well as 'to go to a woman when her husband is absent'. The fourth stem is associated with failing to keep promises. Several different forms have meanings connected with drawing water, apparently because in a caravan those who go to draw water leave behind their goods beside the caravan. Finally the man who comes after another may act on his behalf as a substitute or deputy. This last sense is one that will receive more attention in what follows.

The singular *khalīfa* is found twice in the Qur'ān, once applied to Adam and once to David. The latter is in 38.26/5; 'O David, we have made thee a *khalīfa* in the earth; so judge between men with truth, and do not follow (personal) inclination so that it leads you astray from the way of God . . .' The context gives no help. In the story of how Adam told the angels the names of things there occur the words (2.30/28): 'Thy Lord said to the angels, "I am making in the earth a *khalīfa*"; they said "Wilt thou make in it one (or 'those') who will act corruptly and shed blood, whereas we glorify thee with thy praises and hallow thee?"' The commentators had to deal with a hard problem in discussing these verses. If they emphasized the element of succession in *khalīfa*, they had to say who was being succeeded; but if they said a *khalīfa* was a deputy, was he God's deputy? Apart from other considerations several commentators were anxious to avoid approving the Umayyad caliphs' use of the verse about Adam to enhance their own dignity (a point explained below).

In 38.26/5 Jalālayn have no objection to interpreting *khalīfa* simply as 'one who will direct the affairs of the people' while in 2.30/28 it is one 'who will deputize for me in executing my judgements in it (the earth)'. For 38.26/5 al-Ṭabarī gives only one meaning, 'a successor of the messengers before him as an arbiter between the people'. Al-Zamakhsharī gives a meaning like this in the second place, but puts in first place one like Jalālayn though carefully phrased to express subordination: 'we made thee a deputy (*istakhlafnā-ka*) over the kingdom (*mulk*) in the earth', in the same way as a particular sultan made someone a deputy over a particular land; that is, he has only a part of the sultan's authority. With this qualification al-Zamakhsharī is prepared to accept the phrase 'God's caliphs in his earth'. Al-Bayḍāwī gives the two interpretations briefly without the qualification and without any mention of 'God's caliph'.

Al-Ṭabarī has a long discussion of 2.30/28. First he mentions and rejects a view of Ibn Isḥāq's that *khalīfa* means 'one who settles in or inhabits' (*sākin, ʿāmir*); he also speaks of the earth as having been previously inhabited by jinn, so that Adam is the *khalīfa* or 'successor' of the jinn. Next comes the view of al-Ḥasan al-Baṣrī that *khalīfa* means 'a posterity who will succeed one another'; this avoids the two problems mentioned and the difficulty that Adam as a prophet could not 'act corruptly and shed blood'; but the meaning of *khalīfa* can hardly be supported. The chief remaining view is the one he attributes to Ibn ʿAbbās and Ibn Masʿūd that the *khalīfa* is 'one who will deputize for me in judgement between my creatures'. Al-Ṭabarī's own definition, given at the beginning, is 'one who takes a person's position after him in respect of something'. With this definition *khalīfa* here could mean either 'a successor to the angels' or 'God's deputy'. Al-Zamakhsharī is not dissimilar. He prefers the interpretation that Adam and his progeny are to succeed the angels, but mentions as a possibility the interpretation that Adam is 'God's deputy'. He also notes a variant reading *khalīqa*. There is nothing to commend this reading; it seems to be a feeble attempt to avoid the difficulties raised by the usual text. (The reading is not among the variants listed by Arthur Jeffery in *Materials for the History of the Text of the Qur'ān*, Leiden, 1937).

Before attempting to decide which of these meanings was conveyed to the first hearers of the Qur'ānic verses by the word *khalīfa*, there are some further points to be noticed about the use of the root in the Qur'ān. Prominent in general in the Qur'ān is the thought that contemporary communities live where other communities previously lived which have now disappeared, destroyed by God because of their disobedience. This seems to be the image behind the instances of *khalā'if* and *khulafā'*, plurals of *khalīfa*. It is seen most clearly in 10.14/15 where God, addressing the Meccans says 'We have made you *khalā'if* in the earth after them (*sc.* previous generations which had passed away) to see how you would act'. In 7.69/7 and 74/2 one community is said to have been made *khulafā'* after another. The remaining four instances of these words, however, though they could be intepreted in this way, leave the previous people or community unspecified: 'he it is who made you *khalā'if* of the earth, and raised some above others in rank' (6.165); 'we saved (Noah) and those with him in the ship and made them *khalā'if*' (10.73/4); 'he makes you *khulafā'* of the earth' (27.62/3); 'he made you *khalā'if* in the earth' (35.39/7).

All these instances may thus be referred to the image of a present-day community living where others had lived previously. The phrase 'in the earth' or 'in the land', if not in the text, is always implied. Since the people succeeded are left vague in four instances, the original meaning may not have been far from the 'inhabitants' or 'settlers' suggested by Ibn Isḥāq. A similar emphasis is found in certain other forms from the same root. In 7.129/6 and 11.57/60 *istakhlafa* means 'make successors' of people who are mentioned; but in 24.55/4 it makes an excellent sense when translated 'settled', viz. 'God has promised those of you who have believed . . . that he will *settle* them in the earth as he *settled* those before them, and will establish for them their religion'. The Arabic word, it may be allowed, has a connotation of 'in succession to others', but sometimes this is so slight that it may apparently be neglected in translation.

Another image associated with the root is that of one man performing some function after and as a substitute for another; e.g. where a man (or God) takes the place of a father of a family who has died. It is also used of man going to a woman and occupying the place of an absent husband. This sense is found in the Qur'ān in 7.142/38, where Moses says to Aaron, 'Deputize for me (*ukhluf-nī*) among my people, and act well'. Along with the idea of performing a function, there is the connotation of exercisng authority. The word appears to be used for 'viceroy' in a South Arabian inscription date 543.[40]

Finally there is a verse where the root has the meaning of succession together with engaging in different activity from that of the person succeeded. After the incident of the calf Moses says to the Israelites, 'Bad is your "deputizing" for me after me' (*bi'sa-mā khalaftumū-nī ba'dī*). This appears to show that a man may be called a 'successor' or 'deputy' although his activity differs from that of his predecessor. This is in accordance with al-Zamakhsharī's insistence that the *khalīfa* appointed by a sultan had powers far inferior to those of a sultan. In the early tenth century *khalīfa* could still be applied to an assistant, and presumably inferior, teacher.[41]

This review of the usage of the root gives a basis for a conclusion about the original meaning of *khalīfa* in the two Qur'ānic passages. As applied to David, the word would appear to mean 'a person exercising authority', and to have only the slightest suggestion of succeeding someone else, or God, in this function. In the passage about Adam (2.30/28) the matter is not so clear. On the whole it would seem that the meaning is that Adam was made a settler in the earth but also exercised some authority, namely in instructing the angels. His activity on earth might be thought of as following on the activity of God in creating animals, plants and angels; but succession is not emphasized. Neither is there any emphasis in his deputizing for God. If there is any suggestion of this it is balanced by the implication that his activity and God's are different.

There is also a further conclusion which is strongly supported by this study, though it may also be held on independent grounds. This is that the choice of the word *khalīfa* as a title for Abū Bakr when he became head of state in succession to Muḥammad was not based on Qur'ānic usage or even influenced by it, but was derived from the use of the word in secular affairs. It has been doubted whether Abū Bakr in fact used the title *khalīfat rasūl Allāh*, but there is no good reason for rejecting the standard view. From the present study it is seen that the title meant primarily 'successor of the Messenger of God', with a secondary connotation of exercising some authority. This was helpfully vague and permitted the development of the office. It is virtually certain that it did not connote 'deputy', though it might have suggested 'substitute' or 'replacement'. The report that Abū Bakr was invited to take the title of *khalīfat Allāh*, but refused, cannot be genuine, since there was no question of him succeeding God or of deputizing for him. This point will become clearer in the next section.

2. THE UMAYYAD CLAIMS TO THE CALIPHATE

The difficulties in interpreting the word *khalīfa* experienced by the early Muslim scholars were partly due to the fact that the Umayyad dynasty did what it could to build up the position of caliph, and in particular used the Qur'ānic passage about Adam (2.30/28).[42] This matter will be seen in better perspective after considering how the Umayyads themselves stated their claims. For the most part scholars have accepted anti-Umayyad assertions current under the 'Abbāsids. Virtually no use has been made, for example, of the pro-Umayyad material contained in the works of the poets Jarīr and al-Farazdaq.[43] The material has to be carefully used, for often there is excessive adulation: the mothers of Walīd I and Yazid II are compared to the sun and the Virgin Mary respectively[44]; Sulaymān is called Mahdī[45]; the caliph in general is said to be almost a prophet.[46] Yet by considering what has a degree of realism, and what corresponds to statements of opponents, we can form some idea of the arguments used by the Umayyads to justify the monopoly of the caliphate in their family.

The main claim appears to have been that the Umayyad family, and in particular the Marwānid branch, had inherited the caliphate from ʿUthmān.

> 'They (the Umayyads) are the trustees (*awliyā'*) of ʿUthmān's heritage (*turāth*), – an apparel of *mulk* over them, not to be stripped off'.[47]
>
> 'The sons of Marwān inherited from him (the Caliphate), and from ʿUthmān after a momentous event.'[48]

An interesting verse addressed to Sulaymān regards this inheritance as being not simply in the family of Umayya, but in that of his grandfather (ʿAbd-)Manāf.

> 'You (pl.) have inherited the staff of *mulk*, not as distant relatives, from the two sons of Manāf, ʿAbd-Shams and Hāshim.[49]

(ʿAbd-Shams was the father of Umayya). This mention of Hāshim suggests an attempt to counter Shīʿite propaganda by asserting that the charisma of leadership was not restricted to the clan of Hāshim, but was transmitted in the wider clan-group of ʿAbd-Manāf. Another item of the charge against them was that they had seized the caliphate by force. To this the reply is that ʿUthmān, from whom they have inherited the caliphate, gained it as a result of a decision by an official council.

> 'I saw that the *mulk* of the sons of Marwān had been firmly based by a true council of which their kinsman (*sc.* ʿUthmān) was one.'[50]

The same point is probably made in another verse addressed to Walīd I:

> 'A caliphate sprung from counsel without force.
> whose foundations the Merciful and Bountiful had firmly established.'[51]

This line of argument presumably goes back to Muʿāwiya who gave great prominence to his claim to be the avenger of blood for ʿUthmān. ʿAlī, though accepted as caliph by most of the Muslims, refused to take action against those of the murderers who were among his supporters. This probably strengthened Muʿāwiya's case at the Arbitration, and he presumably also made the most of the tendency for the heir and the avenger of blood to be one and the same.[52]

A subordinate line of argument is that the Umayyad family is worthy of the caliphate because it has many noble deeds to its credit.

> 'The caliphate, because of the fair deeds you have done, is among you; its *mulk* will not be turned away (from you).'[53]

The noble acts are frequently made more specific as fighting on behalf of Islam.

> 'When the sons of Marwān meet (enemies), they unsheath
> for God's religion angry swords
> (And) sharp, by which they defend Islam;

The word *mulk* has been left untranslated because it appears to connote both 'kingship' and 'possession', with the emphasis sometimes on the one, sometimes on the other. Where *mulk* is closely associated with inheritance there is emphasis on possession; and part at least of the objection to Umayyad rule[55] seems to have been that it was something heritable, and indeed only to be inherited within the family. On the other hand, the Umayyads did not object to being called 'kings'. Yazid II is described as

> 'The scion of kings (*mulūk*) in an inheritance (*mawārith*) in which not a king (*malik*) dieṣ, but he bequeaths (*awratha*) a *minbar*'[56]

In the Qur'ān *mulk* has a similar double connotation. It may be that after the Umayyads had disappeared it was more tactful to emphasize the aspect of kingship, since the 'Abbāsids also kept it as a possession within the family.

The second main line of argument is that the caliphate has been bestowed on the Umayyads by God:

> 'The earth is God's; he has entrusted it (*wallā-hā*) to his *khalīfa*: he who is head in it will not be overcome.'[57]
>
> 'God has garlanded you with the *khilāfa* and guidance; for what God decrees (*qaḍā*) there is no change.'[58]

This is more than a verbal compliment, for important religious functions are ascribed to the caliphs.

> 'We have found the sons of Marwān pillars of our religion as the earth has mountains for its pillars.'[59]
>
> 'Were it not for the caliph and the Qur'ān he recites, the people had no judgements established for them and no communal worship.'[60]

The ideas of the invincibility and unchanging character of the Umayyad caliphate lead on to the corollary of this assertion, namely, that disobedience to the caliph and his subordinate officers is a refusal to acknowledge God and so tantamount to unbelief. Al-Ḥajjāj is addressed as follows.

> 'You regard support of the Imam as a duty laid upon you; while they cover their religion with doubt.'[61]

Al-Ḥajjāj, in dealing with the men taken prisoner in the rising of Ibn al-Ash'ath, made them, before he would free them, confess that they were unbelievers; those who refused were executed.[62] In a poem the enemies of al-Ḥajjāj are referred to as 'opposing the religion of the Muslims'.[63] Other terms applied to the enemies of the Umayyads are *mulḥidūn, munāfiqūn, mushrikūn, kuffār*.[64]

In view of all this material, especially the phrase about God entrusting the earth to 'his *khalīfa*', it is not surprising to find the phrase *khalīfat Allāh* being used both by Jarīr and by a number of other persons.[65] In these cases the meaning must be 'the deputy appointed by God'. Goldziher's suggestion that 'God's caliph' meant 'the caliph or successor of the Prophet approved by God' is incompatible with the further material here presented.[66] The same scholar's earlier remarks[67] on the differing attitudes of the Umayyads and ʿAbbāsids towards this title require some revision. He asserts that because of the more theocratic interpretation of the function of the ruler under the ʿAbbāsids, this title and other similar ones like 'shadow of God on earth' were more frequently used; and he further maintains that, whereas for the Umayyads the title was an expression of their absolute power, for the ʿAbbāsids it had a 'theocratic' (or perhaps rather 'theological') content. In view of the material quoted above and much other material from the Umayyad period in the historians, what Goldziher said about lack of theological content under the Umayyads is hardly convincing. A more serious objection to his remarks is that, while other titles with a reference to God become more frequent under the ʿAbbāsids, the title of 'God's caliph' seems to be less frequently used. The evidence for this is not altogether clear, but the reduced frequency, besides being probable on the available evidence, is what might be expected in view of the points about to be made.,[68]

A further point of great importance is contained in the report that al-Ḥajjāj asserted that the caliph was superior to angels and prophets and adduced in proof the Qur'ānic passage about God making Adam a *khalīfa* in the earth and enabling him to instruct the angels.[69] The story implies that by the time of al-Ḥajjāj *khalīfa* was being understood as 'deputy', and also shows that the Umayyads or their supporters produced theological reasons to justify their claims.

The familiar story that Abū Bakr was addressed by the title *khalīfat Allāh* and objected to it, saying he was only the *khalīfa* of the Messenger of God is almost certainly an invention made to oppose the Umayyad claims (as are also some of the interpretations of the verse about Adam). We are told that the propriety of the title 'God's caliph' was discussed by scholars, and that on the whole they thought it improper.[70] The earliest version of it so far traced is that in the *Musnad* of Aḥmad ibn Ḥanbal,[71] where the earliest source named in the *isnād* is Ibn Abī Mulayka. Since this man, who died in 735, was a *qāḍī* under Ibn al-Zubayr during the latter's rebellion against the Umayyads,[72] the probability is that the story was invented in Mecca about this time.

From a modern historical standpoint the alleged absence of a theological justification for the Umayyad claim to the caliphate, cannot be regarded as a factor in the dynasty's downfall. It might perhaps be held that their theology contained an undue emphasis on pre-Islamic ideas of predestination. Yet the chief ideological failure must be that their primary claim to the caliphate was based on the Arab idea of blood-revenge, and the associated idea that the heir was the avenger of blood. The essentially Arab basis of their rule made it difficult for them to adjust the governmental institution to the needs of a vast empire.

A9. Reflections on some Verses of Sūrat al-Ḍuḥā

European and American orientalists have often given offence to Muslims by treating the Qur'ān as if it were a book consciously composed by Muḥammad. It is worth noting, however, that the Muslim, who faithfully adheres to the belief that the Qur'ān is the revealed speech of God communicated to Muḥammad by an angel, is still able to learn from the Qur'ān about conditions in Arabia in the time of Muḥammad. He can even learn about the beliefs of the pagan Arabs, as in the verse: 'They say, there is only this present life of ours; we die and we live, and only Time (*al-dahr*) causes us to perish' (Sūrat al-Jāthiya, 45.24/3). In a similar way the Qur'ān gives some understanding about the early life of Muḥammad and his attitude to the hardships he experienced.

What may be learnt from the Qur'ān in this way confirms recent psychological discoveries. As a result of the work of psychologists it is now generally accepted that happenings in the first years of life influence the conduct of the mature man. If a child is deprived of parental affection and support through the death of one or both the parents, or for some other reason, this creates in him a pattern of response to situations which continues into adult life. The pattern varies according to the precise circumstances of each child. Sometimes the search for a substitute for the missing parent will be prominent. Sometimes there will be a tendency to feel bitterness towards the world in general or towards some particular persons, who are – often unjustifiably – felt to have been responsible for the various deprivations and hardships the man has endured.

In the biographies of Muḥammad, we learn that he was an orphan whose father was dead before he was born, and whose mother died when he was six years old. In the conditions of life in Mecca at that period, this must have meant great hardship for Muḥammad. It would not have been surprising had he become embittered and cynical. Yet there is no trace of this in the records of his life. On the contrary, everything suggests that he triumphed completely over the unfortunate aspects of his early life.

Some idea of how he did this may be gained from Sūrat al-Ḍuḥā (93), especially the verses:

> Did he not find you an orphan and give you a home? . . .
> So as for the orphan, do not oppress him. . .

And as for the favour of your Lord, tell of it.

These are commands to Muḥammad and it may be that the Qur'ān in this way first directed him to the proper attitude to his early deprivations; or it may be that these commands merely encouraged him to continue along a path he had already begun to follow. In either case we see various points which are valuable in guiding us to finding a mature attitude to our experiences of deprivation and hardship in early life.

Firstly, Muḥammad is made to realize that, despite the deprivation of being an orphan, life was made possible and indeed tolerable for him. This came about through the care of his mother's family and of his father's father and brother, ʿAbd al-Muṭṭalib and Abū Ṭālib. But the kindly actions of these people are further shown as coming from God. Ultimately it was God who was responsible for providing Muḥammad with a home and some measure of kind treatment. This teaches us that we must try to look away from our experiences of deprivation and hardship and see how they have been overcome or transcended by experiences of good. We must not, of course, simply forget the painful experiences and shut them out of our minds. That is repression, which, as it were, causes the evil thing to fester under the surface and to have undesirable effects on our conduct. The view we have to try to keep before us is that there have been painful experiences, some lasting many years, but that these are only parts of a greater whole, and that this whole is ordered by God who is the Merciful. The bitter experiences of Muḥammad as an orphan must have made him more aware of the troubles and problems of Mecca in his time, and so fitted him for the role of Messenger of God.

Secondly, Muḥammad was commanded to be specially concerned not to cause for others any sufferings of the kind he himself had known, but to be zealous for the prevention of all oppression. We know from the Sīra that this was done. It is also something we ourselves can do in so far as we have opportunity; and perhaps any relief we can bring to the sufferings of others will help to heal old wounds in ourselves.

Finally, Muḥammad was instructed to be constantly aware of God's favour and kindness to himself and to talk about it to others. There is clearly a very great gain in directing our attention chiefly to this aspect of our lives, so that quite naturally, we often speak about it. In this way we are helping our fellow-men to overcome their bitterness and resentment and to advance to a mature attitude which sees, behind all the deprivation and pain of the world, the mercy of God.

A10. The Christianity criticized in the Qur'ān

The aim of this paper is a very simple one. It is to take a fresh look at the criticisms or apparent criticisms of Christianity to be found in the Qur'ān, and to consider whether these are attacks on orthodox Christianity, or whether they should not be regarded as attacks on Christian heresies which orthodox Christians would themselves criticize. The present paper was conceived before the appearance of the scholarly and eirenic work of Geoffrey Parrinder, *Jesus in the Qur'ān* (London, Faber, 1965), and many of the points to be made have been anticipated by him. Yet it still seems worth while to devote attention to the specific question: Was the Christianity attacked by the Qur'ān orthodox or heretical?[73]

It is natural for the occidental scholar to approach the Qur'ān with the assumption that it attacks Christianity, since there was hostility between Muḥammad and Christians in the closing years of his life. At first he had been amicably disposed towards Christians. When he began to receive revelations, Khadīja's Christian kinsman, Waraqa ibn-Nawfal, is said to have given him encouragement. A little later the Negus of Abyssinia provided a secure refuge for the Muslim emigrants from Mecca; they may indeed have hoped for some more active help from him, and in this been disappointed, but on the other hand he refused to help the pagan Meccans against them. After the Hijra to Medina the hostility of the Jews there became an important factor in the experience of Muslims; and the contrast between Christian friendliness and Jewish hostility is reflected in the verse (5.82/5):

> Indeed you will find the most hostile of the people to the believers are the Jews and the pagans, and you will find the closest of them in love to the believers are those who say, 'We are Christians'; that is because among them are priests and monks, and they are not proud.

It was probably after the conquest of Mecca (January 630) and more particularly after the expedition to Tabūk (October to December 630) that Muḥammad realized that he would have to face military opposition from the Christian tribes towards the Syrian border – the direction in which it was necessary for the Islamic state to expand. Christians are presumably included among the opponents against whom fighting is prescribed in sūra 9.29. If one assumes that the Qur'ān was revised – and this assumption does not contradict the Muslim conception of revelation, since the revisions could have been revealed as a form of *nāsikh* – then it is probable that many verses which at first only criticized Jews, were now revised to apply to both Christians and Jews. So far as the Qur'ān itself is concerned, it does not appear to assert any general corruption of Jewish and Christian scriptures;[74] after the conquest of Iraq, Syria and Egypt, however, the doctrine of *taḥrīf* or 'corruption' was elaborated in various ways to give the Muslim Arabs a defence against the better-educated Christians with whom they were now mixing. From this period onwards Islam and Christianity have been rivals, and this has made it natural to suppose that the criticisms of Christian doctrines in the Qur'ān have a hostile, that is, anti-Christian, intention. With the thought in mind that this is probably a mistaken assumption let us look in detail at some of these criticisms.

The obvious point at which to begin is the apparent attack on the Christian doctrine of the Trinity.

> Disbelieved have those who say that God is the third of thee; there is no deity except one deity. . . (5.73/7).
>
> O people of the book, do not be extreme in your religion, and of God say only the truth; the Messiah, Jesus son of Mary, is the messenger of God and his word which he cast into Mary and a spirit from him; so believe in God and his messengers, and do not say 'Three'; desist and it will be better for you; God is only one deity; sublime is he beyond having a son. . . (4.171-69).

Now, if these passages are examined without *parti pris*, it is clear that they are not attacking the orthodox Christian doctrine of the Trinity, but the misinterpretation of that doctrine sometimes called 'tritheism'. The great body of Christians officially deny that they believe in three gods, and in their creeds profess their belief in God who is one. They officially claim to be monotheists, and would indignantly repudiate the charge that they are tritheists. There may indeed be simple-minded Christians who fall into something like the error of tritheism in practice, but in so far as they are tritheists they are heretics. It is not part of the purpose of this paper to look for sources for the criticisms being discussed; but it may be noted in passing that they might well be derived from Christians.

Closely connected with this attack on tritheism is the apparent attack on the divinity of Jesus. Two aspects may be distinguished here, the denial of divinity, and the assertion of humanity and creatureliness. Now it must be admitted that there are verses which could be applied to orthodox Christian doctrine on this point, such as the words in 9.30: 'the Christians say that the Messiah is the son of God'. It may be argued, however, on the basis of other verses that this was not intended as an attack on the orthodox Christian conception of the sonship of Christ, but on something else. Thus there is a clear denial that Jesus is to be regarded as one deity in three, in line with the tritheistic conception already discussed:

> God said, 'O Jesus, son of Mary, didst thou say to the people, "Take me and my mother as two deities apart from God"?' He said, 'Sublime art thou; it is not for me to say what I have no right to say; if I said it, thou hast known it; thou knowest what is in me, and I do not know what is in thee; thou art knower of the unseen'. (5.116).

Let us ignore the complication here that Mary is apparently regarded as the third hypostasis of the Trinity; the view may have been held by badly instructed Christians. The assertion that Jesus is a deity apart from God is definitely heretical from the standpoint of Christian orthodoxy. In the light of the Qur'ānic attack on tritheism, it seem certain that the denial that the Messiah was the son of God was a denial that he was a deity separate from God; and this is confirmed by the later part of 9.30 which identifies what is denied with the views of 'former unbelievers' (*qawl alladhīna kafarū min qabl*), that is presumably of the pagans.

Yet another form of Christian belief in the divinity of Jesus is denied in two verses (5.17/9, 72/6) in the words:

> Disbelieved have those who say 'God is the Messiah, the son of Mary'.

The first of these verses continues with an argument which might well have been familiar to some of the original hearers as a result of contact with Christian sources:

> Say: 'Who then would overrule God at all, if he willed to destroy the Messiah, the son of Mary, and his mother and all the earth? for God's is the sovereignty of the heavens and the earth and what is between them, creating what he will, seeing he has power over everything.

What is denied here is the assertion of complete identity between Jesus and God, an assertion sometimes made by Christians but generally regarded as the heresy of confusing the hypostases. Once again the Qur'ān is attacking Christian heresy and not Christian orthodoxy. It is also noteworthy that the Qur'ān takes cognizance in this way of divergent Christian views.

Complementary to these attacks on the divinity of Jesus is the assertion of his humanity and creatureliness.

> The likeness of Jesus in God's sight is as the likeness of Adam; he created him of dust, then said to him 'Be' and he is (3.59/2; cf. 47/2).

The creation of Jesus is, of course, to be understood as his creation in the womb of his mother. The initiation of his individual existence there is the result of God's word 'Be' and not of the act of a human father; but there is no suggestion that the later development there takes place by other than, in modern terms, natural processes. Now most of what is asserted or implied here is not contrary to Christian orthodoxy, for, as the Athanasian creed put it, 'he is man, of the substance of his mother, born in the world'. Similarly there is nothing heretical in such sayings put into the mouth of Jesus by the Qur'ān as: 'serve God, My Lord and your Lord'(5.72/3).[75] Indeed there is almost a New Testament ring in the verse (4.172/0):

> The Messiah will not disdain to be called a servant to God, nor will the angels, the cherubim.

'The servant of God' was an honoured title in the Old Testament, and Paul goes so far as to say that Jesus humbled himself and took the 'form of a servant'.[76] Thus in this respect, as in several others, the Qur'ān is asserting one strand in Christian orthodoxy.

Some reference to the Virgin Birth is relevant here. As is well known the Qur'ān teaches the Virgin Birth but interprets it simply as a miracle on somewhat the same level as the miraculous birth of John the Baptist. Perhaps it is not even accurate to say that the Qur'ān gives this specific interpretation, but only that it provides materials on the basis of which later Muslim scholars have adopted this interpretation. The point is difficult to discuss, because there has been much confusion in recent Christian thinking on the subject, perhaps as a result of opponents of Christianity thinking that, if they showed that birth from a virgin was scientifically impossible, this disproved the divinity of Jesus. In this way many Christians came to think that to maintain the literal truth of the Virgin Birth was a central point in the defence of Christianity. It is rather the case that the Virgin Birth is no part of the *proof* of the divinity of Jesus, just as it played no part in the earliest Christian preaching. What should be held is that, once the divinity of Jesus is believed in on other grounds, the conception of the Virgin Birth is seen to be appropriate. The very fact that millions of Muslims believe in the Virgin Birth of Jesus but deny his divinity should make it clear that, contrary to the view of many Christians, there is no necessary connection between Virgin Birth and divinity.

To some readers it might seem that the most important item of the attack or apparent attack of the Qur'ān on Christianity was its denial of the crucifixion. Yet careful examination of the precise wording of the Qur'ān shows that this is not a direct attack. The passage[77] tells of God's punishment of Jews for various faults and among other things:

> for their saying, 'We killed the Messiah, Jesus son of Mary, the messenger of God', when they did not kill him and did not crucify him, but a resemblance was made for them. . . and they certainly did not kill him, but God raised him to himself.

Once again the primary denial is of something heretical, namely the Jewish contention that the crucifixion had been a victory for them; and this same denial would of course be most vigorously affirmed by Christian orthodoxy. Unfortunately the denial is linked with a positive assertion which is unacceptable to orthodox Christians, contained in the rather vague phrase here translated 'a resemblance as made for them' (*shubbiha la-hum*). In the present context there is no need to speculate on the possible gnostic origin of the positive conception. The point to be insisted on here is that the Qur'ān is not attacking Christianity, but rather defending it against Jewish attacks.

This verse also illustrates how there are many Christian doctrines of which the Qur'ān has no positive appreciation, for it makes virtually no assertion corresponding to the Old Testament ideas of sacrifice, and consequently cannot refer to the link between these and the crucifixion. It is perhaps because of this that it minimizes the 'work' of Jesus: he is spoken of as only one messenger among many (5.75/9; 3.49/3), and as *a* word from God (3,45/40; cf. 4.171/69), instead of *the* word of God as asserted by Christians.

In conclusion it may be suggested that, if the main contention of this paper is sound, namely, that there is no primary attack on Christianity in the Qur'ān, then a widespread realization of this point has profound implications for the present and future relations of Islam and Christianity.

A11. Two Interesting Christian–Arabic Usages

The starting-point of this article[78] is constituted by two passages from the *Risāla* of ʿAbd al-Masīḥ al-Kindī (London, 1880, etc.). In the first (p. 42), after speaking of Abraham worshipping the idol as a *ḥanīf*, he goes on to say that 'he abandoned the *ḥanīfiyya* which is the worship of idols (*wa-huwa ʿibādat al-aṣnām*), and became a monotheist and believer, for we find that the *hanīfiyya* in the revealed books of God is a name for the worship of idols'. The second passage (p. 101 foot) is less immediately striking; after telling of the misfortunes which befell the wicked Persians he concludes with the remark 'and they perished through the anger (*sukhṭ*) and *rijz* (or *rujz*) of God'. The interest is in this usage of the word *rijz* or *rujz*.

The important question which these passages raise is whether there persisted for some centuries[79] among Christian Arabs an independent Arabic linguistic tradition reaching back into pre-Islamic times. It is commonly held by European scholars[80] that the word *ḥanīf* in pre-Islamic poetry means 'heathen'; and this is in accordance with the meaning of the corresponding Syriac word. It follows that al-Kindī's definition of *hanīfiyya* as 'idolatry' – which can be illustrated from other Christian writers[81] – goes back to pre-Islamic roots. It certainly cannot come from Muslim sources, since *al-hanīfiyya* is one of the names given to the religion of Islam. On the other hand, it might be argued that this usage of *ḥanīf* and *hanīfiyya* by Christian Arabs is something isolated and exceptional, due to the polemics between Muslims and Christians. If the word suggested some inferior form of religion close to heathenism, it would be natural for Christians to apply it to Muslims (though it was not appropriate) in order to express their contempt for the religion of their rulers. This Christian application might also be a reason for the abandonment of the name by Muslims.

Let us turn, then, to the other passage from al-Kindī and ask whether it confirms the view that certain pre-Islamic usages which had been forgotten by Muslims were retained by Christians. A *prima facie* case can be made out for an affirmative answer. The word *rujz* occurs once in the Qur'ān (74. 5), and, as Richard Bell and others have pointed out, almost certainly represents the Syriac *rūgzā* and means 'wrath' or, more particularly, refers to the outpouring of God's wrath at the end of the world.[82] There is no trace of this meaning, however, in the Muslim commentators. Yet the meaning which they had forgotten is seen – so the argument will run – to have remained alive among the Christians, since the parallel with *sukhṭ* in the passage from al-Kindī shows that his word is *rujz* and means 'wrath'.

This *prima facie* argument, however, can be countered. The word in al-Kindī, it may be said, is *rijz*, and it means 'punishment' – a sufficiently close parallel to 'anger'. This is the meaning commonly assigned to the Qur'ānic word by commentators like al-Ṭabarī. The passage is, therefore, no evidence of the persistence of Arabic usages among Christians independently of the tradition of Muslim scholarship.

In order to decide between this argument and counter-argument it is necessary to look into the interpretation of the words *rijz* and *rujz* in the Qur'ān, particularly the early interpretations recorded by al-Ṭabarī. In the usual texts *rijz* occurs nine times and *rujz* once, and the root is not found in any other form. It soon becomes clear, however, that no importance can be attached to the distinction between the two forms. *Rujz* is mentioned as a variant for *rijz* by al-Bayḍāwī at its first occurrence (2. 59/56), and he read *rijz* where *rujz* is normally read (74. 5), though again giving *rujz* as a variant.[83] Both he and al-Ṭabarī, as well as the lexicographers,[84] treat the difference of vowel as without significance.[85] The problem of the different vowels thus changes into that of why the normal text retained *rujz* in one instance and not in others. Perhaps it was because the usual early interpretation, namely 'punishment', was not suitable in this instance; the words 'flee the *rujz*' are addressed to Muḥammad, and he could not be supposed to be liable to punishment from God; the form *rujz* would give greater latitude to the exegetes. On the other hand, it might have been realized by some Muslims that *rujz* was closer to the pre-Islamic usage of the Christian Arabs, based on Syriac. It is not necessary here, however, to solve this problem.

Of the instances of *rijz* one is quickly seen to be irrelevant to the present investigation. This is in the passage, traditionally associated with Badr, where God sends down water from heaven on the Muslims to purify them and remove from them *rijz al-shayṭān* (8. 11). The earlier interpreters, both those reported by al-Ṭabarī and Ibn Isḥāq,[86] are unanimous in saying that this means the whisper (*waswasa, waswās*) of the devil in their hearts, suggesting that God was not with them, and making them afraid. There is no strong reason for rejecting this. Lane gives various verbal forms from the root RJZ as meaning to make a sound, especially a continuous sound, and referring to wind, thunder and the sea. The *rijz* of the devil could thus very well be his persistent murmur or whisper in their hearts. It is true that some later commentators, including al-Bayḍāwī, prefer the meaning 'filth'. This might be only an inference from the context, but it is supported by the assertion that *rijz* is equivalent to *rijs*. An examination of Lane shows that there is indeed some confusion between the two roots.[87] A modern Western scholar, however, would not be justified in following this later view unless it could be shown that there was in the Jāhiliyya a whole set of ideas with which this conception of satanic pollution was in harmony.

The remaining instances of *rijz* may be reduced to four distinct cases. First (in 7. 134/131, 135/131) there are three instances in the story of Moses and the plagues which were inflicted on the Egyptians. The *rijz* is said to have fallen on the Egyptians, they asked Moses to pray and remove the *rijz*, and God removed the *rijz*. Five plagues have been mentioned in the previous verse. Al-Ṭabarī's authorities are divided between taking the *rijz* in a general sense as the punishment, and taking it in a particular sense as 'pestilence'. According to the former interpretation it would presumably refer to the five plagues mentioned; according to the latter it would constitute a sixth. Secondly, two instances (2. 59/56; 7. 162) refer to Jews who changed a word God had commanded them to pronounce; God sent upon them a *rijz* from heaven. This is commonly interpreted as punishment or a specific punishment. Somewhat similar (thirdly) is one version of the story of Lot, where God threatens to send down a *rijz* from heaven on Lot's townsmen for their evil conduct (29. 34/33). Lastly, in two passages (34. 5; 45. 11/10) those who disbelieve in God's signs are threatened with 'a painful punishment of a *rijz*'.[88]

Thus, when we set aside the passage about the *rijz* of the devil, the word *rijz* is found only in contexts which are based on Judaeo-Christian material and ideas. It is in fact always a punishment inflicted by God or a manifestation of his wrath. Since the word is frequently indefinite, it cannot simply have meant 'wrath'. Al-Ṭabarī is thus justified in regarding its general meaning as 'punishment', while also noting that not all punishment is *rijz*. We might perhaps go on to say that the differentia of *rijz* is not its severity[89] or its particular nature but its being inflicted by God in wrath at evil-doing. The interpretation 'pestilence' is probably the result of a false inference, slightly supported by the application of *rajaz* to a disease of camels; the most probable interpretation of the passage about the Egyptians is thus that the *rijz* consists of the five plagues named, regarded as a manifestation of God's wrath.

The conclusion now seems unavoidable that, always leaving out of account 8. 11, *rijz* no less than *rujz* represents the Syriac *rūgzā*. It has suffered a slight transformation of meaning – if indeed it is a transformation – by coming to denote the outward expression of anger rather than the feeling itself, and by being used on occasion indefinitely; this is only a very slight change. The view of the Muslim scholars that there was no essential difference between *rijz* and *rujz* is thus shown to be sound. *Rujz* in the verse 'flee the *rujz*' (74.5) will be either the manifestations of God's wrath in general, or that impending on the Meccans, or the supreme manifestation, that is, condemnation on the Last Day; and the interpretation of the verse must be 'flee what leads to such punishment'.

This conclusion is reinforced by observing that al-Ṭabarī and his authorities sometimes show themselves aware that *rijz* and *rujz* meant 'anger'. The exegete Abū 'al-'Āliya, cited by al-Ṭabarī in his first discussion of *rijz*[90] gives the meaning as *ghaḍab*, 'anger'; while in the next passage[91] al-Ṭabarī himself speaks of the word as meaning *'adhāb* and *sukhṭ*, 'punishment' and 'anger'. Most interesting is the first citation on 74. 5 where Ibn 'Abbās says *al-rujz* means *al-sukhṭ wa-huwa 'l-aṣnām*. This remark also shows that the two meanings for *al-rujz* here which al-Ṭabarī found in his authorities, namely, 'idols' and 'sin', are not meanings in the strict sense but interpretations showing the precise reference or application.

From this examination of the Qur'ānic passages we may now return to al-Kindī. The *sukhṭ* and *rujz* of God of which he spoke must be God's anger and wrath. He is thus using the word in a sense close to that of the Syriac word from which it was derived. This usage was presumably current in certain Arab circles in Muḥammad's time and must have been the result of Christian (or, less probably, Jewish) influence. It is significant in this connexion that al-Kindī comes from the tribe of Kinda which was partly Christian in the Jāhiliyya. The use of the word in this sense cannot have been widespread, however, since it caused so much dispute among the commentators and had been almost forgotten by the time of al-Ṭabarī. This is readily understandable if the word was current chiefly among Christian Arabs.

The result of our investigation may be summarized as follows. There was among Christian Arabs a peculiar linguistic tradition. This tradition influenced the language of the Qur'ān in certain points. Independently of Muslim scholarship some parts of this tradition persisted at least until the tenth century A.D. Finally one might note the possibility that this persistence of a peculiar Christian linguistic tradition is due to an Arabic version of the New Testament.[92]

Part B

Early Islamic Thought

B1. The Early Development of the Muslim Attitude to The Bible

I. THE QUR'ĀN

A study of the Muslim attitude to the Bible must commence with the Qur'ān, but in doing so it must try to limit itself to what the Qur'ān actually says and exclude all later interpretations. There are four assertions of the Qur'ān that have to be specially considered.

(1) The general position of the Qur'ān is that it confirms previous revelations, and in particular (to adopt a convenient rendering of the Arabic terms) of the Torah and Evangel. This position ought to have had as its corollary an acceptance of the Old and New Testaments, but the Muslims soon discovered that there were serious differences between these and the Qur'ān. The Jews of the time, too, could not or would not find a place for Muḥammad in their doctrinal system, and the same later held of the Christians. This made it difficult for the Muslims to reconcile their presuppositions about the Bible with the actualities of the situation.

(2) The Qur'ān often implies and in one verse (7.157/156) definitely states that Muḥammad was foretold in the Bible. It seems probable that the Muslims had some grounds other than the words of the Qur'ān for thinking that this was so. It may be, as is suggested by some of the stories to be considered later, that the men of Medina had learned something of the Messianic hopes of the Jews and thought that Muḥammad was the expected Messiah. On the other hand, such stories may be mainly later inventions. Yet, whatever the explanation, the Muslims certainly believed that there were references to Muḥammad in the Bible.

(3) There are a number of verses in which the Jews are explicitly or implicitly accused of concealing some part of their scriptures, or are commanded not to do so.[93] The primary reference in these verses is to passages of the Old Testament allegedly foretelling Muḥammad's coming, but the Muslims who first heard them may have had other matters in mind also; one point frequently mentioned is the Mosaic prescription of stoning for adultery, but it is open to grave suspicion (as will be seen later). The accusation of 'inventing falsehood about God'[94] is perhaps only the corollary of the charge of concealing things, since concealing one thing often implies asserting something else that is false; but, since more is said about inventing falsehood than about concealing, it may

also have been applied to other matters, such as the Jewish oral law.[95]

(4) There are four passages which speak of the Jews deliberately 'corrupting' or 'altering' the scriptures. The meanings ascribed to the word *yuḥarrifūna* in commentaries and dictionaries are the outcome of the subsequent discussions and do not necessarily give much insight into the meaning of the passage at the time of revelation. One of the four passages, however, gives examples (4.46/48f.). After the general statement that the Jews 'alter the words from their sets' (which may be either 'places' or 'meanings'), it goes on to allege that they say 'we hear and disobey' instead of 'we hear and obey', 'hear something not audible' instead of simply 'hear', and 'show regard for us' instead of 'consider us'. The second example is obscure and will be left aside here. The first example involves a play on the Hebrew and Arabic phrases, *shāmaʿnū we-ʿāsīnū* and *samiʿnā wa-ʿaṣaynā*, meaning respectively 'we hear and do' and 'we hear and disobey'.[96] Similarly in the third example there is some play on the resemblance between *rāʿi-nā*, which means 'show regard for us' in Arabic, and the Hebrew root *raʿ*, 'evil'.[97] In the latter case this looks like a piece of Jewish mockery of Muḥammad, whereas in the former it is rather a linguistic confirmation of the rebelliousness of the Jews – they seem to say the Hebrew *ʿāsīnū*, but their actions show that they have in fact said the Arabic *ʿaṣaynā*.

The remaining passages with *yuḥarrifūna* throw little further light on its use; 'a section of the Jews were hearing the word of God and altering it wittingly' (2.75/70); 'they alter the words from their sets' (5.13/16); 'they alter the words after their sets and say "If this is given you accept it, but if it is not given you beware"' (5.41/45).

Some other passages containing similar ideas are also relevant. There are two references (2.58/55; 7.161) to a mysterious incident; God had told the Jews that, if they entered a certain town fulfilling certain conditions, they would be forgiven and prosper, and one of the conditions was that they should say *ḥiṭṭah* (said to mean 'forgiveness'); but they substituted another word. Another verse [98] speaks of some of them 'twisting their tongues in the Book' so that people may think a passage belongs to the Book when it does not, and saying 'It is from God' when it is not.

The conclusion of this examination of passages is that the Qur'ān does not put forward any general view of the corruption of the text of the Old and New Testaments. It makes clear allegations of the concealment of passages. It also makes the accusation of *taḥrīf* ('corruption' or 'alteration'), but by this does not mean tampering with the written text (except perhaps in copying it),[99] but – to judge from the examples – means the employment of various tricks in the course of dealings with Muslims.

2. THE FIRST PHASE OF DEVELOPMENT

The next lot of material bearing on the Muslim attitude to the Bible consists of a number of stories in the biographies of Muḥammad by Ibn Isḥāq (d. 768/151) and Ibn Sa'd (d. 844/230). Most of the items of this material are provided with a chain of authorities, but scrutiny of these chains has not so far revealed to me anything significant about the circles in which the various developments took place. It is almost certain, however, that the developments here called the first phase had occurred not later than the early 8th/2nd century. This phase can further be distinguished as being directed towards illiterate people with no knowledge of the Bible.

The Qur'ānic assertion that parts of the Bible had been concealed was supported by some crude stories, which could hardly have been believed except by people to whom writing was a mystery savouring of the magical. One story was that a Christian orphan, being brought up by an uncle, was one day reading in his uncle's copy of the Evangel when he came across a thick page, which proved to be two pasted together; he separated them and discovered a description of Muḥammad, which mentioned such points as that he was of medium height, of a fair complexion, of the seed of Ishmael and called Aḥmad. The uncle found the boy and beat him, and when the boy said, 'This has the description of the prophet Aḥmad,' replied, 'He has not yet come' [100] A similar story is told of a learned Jew, al-Zubayr b. Bāṭā; he found a book which his father had kept hidden in which there was a description of a prophet Aḥmad, but when Muḥammad began to proclaim his message at Mecca al-Zubayr obliterated this passage and denied its existence.[101] A man's attempt to conceal a legal prescription by putting his hand over it is described in an addition to the main story about the 'verse of stoning'.[102]

These stories of the physical concealment of verses help to buttress the chief point Muslims were anxious to maintain, that Muḥammad was foretold in the Jewish and Christian scriptures, but there were also other ways of doing this. A number of passages assert or imply that the Jews of Arabia immediately before Muḥammad's appearance were expecting a prophet. A man of Medina who fought at Badr is reported to have said that he remembered a Jewish neighbour speaking of a prophet that was expected from the south[103]; while other men of Medina are said to have become Muslims because they thought Muḥammad was the prophet expected by the Jews and wanted to be before the Jews in acknowledging him.[104] A Meccan Muslim told how he had heard a description of the external appearance of the prophet from various sources; the Meccan opponents of Muḥammad inquired of the Medinan Jews about him and learned that these had a description of the prophet which tallied with that of Muḥammad; a Muslim of Jewish stock spoke of a revelation to

Jacob about a *ḥaramī* (sc. Meccan) prophet who would be the seal of the prophets and would be called Aḥmad.[105] It is further implied that this Jewish expectation of a prophet was familiar to many Arabs, for it is alleged that a number of men in the 'times of ignorance' gave the name Muḥammad to a son in the hope that he would be the expected prophet.[106]

Another line of support for the same point was the assertion that various Jews admitted the truth of the claim that Muḥammad was foretold in the Old Testament. There are stories of Jews who realized that Muḥammad fulfilled the prophecies and who therefore became Muslims.[107] In addition to these it is alleged of several prominent Jews that they were aware that the descriptions they had of the expected prophet applied to Muḥammad, but that out of envy or for some other reason they refused to acknowledge him.[108] It is even said that at a much earlier period when Tubbaʿ (a former king of Yemen) was threatening Medina, a Jew Sāmawal told him about the prophet who was to come and about the futue glory of Medina, and so impressed him that he withdrew.[109]

A similar result is also obtained from stories about Christians who knew that Muḥammad was described in the Bible. There is the famous story about the monk Baḥīrā who, when the young Muḥammad accompanied his uncle Abū Ṭālib on a caravan to Syria, recognized his prophethood from descriptions in the books in his possession.[110] In the story of the conversion of Salmān the Persian various Christians are mentioned who knew about the coming of Muḥammad.[111] Less apparently legendary is the bishop who came with the deputation from Najrān, Abū 'l-Ḥārith b. ʿAlqama b. Rabīʿa, who agreed that Muḥammad was one of the apostles (*mursalīn*), that ʿĪsā had foretold him, and that he was in the Torah, but refused to accept him, though his brother did so.[112]

When we turn back to consider this material as a whole, we notice, apart from the many inherent improbabilities, that the stories are full of contradictions. This may be illustrated from those dealing with the messianic expectations of the Jews. Some imply that the coming of a prophet is widely known; one even suggests that many Arabs knew what his name was to be. Yet from the account of the conversion of three Jews [113] it is to be inferred that the advent of a prophet would have been unknown to these Medinan Jews but for the coming of a coreligionist, Ibn al-Hayyabān, from Syria. That Jews at many periods have held messianic hopes is well known, but it is not clear whether, apart from this Arabic material, we have any means of deciding to what extent such hopes were entertained in Arabia or Syria at this time.

The most important part of the material under review is that about the concealment of the 'verse of stoning' in the Torah (Deut. 22. 22), since this verse, along with the prophecies of Muḥammad, continues to be given as an illustration of what the Qur'ān means by concealment, long after the other stories have ceased to be mentioned. The reason for this is presumably that the Tradition about Muḥammad ordering a man and woman to be stoned for adultery was acknowledged as sound, because it was necessary to retain it as the justification for the prescription of this punishment in certain parts of the Islamic world. It is even asserted by some Muslim writers that there was a verse in the Qur'ān prescribing stoning; but this is almost certainly not so.[114] In Ibn Isḥāq's account [115] some Jews brought an adulterer and adulteress to Muḥammad and asked him to pass sentence; he asked for a learned Biblical scholar, verified that the Torah prescribed stoning, and had the sentence carried out. It is unlikely, however, that Medinan Jews would acknowledge Muḥammad's authority to this extent, even if they only wanted to test his prophethood. To judge from the case of Ka'b b. al-Ashraf, the son of an Arab father who was reckoned as belonging to his Jewish mother's tribe, the Jews of Medina observed in part the matriliny which was widespread among their Arab neighbours, and with which a loose sexual ethics was associated. It is therefore unlikely that any Jews would have tolerated the infliction of such a severe punishment as stoning or that Muḥammad would have prescribed it.

On the whole, then, there is hardly any historical fact behind the material here considered. Presumably some Jews and Christians became Muslims. Beyond that, however, the stories contain nothing of which we can be certain. They appear to be the work of those pious story-tellers, *quṣṣāṣ*, who were so fiercely attacked by later Muslim scholars.[116] These scholars must have realized that the material was useful in defending Qur'ānic positions only in so far as one was dealing with illiterate people (such as many nomadic Arabs and perhaps some of the poorer Ahl al-Kitāb in 'Irāq and Syria) who had no real knowledge of the Bible (apart from the fact that some Jews expected a Messiah). To such people it gave readily understood answers to the arguments against Islam which they might hear advanced by Jews or Christians, even though it was not an exact expansion of the assertions of the Qur'ān.

Slightly in advance of the *quṣṣāṣ*, but not much, were the early commentators on the Qur'ān as reported by Al-Ṭabarī. Most prominent is Mujāhid, who died about 721/103. He seems to have interpreted the Qur'ānic verses with *yuḥarrifūna* as applying to the Torah in general, and, when 'a section of the Jews' or 'some of them' were mentioned, to have taken these to be the rabbis.[117] The interpretations of al-Suddī (d. 744/127) were similar. As will be seen presently, this general condemnation was found by later scholars to be inadequate.

3. THE ATTEMPT TO FIND BIBLICAL PASSAGES FORETELLING MUḤAMMAD

The next phase of the development may be said to consist in the earlist attempts to find Biblical passages in which it could be maintained that Muḥammad was foretold. The description of the Messiah in Isaiah 42 early attracted attention. None of the versions in which it is found reproduces the Old Testament exactly, though they seem to have a common origin. A typical one is:

> ʿAbdallāh b ʿAmr b. al-ʿĀṣ, when asked about the description of the Prophet in the Torah, said: Yes, by God, he is described in the Torah with the description in the Qur'ān, 'O prophet, We have sent thee as a witness, an announcer and a warner' (33.45/44; cf. 48.8). In the Torah it runs, 'O prophet, We have sent thee as a witness, an announcer, a warner and a refuge for the Gentiles (*ummiyyīn*); thou art My servant and My messenger; I have named thee thy name, the trusting; he is not harsh nor rough nor crying in the streets (*aswāq*); he does not reward evil with evil, but pardons and forgives; We shall not take him (sc. he shall not die) till by him We have caused the crooked people to say 'There is no god but God' and by him We have opened the blind eyes, the deaf ears and the uncircumcised hearts.[118]

It is interesting that a messianic prophecy, even in this distorted form, should be applied to Muḥammad; but it is no more than a logical development of the claim that he was the prophet expected by the Jews.

In contrast to this inaccurate reference to the Old Testament, there is a fairly exact translation of John 15. 23-16.1 in the *Sīra* of Ibn Isḥāq (d. 768/151).[119] After the quotation there is a comment, presumably by Ibn Isḥāq and not by his editor, Ibn Hishām, to the effect that Muḥammad is linguistically equivalent to the Syriac MNḤMNĀ and the Greek BRQLĪṬS. This comment seems to presuppose the confusion between *paraklētos* and *periklutos*.

It is noteworthy that Ibn Isḥāq does not mention sūra 61.6 in this connexion. The explanation would seem to be either that the words 'his name is Aḥmad' did not stand in the Qur'ān at that time but were later interpolated,[120] or that they stood in it but were taken to mean 'his name is more worthy of praise' (with *aḥmadu* as an adjective).[121] From the absence of occurrences of the name Aḥmad before about 740/123 and the absence in the *Tafsīr* of al-Ṭabarī of early interpretations of 61.6 in what is now the normal sense, it would seem that the interpolation or (more probably) reinterpretation took place round about 730/112. The linking up of the New Testament promise of the Paraclete with sūra 61.6 greatly strengthened the Muslim case at this point. The name Aḥmad soon became very popular, while in the material from Ibn Saʿd (d. 844/

230) just considered many of the alleged prophecies of Muḥammad contain the phrase 'his name is Aḥmad' (though this could be an addition to the original text).

The next figure in chronological order is the caliph al-Mahdī, who about 782/166 had a discussion with the Nestorian Catholicos Timothy, which has been reported from the Christian side. Besides asserting that there had been a general 'alteration' of the scriptures and an omission of testimonies to Muḥammad, the caliph mentioned three Biblical passages which he alleged to refer to Muḥammad. There was the promise of the Paraclete (again without any mention of Aḥmad), the 'rider on the camel' (a variant translation of Is. 21.7), and the promise of a prophet like Moses (Deut. 18.18).[122] After this Muslim scholars seem to have devoted much attention to the text of the Bible to discover passages which might serve their purpose. Ibn Qutayba (d. 889/276) had a sizeable list of such passages,[123] while the convert ʿAlī al-Ṭabarī, writing in 855/241, produced 130.[124]

This new phase in the Muslim attitude to the Bible and in Muslim polemics against the 'people of the Book' is in part an expression of the widening of interests and of the outburst of intellectual activity which took place about the time of the caliph al-Ma'mūn (813/198–833/218). It also implies closer contacts between Muslims and Christians, and this would be in accordance with the (perhaps exaggerated) picture drawn by al-Jāḥiẓ (d.868/255) in his *Radd ʿalā 'l-Naṣārā,* where he speaks of their high social position and neglect of the outward marks which distinguished them from Muslims. In such circumstances the naïve attitude of the earlier phase was no longer possible. An educated audience in contact with educated Christians (and to a lesser extent Jews) required arguments at a higher level. It is thus not surprising that ʿAlī al-Ṭabarī has an introductory chapter on logical principles. In particular it was necessary to replace the former vague references to descriptions found in the Torah by exact quotations. Much was achieved in this direction, but, as Goldziher has pointed out, even the best Muslim scholars still had a very slight acquaintance with the Bible, and they still retained some of the old fables.[125]

4. THE AVOIDANCE OF INFORMATION FROM JEWS AND CHRISTIANS

Complementary to the material so far considered are the traditions regarding questioning 'people of the Book' and using copies of the former scriptures. Some of this material is found scattered through the canonical collections, but it will be sufficient here to confine our attention to the traditions and anecdotes brought together by the Andalusian scholar, Ibn ʿAbd al-Barr (d. 1070/463).[126] Though this work is late in date, the presumption is that the material had not been much altered in the previous

200 or even 300 years, but the study of the chains of authorities has not progressed sufficiently to enable us to say whether any of it had its present form at a still earlier period. The fact that most of Ibn ʿAbd al-Barr's material envisages Muslims conversing with Jews and Christians but not reading their books suggests that it belongs to the 'first' phase (§2).

Some of the traditions express a moderate attitude, according to which the questioning of Jews and Christians seems to be permitted, but Muslims are told to adopt a non-commital attitude to what they hear or to test it by the Qur'ān.

> (After a Jew had made a palpably false statement in Muḥammad's presence) the Messenger of God said, Whatever the people of the Book relate to you, neither believe them nor disbelieve them, but say, We believe in God and His books and His messengers; if it is true, you have not disbelieved them, and if it is false, you have not believed them.[127]
>
> He (ibn ʿAbbās) said, If you are asking them, that is that; but see what agrees with the Book of God, and accept it, and what is contrary to the Book of God, and reject it.[128]

Along with this moderate attitude to the people of the Book goes the view that the Muslims form a community parallel to the Jews and Christians, and that they should therefore remain loyal to Muḥammad and the Qur'ān.

> (Muḥammad) said, There is a people sufficiently foolish or misguided to turn away from what their prophet brought them to a prophet who is not theirs or a book which is not theirs. Then God revealed. . . (29.51/50) [129]
>
> (Muḥammad) said, By Him in Whose hand is Muḥammad's life, if Moses came among you and you followed him and left me, you would err; you are my portion among the peoples, and I am your portion among the prophets.[130]

Most of this section in Ibn ʿAbd al-Barr shows a stricter attitude, however. The questioning of Jews and Christians is discouraged or forbidden. They are in error or have deliberately corrupted the scriptures, so that one never knows when they are to be relied on.

> ʿAbdallāh b. Masʿūd said, Do not ask the people of the Book about anything, for they will not guide you aright, seeing they have misled themselves, and you will (find yourselves) disbelieving something true and believing something false.[131]
>
> Ibn ʿAbbās said, How do you ask the people of the Book about anything while your book, which God revealed to His prophet, is among you?. . . Did God not inform you in His book that they have changed and altered (*ghayyarū, baddalū*) the book of God? and have written the book with their hands and said, This is from God, that thereby they may make a small gain (2.79/73)? Does He

> not forbid you the knowledge that comes to you from questioning them? By God, we never saw a man of them asking you about what God revealed to you.[132]

In the last quotation it is implied that all the sound knowledge of religious matters necessary for a Muslim can be gained from the Qur'ān.

Another anecdote, which also mentions the use of non-Muslim scriptures, goes so far as to assert the superiority of Islam to Judaism (contrary to the earlier doctrine of parallelism).

> (When 'Umar b. al-Khaṭṭāb came to Muḥammad with a book belonging to some of the people of the Book), he was angry and said, Are you all amazed about them (? these books), O Son of al-Khaṭṭāb; by God, they were brought to you white and pure; do not ask them (those people) about anything; they will tell you something true and you will disbelieve it, or something false and you will believe it; by God, even if Moses was alive, nothing would be open to him but to follow me.[133]

The material thus conveniently collected by Ibn 'Abd al-Barr emphasizes the importance for Muslims of avoiding discussions with Jews and Christians.[134] The people of the Book held views which were contrary to certain fundamental Islamic conceptions and which, if given free play, would in course of time have so eaten away these conceptions that the whole structure raised upon them would have collapsed. These traditions and anecdotes probably did not so much help to form a new attitude as give expression to the attitude already formed. They are complementary to the material already considered in that they presuppose a general corruption of the Bible as held by the early commentators on the Qur'ān [135]

ADDITIONAL NOTE

Before writing the article, I was unable to consult the important discussion of *Taḥrīf* by Monsignor Di Matteo in *Bessarione*, Volume xxxviii, but I have since done so. The chief additional point to be derived from it is that there are a number of passages in the Qur'ān which imply that the Scriptures actually in the hands of Jews and Christians are authentic.

B2. Some Muslim Discussions of Anthropomorphism

The general course of Islamic thought on the subject of anthropomorphism is well known, and is conveniently expounded by Strothmann in the article on *Tashbīh* in the *Encyclopaedia of Islam*. The aim of this paper is to provide an interpretation and appreciation of the questions at issue and the answers given.

I. THE DOCTRINE OF *BALKAFIYYA*

The problems implicit in the anthropomorphic conceptions of the Qur'ān did not begin to thrust themselves upon the awareness of Muslim thinkers till towards the close of the second century of the Hijra. The point was apparently raised first by the heterodox groups of the Muʿtazila and Jahmiyya, and they raised it in a fashion that could not be ignored, by accusing the main body of the faithful and the 'orthodox' doctors of the heresy of *tashbīh*, of likening God to creatures or, as it is usually translated, anthropomorphism. The Muʿtazila and Jahmiyya – at this period probably not entirely distinct from one another – had come under the influence of Greek philosophy, but the idea of most nineteenth-century Orientalists that their dislike for anthropomorphism sprang from a desire to hellenize and rationalize Islamic theology is unsound. It is now realized that they devoted much time and energy to apologetic for Islam against Manichaeanism and various Indian religions and that they were not primarily hellenizers and rationalists but primarily Muslims who found in the armoury of Hellenistic thought useful weapons against their opponents. It seems likely, therefore, that their hostility to anthropomorphism was on account of the apologetic difficulties to which it led.

There is some confirmation for the view that their motive was Islamic and not rationalistic in the way in which they supported their doctrines by quotation from the Qur'ān. The phrase 'There is nothing anything like Him' (42. 9) was in constant use, while such a verse as 'Sight reacheth not to Him' (6. 103) seemed to disprove any physical vision of God. Now it is conceivable that the Muʿtazila and Jahmiyya were simply trying to meet their orthodox opponents on their own ground, and did not take the appeal to the Qur'ān seriously; it was this same group which denied that the Qur'ān was the eternal and uncreated Word of God. The tone of the discussions, however, shows that they claimed to be expounding the religion of God and Muḥammad, not to be setting up a new religion. And – what is more important – in emphasizing that God is different from everything corporeal and material they were, in fact, developing one factor in the Qur'ānic conception of God. We in the West tend to speak of Islam as stressing the transcendence of God, but it has to be remembered that, while for the West the chief aspect of transcendence is probably God's might and majesty, for Islam it is rather His otherness from His creatures. This aspect is present in the Old Testament – 'My thoughts are not your thoughts, neither are your ways My ways, saith the Lord' – but in the Muslim outlook its relative importance is greater. Among later theologians God's otherness or difference, *mukhālafa*, is a point included in the creed. In accordance with this, too, the heresy we are considering is called 'making God like', that is, denying His otherness.

Modern Orientalists, assimilating the rationalism of the third and fourth centuries of Islam to the rationalism of nineteenth-century Europe, have expressed surprise that al-Ashʿarī, the founder of the rationalistic school of orthodox theology who turned the intellectual weapons of the Muʿtazila against themselves, should in his extant works devote himself mainly to arguments from the text of the Qur'ān and not to purely rational arguments. Yet, when the rationalism of the Muʿtazila is properly understood, the preoccupation of al-Ashʿarī with textual arguments is not surprising. The teachings of the Muʿtazila had a solid substructure of Qur'ānic exegesis, and therefore a man like al-Ashʿarī who professed an orthodoxy in accordance with Qur'ān and Traditions, had first and foremost to dispute the exegesis of his opponents. In particular, the Jahmiyya and Muʿtazila had invented the method of *ta'wīl* which may be roughly translated 'metaphorical interpretation'. They argued, for instance, that the verses which said that the faithful would 'see' God on the day of resurrection really meant that they would 'know' Him, and in defence of this interpretation they could quote other verses where the word 'see' was used of men although there could be no reference to physical sight. Again, they could show that the word for 'hand' sometimes in good Arabic had the meaning of 'grace' (*niʿma*) – a rough equivalent is our coloquial phrase 'I'll give you a hand' – and on this basis they held that when God was said to create by His hands (38. 75)) that really meant by His grace. Similarly, the face of God which alone endures (55. 27) they asserted to be His essence. These examples show that the word *ta'wīl* had a much narrower sense than our word 'metaphor'; the method of *ta'wīl* was to interpret single words of the sacred text according to secondary or metaphorical meanings found elsewhere in the Qur'ān or in good poetry. There was no question of novel metaphors or of the metaphorical interpretation of whole phrases.

The adoption of such *ta'wīl*, however, was not the only attitude found among the opponents of anthropomorphism. There were also some who preferred the *via negativa*, and who apparently denied that we could say anything positive about God except that He was Divine, and interpreted the positive attributes as denials of the contrasting imperfections; thus to say God is knowing or generous is not to attribute any quality to Him positively, but to deny ignorance and meaness of Him. Some extremists in this line went so far in their agnostic attitude that they refused either to affirm or to deny that God is a thing.

On the whole, however, and especially among the Muʿtazila proper, a more moderate attitude prevailed, and they were prepared to admit that 'God is a thing' with the proviso that 'He is not as the things' (*shay' lā ka 'l-ashyā'*). That is to say, there is a certain relation of God to things or creatures which enables us to employ mundane and creaturely predicates of Him. These predicates are not used in precisely the same sense of God and of man; on the other hand, they are not used in completely unrelated senses; but the exact relation of the two senses is not defined. The majority of the Muʿtazila rejected the attribution to God in a literal sense of anything that suggested that He had a body – hands, face, sitting on a throne, being seen, hearing, seeing – but they permitted the statements that He is knowing, powerful, and living.

This, then was the background against which was formulated the doctrine of *balkafiyya*, that is, the doctrine that we are justified in using mundane predicates of God *bi-lā kayf*, without explaining exactly how they apply to Him. The doctrine is specially connected with the name of Aḥmad ibn Ḥanbal (d. 243/855), but he was doubtless building on the foundations of earlier men. The most accessible early expositions of the doctrine by thinkers who accepted it are *Kitāb Ta'wīl Mukhtalif al-Ḥadīth* by Ibn Qutayba (d. 276/889) and *Kitāb al-Ibāna ʿan Uṣūl al-Diyāna* by al-Ashʿarī (d. 324/935). Let us now therefore turn to the doctrine itself and consider its import and bearings.

Orthodoxy had been accused of making God similar to men. This charge they indignantly denied, and they inveighed against *tashbīh* as vehemently as the Muʿtazila. They agreed that God was not corporeal and that He transcended and was different from all creatures; and in this they were quite genuine, for it was one side of the traditional Islamic outlook. At the same time, however, they clung to the text of the Qur'ān, which they regarded as the very words of God. If the Qur'ān spoke of God's hands and face, then God must have hands and a face. How God Who is incorporeal has hands and a face may be difficult to understand, but this difficulty is not a valid reason for rejecting the phrases of Scripture or explaining them away by the method of *ta'wīl*. One must maintain both the authority of Scripture and the incorporeality of God, even if one cannot reconcile them intellectually. In the doctrine of *balkafiyya* this position was regularized and a formal acknowledgement made of the limits of the human intellect.

The essence of the doctrine is that the terms and phrases of Scripture are to be accepted *bi-lā kayf*. God 'has two hands *bi-lā kayf*. . . He has two eyes *bi-lā kayf*' says al-Ash'arī in his creed, quoting appropriate verses from the Qur'ān. It is implied that the hands and eyes are not corporeal, and the phrase *bi-lā kayf* further suggests that no attempt is to be made to substitute something else for 'hands' and 'eyes'. There is also an important corollary which is formulated several times by Ibn Qutayba: we must not argue by analogy from what occurs in Scripture to what does not occur there; that is to say, we must not argue that because God has hands He has flesh, blood, and bones.

What are we to make of such a doctrine? It has often been derided as mere obscurantism; but that is very far from being the case. The doctrine of *balkafiyya* is a serious and by no means unsuccessful attempt to grapple with the problem of the relation of the picture-language of religious intuition to the metaphysical theology connected with it. The Mu'tazila had tried to translate some of the picturesque terms of religious intuition into abstractions that were more tractable theologically. In effect, they said, 'God's hand does not really mean God's hand but something else'. That, however, is the beginning of the process of discrediting the Scriptures, and the end of such a process is their abandonment. Ibn Qutayba was expressing one of the deepest and truest insights of his party when he said that the integral acceptance of the Scriptures was the foundation of the unity of the Islamic community.

Thus the achievement of the upholders of *balkafiyya* in the third and fourth centuries of the Hijra was that they preserved for their community its essential bond of unity. A subtle attack had been made upon the Qur'ān in the name of a principle expressed in the Qur'ān itself. If Islamic orthodoxy, because it believed in the otherness of God, had admitted *ta'wīl* or metaphorical interpretation as a general principle of exegesis, it would tacitly have abandoned the authority of religious intuition (or revelation) for that of reason, and the disintegration of Islam would probably have followed.

The weakness of the doctrine of *balkafiyya* was that, while limiting the authority of reason in the interpretation of the Scriptures, it did not show how reason in its theological or metaphysical use is connected with religious intuition. It was clear, as Ibn Qutayba had seen, that the various conceptions of religious intuition cannot be formed into one harmonious whole; according to one conception God must be at rest, but according to another He moves, and yet the principle of *bi-lā kayf* permits us to accept both conceptions as true without harmonizing them. On the other hand, a thinker like al-Ash'arī who admitted a proper theological use of reason could not rest content in the acceptance of this disharmony in our theological conceptions. He himself, though admitting *balkafiyya*, never, so far as I am aware, went so far as Ibn Qutayba in emphasizing the disharmony of the Scriptural conceptions; and the development of doctrine among his followers was largely guided by the ideal of finding harmony and system in the main conceptions of Scripture.

2. THE SUCCESSORS OF AL-ASHʿARI

Al-Ashʿarī was a supporter of *balkafiyya.* He was also interested in metaphysical theology, however, and in his *Ibāna* introduces purely rational arguments alongside the textual arguments. His later oral teaching may have developed the metaphysical side of his thought much further than the *Ibāna*. Within a century from the death of al-Ashʿarī in 324/935 the school which took his name had abandoned the doctrine of *balkafiyya* on most of the points on which al-Ashʿarī had contended for it and had adopted views similar to those of his opponents among the Muʿtazila. Examples of this new attitude are *Kitāb Uṣūl al-Dīn* of al-Baghdādī (d. 429/1037) and *Kitāb al-Irshād* of al-Juwaynī, Imām al-Ḥaramayn (d. 478/1085).

The precise extent of the change must first be noted. The two theologians named agree in saying that the hands of God mean His power, His eyes mean His seeing, and His face means His essence or existence; and neither takes the sitting on the throne literally or *bi-lā kayf*. On the other hand, they held that God would be seen by the faithful on the day of resurrection, even considering that they could give a rational proof of the possibility of God's being seen; this alleged proof presupposed, of course, that God was not corporeal. They also held that Life, Hearing, and Sight were among the attributes of God. The attitude of men like al-Ghazālī (d. 505/1111), al-Shahrastānī (d. 548/1153), and Fakhr al-Dīn al-Rāzī (d. 606/1209) to the question of anthropomorphism was in the main that of al-Baghdādī, except that they did not consider it worth while discussing in detail the interpretation of the hands of God. The *Mawaqif* of al-Īji (d. 756/1355) as commented by al-Jurjānī (d. 816/1413) perhaps comes back closer to the al-Ashʿarī of the *Ibāna*, but definitely does not return to the doctrine of *balkafiyya*. How is this right-about-turn in the school of al-Ashʿarī to be explained? And is it to be regarded as advance or regression?

It has been noted earlier that the doctrine of *balkafiyya* can only be maintained if one renounces the attempt to form one's intuitional conceptions into a harmonious system. This the theologians of the Ashʿariyya could hardly be expected to do since their intellectual energies were devoted to the task of systematizing their religious beliefs. For instance, al-Juwaynī, writing against those whom he calls the Ḥashwiyya, whose attitude was presumably similar to that of Ibn Ḥanbal and Ibn Qutayba, points to the contradiction between the conceptions that God 'is with you wheresoever you are' and that he 'seated Himself on the throne'; if God is on the throne, He cannot be with all the Muslims. From this contradiction al-Juwaynī draws the conclusion that the method of *ta'wīl* cannot be avoided in some cases, and in particular that God's presence with the believers must mean His knowledge of their secrets. In this he is assuming that there must be a harmonious rational interpretation of the Scriptural phrases, and apparently his opponents were not capable of defending the opposite view.

From the principle that *ta'wīl* or metaphorical interpretation is permissible, al-Juwaynī argued that there was no point in attributing to any verse a sense which implied contingency in God (*ḥadath*). When we remember that for both the Ash'ariyya and their chief opponents, the Mu'tazila, corporeality involved contingency, we begin to understand what impelled them to adopt metaphorical interpretations of the bodily attributes of God. They had accepted a natural or rational theology in which the contingency or temporal character of the world was made the basis of the proof that the world has a non-contingent or necessary and eternal Creator. Thus, it was the form taken by their proof of the existence of God which made it so urgent for them to avoid ascribing any bodily attributes to God.

It was not possible for them, however, to explain away all the bodily characteristics in the Qur'ānic conception of God. It seems probable that what led them to treat some cases differently from others was the place they occupied in popular religion. The conception of God's hands, for instance, was not a vital factor in the religious intuition of Islam, whereas to say that God was not to be described as 'hearing' might have undermined the practice of prayer, since it would have implied or at least suggested that God did not hear prayers, and similarly to deny that God would be seen by the believers on the day of resurrection would possibly have weakened belief in the future life and the day of Judgement. Consequently, orthodox theologians tried to find rational accounts of God's hearing and sight and of the vision of God which avoided asserting that these were metaphors and so not quite real.

One of the things which made the abandonment of *balkafiyya* possible was the very success of the Ash'ariyya. That doctrine had originally been part of an attempt to maintain the authority of the Scriptures. In this struggle orthodoxy had been victorious, and the Ash'ariyya, for all their rationalistic tendencies, loyally acknowledged the primacy of the Scriptures. Because of the wide agreement about this, more liberty could be taken in the actual work of exegesis. We must be careful, however, not to exaggerate the liberty in interpretation claimed by men like al-Juwaynī. The conceptions which they interpreted metaphorically were few in number, and even to these they applied the metaphorical interpretation only in order to bring them into harmony with principles which long discussion had convinced them were thoroughly in accordance with the sacred texts.

Moreover, the school of al-Ashʿarī were in contrast with other exponents of the method of *ta'wīl* in yet another way. In their case the doctrines with which *ta'wīl* was associated were thoroughly orthodox, whereas in the case of the Jahmiyya, for example, the denial that God sits on the throne was coupled with the assertion that He is omnipresent in a pantheistic sense, and it was the pantheism as much as the belittling of the Scriptures which provoked the counter arguments of al-Ashʿarī. Much of the objection to the *ta'wīl* of the early Muʿtazila was perhaps due to the connection of their *ta'wīl* with their preference of the authority of reason to that of the Scriptures.

These various points, then, show how it was possible for the Ashʿariyya to make this right-about-turn on the question of *balkafiyya*. How far were the results of the change gain and how far loss?

The new position of the Ashʿariyya was an advance in that it recognized distinctions within the conceptions of religious intuition. Some were devotionally important, that is, important in the day-to-day religious life of ordinary men; others not so important. Some were theologically acceptable and others theologically objectionable. Further, those which were theologically acceptable were treated as primary and fundamental, and it was assumed that they were adequate to their subject-matter, the nature and attributes of God; no difficulty was felt, for instance, in saying that God was knowing and powerful and living. Yet, if God is absolutely other, there is a difficulty in characterizing Him thus, and at a much later time we find Muslims becoming aware of this. In the early nineteenth century al-Fuḍālī maintained that God's hearing is connected not merely with sounds but also with essences, although we do not know the manner (*kayfiyya*) of this connection; this is an application of the principle of *balkafiyya* to those fundamental attributes of God which had been tacitly excepted from its scope by al-Ashʿarī.

This illustrates how there was also an element of loss in the new position of the Ashʿariyya. The truth which had been seen by the upholders of *balkafiyya* was now lost sight of. It did not occur to those later men that there could be a use of words which was neither literal nor metaphorical, as the terms were currently used. Al-Ījī and al-Jurjānī had some awareness of the differences between al-Ashʿarī and the majority of his followers, but their description of al-Ashʿarī's views shows that they had no appreciation of his standpoint in this matter. His statement that God has a hand *bi-lā kayf* was translated into the assertion that God's hand is an attribute distinct from His essence but otherwise unknown. Al-Ashʿarī was supposed to hold the same about the Face of God; and then it was easy for later expositors to argue that such a view was untenable, since taken with the verse that nothing endures but the Face of God it leads to the conclusion that a single attribute of God endures and that the other attributes and His essence perish; and that is absurd. It did not even occur to them that al-Ashʿarī might have meant something quite different by his *balkafiyya*.

The failure to appreciate this aspect of ancient teaching was symptomatic of the rationalism which had come to dominate orthodox theology apart form the followers of Ibn Ḥanbal. It was not a rationalism in which reason was set above the revealed Scriptures, but one in which reason was assumed to be competent to understand and interpret the main truths contained in the Scriptures, and with these as basis to fathom the mystery of the Divine nature. That is to say, it was argued that, though the conceptions of religious intuition could not be reached by purely rational procedures yet, once they were reached, they were thoroughly rational conceptions, forming a harmonious system.

Al-Ghazālī was possibly the theologian most aware of the difficulties caused by the gulf between the intellectual and intuitional aspects of Islamic religion. Early in his career he realized the importance of confirming the ordinary man in his simple, childlike acceptance of the intuitional conceptions for which the intellectuals had subtle interpretations; and to the end he insisted that the intellectual should not despise the naïve attitude of the ordinary man, but should accept scriptural statements at their face value and practise them. Since Muḥammad had said that the angels of God do not enter a house where there is a dog, the truly pious intellectual should not merely drive the dog of wrath from the house of his heart but should see that his physical dwelling had no canine inhabitants.

Al-Ghazālī also tried to find a place for the intuitional aspect by adding to the two groups of ordinary men and intellectuals a third group, those who had had direct experience of God by *dhawq* or 'taste'. By placing this third group above the intellectuals he suggested that such direct experience of God was something superimposed on the rational beliefs of the intellectual, as if a man could not taste and see that God is good until he had had a university course in systematic theology. The possibility of the unlettered man attaining the insight of the saint presupposes that the essential truths contained in the simple and crude scriptural conceptions can be apprehended without any training in subtle rational exegesis. The weakness of both these attempts seems to indicate the need for something like the doctrine of *bi-lā kayf*.

B3. Created in His Image: A Study in Islamic Theology

I

It is now a commonplace among Western scholars of Islam that in the early formative period – the period of about two hundred years after the conquest of Syria and Iraq – the new religion incorporated into itself the quintessence of the inherited wisdom of these lands of ancient culture. The Qur'ān already presented in its distinctive way much of the deepest insights of Judaism and Christianity; but it was a presentation suited in the first place to the restricted horizons of Mecca and Medina. The conquests, and the subsequent conversion of many of the inhabitants of the conquered lands, led to a different situation. The new Muslims were more cultured than the old, and had various conceptions in matters of religion. In due course they found a way of incorporating their ideas into Islam. All they had to do was to invent an anecdote in which the ideas were put into the mouth of Muḥammad on a specific occasion. The anecdote insinuated itself into the vast body of Traditions about Muḥammad which constituted part of the revelational basis of the community. By this method Jewish, Christian, Gnostic and other non-Islamic doctrines and practices were brought into Islam. Muḥammad is even depicted as exhorting his followers to use a prayer which is essentially the Christian pater-noster.[136]

This process by which Islam has taken into itself the old culture of the Middle East, and has tried to become the sole bearer of that culture, is a fascinating subject of study, which has attracted attention and will continue to do so. Here, however, we are concerned with only one small facet of the whole. An attempt was made to introduce into Islam the conception from the book of *Genesis* (i. 26 f.) that God created man in his own image; but the conception came up against strong resistance and after some vicissitudes may be said to have been rejected by Islamic orthodoxy. To look for a little at the different attitudes adopted by Muslims on this point will perhaps contribute to an understanding of some theological developments.

The first step was taken when a Muslim, presumably one from a Jewish or Christian background, alleged that Muḥammad had once said that 'God created Adam in his image'. There does not seem to be any direct evidence for this invention of the Tradition by a convert, but the inferential arguments for it are conclusive. It is necessary in order to explain the later elaborations of the Tradition, and it is virtually accepted by later Muslim writers such as Ibn Qutayba (d. 885). This simple form of the conception from *Genesis* must have been in circulation as a Tradition soon after 700 A.D.

The second step is the reinterpretation of this Tradition as it stands by the assertion that the pronoun 'his' refers to Adam. That is, the words mean that God created Adam in Adam's image or form.[137] (The Arabic word is *ṣūra*, and in what follows the rendering 'form' will usually be more convenient than the 'image' of *Genesis*. The word also suggests 'face' in some contexts.) This reinterpretation must have taken place before the Tradition was expanded in the way that is to be described as constituting the third step. The chief difficulty about interpreting the words in this way is that they do not seem to have much point, as was remarked by Ibn Qutayba. Later writers tried to deal with this objection in various ways. The most successful was to say that it meant that Adam was created in the Garden (or Paradise) in precisely the form he was later to have on earth.[138] This would have a certain point. Indeed, it could be construed as the denial of various views that were actually held, or might be held, within the Islamic world. It was a denial that Adam was changed, like the serpent or peacock, when he was expelled from the Garden; it was a denial that he came into being through natural processes, whether physical or embryological, and had to undergo development in order to reach maturity. It could even be regarded as a denial that the form or conception of humanity was a mere abstraction of the human intellect.[139] For the exponents of these views and for the more intellectual Muslims this might be a satisfactory way of dealing with what they felt to be objectionable in the assertion that God created Adam in his image or form; but such subtleties of interpretation could hardly have appealed to the ordinary man.

It is not surprising, therefore, to find that an alternative explanation was put forward by members of that central or conservative body of opinion, close to the outlook of ordinary Muslims, and usually called the Traditionists. These Traditionists (*muḥaddithūn*) were not the only persons involved in handing on Traditions, but that section of them who were accounted reliable by later Tradition-critics. This may be called the third step. Like the more intellectually-minded persons responsible for the second step, some of these Traditionists must have been seriously perturbed when Muslims accepted the assertion that God created Adam in his form and understood this in the usual Jewish and Christian sense. At the date when this third step was being made, probably a little before 750,[140] there was no science of Tradition-criticism which could be invoked to impugn the objectionable doctrine. As has been the case in many other places and periods, once a statement or story or slander has come into circulation, a mere denial does not scotch it. So the opponents of the conception of man's creation in the form of God thought of an ingenious way of reinterpreting the words so that they did not imply this conception.

The method consisted in giving a context to the words in such a way that the pronoun 'his' attached to the Arabic word *ṣūra* referred neither to God nor to Adam himself but to a third person. Muḥammad is alleged to have given a command or counsel, 'Do not say, May God make foul his face and a face like his, for God created Adam in his form'. A variant was, 'If you are beating anyone, avoid his face, for God created Adam in his form'.[141] The pronoun 'his' here naturally refers to the man cursed or beaten; and, in the case of the cursing, it could be said that the point of the prohibition was to prevent men cursing Adam and the prophets.[142] The form which spoke of not beating the face was expanded into a little story. Muḥammad once passed a man who was beating his servant on the face, and said to him, 'Do not beat his face, for God created Adam in his (or its) form'.[143] This version of the Tradition seems to have been the most widespread at certain later periods. It must have been in circulation by about 875 at latest (since Ibn Qutayba died in 885 or 889), but it was not noticed by Ibn Khuzayma (d. 923). Yet al-Ghazālī two centuries later implies that it was the familiar form in his day. It was certainly the most likely to appeal to the ordinary man, since it gave an easily pictured context in which the dubious words had a clear and inoffensive meaning. For intellectual Muslims, however, it was somewhat pointless, and it is not surprising that it was neglected altogether in the elaborate treatment of the question by Fakhr-al-Din al-Rāzī (d. 1209).[144]

What may be called the fourth step in the history of the Tradition consists in the attempt by a section of the Traditionists to prevent the whittling away or transformation of the original Jewish-Christian meaning of the statement (here described as the second and third steps). Those responsible for this fourth step, however, must not be thought of as in any way disloyal to Islam or advocating a return to Judaism or Christianity. They are rather representatives of a definite trend within Islam, usually called *tashbīh* or anthropomorphism. In part this indicates the persistence of very primitive ideas within Islam – ideas which had continued to exist on the fringes of Judaism and Christianity, though not fully taken up into these religions. Among those of the Traditionists inclined to anthropomorphism there became current a form of our Tradition which began: God created Adam in his form, his height being sixty ells.[145] This is not the place to study all that is involved in this conception of Adam as a gigantic angel;[146] and it will be enough to point out that the addition of the words 'his height being sixty ells' excludes the application of the basic statement to a man who was being beaten or cursed.

Along with this version of the Tradition may be classed another which has the same effect of excluding the application of the pronoun 'his' to a man beaten or cursed, or even to Adam himself. In its simplest form this version simply substituted *al-Raḥmān*, the Merciful: God created Adam in the form of the Merciful.[147] Another version justified the prohibition of the cursing of the face by the words 'for the son of Adam is created in the form of the Merciful'.[148] Any of the versions with the words 'the Merciful' makes it clear that the form or *ṣūra* is God's. Yet even this did not end the debate, where it was accepted, for some men still maintained that the Merciful's form was not the form in which God himself existed or appeared, but one which he possessed in the same way as he possessed forms or models for other things which he created.

Among the Traditionists, too, there continued to be a section which accepted the standard interpretation, that Adam was created in the form or image of God. A representative of this section is the Ḥanbalite theologian, Ibn Baṭṭa (d. 997), in whose creed there is a brief reference to the version of the Tradition which prohibits cursing the face; this is then followed by another Tradition in which Muḥammad says, 'I saw God in such and such a form (*ṣūra*)'.[149]

This, then, in outline appears to be the history of the Tradition that God created Adam in his image. Though the presentation here has been largely based on conjectures made in accordance with the latest Western theories of the growth of Tradition, it is worthy of note that all the main points were anticipated by Ibn Qutayba in the ninth century. And he is usually reckoned a Traditionist!

II

It remains to consider something of what lies behind this vast expenditure of intellectual effort. Why were all these resources of ingenuity brought to bear on this little point? Why was there so much interest in the question? Why was it so important for many Muslims to prevent the conception of man's being created in the image or form of God, from finding *droit de cité* in Islam?

These questions are made more urgent when one looks at Ibn Qutayba's own attitude on the point. He outlines the versions and interpretations of the Tradition in much the same way as has been done above. Then he goes on to say that he finds all these unsatisfactory, since he has read the account of the creation of Adam in the *Torah*, and he knows that it meant 'in the *ṣūra* of God himself'. He finds no special difficulty in the word, however, and does not consider that it implies anthropomorphism. God may be regarded as having a *ṣūra* in the same way as he has a hand. His hand is not like a human hand, but we accept the fact of his having it and understand it *bi-lā kayfiyya*, that is, without explaining the precise manner of its existence.[150] In this view of Ibn Qutayba's, then, there is apparently a simple way of accepting the Tradition in its original form and meaning into Islam, while making it innocuous to generally accepted Islamic doctrine. This makes it all the more puzzling to say why the original meaning should on the whole have been rejected.

Before attempting a direct answer to this question it is worth while looking at some of the heretical groups and individuals within Islam who made use of the conception of man being in God's form or image. One man, who is reckoned a Murji'ite and flourished about 750, held that God is in the form of a man, and quoted in support of this view the Tradition about the creation of Adam in the form of the Merciful.[151] About the same time and a little later similar views were held by several members of the Rāfiḍite or Imāmite branch of the Shīʿites;[152] to support their views they quoted, in addition to the Tradition, a verse from the Qur'ān.[153] Another man, clearly much under Christian influence, though described as a Muslim sectary belonging to the extreme Shīʿites, regarded Christ as a kind of demiurge under God and held that Christ had created Adam in his (own) form.[154] This latter view cannot have been widespread, but crude anthropomorphism undoubtedly was, and this fact constitutes an important part of the background of the discussion and manipulation of the Tradition about the creation of Adam.

A completely different use of the word *ṣūra* was meanwhile being made in the philosophical movement among the Arabs, based on the translations of the Greek philosophers. Here *ṣūra* was used for the Aristotelian 'form' or *eidos*, and was contrasted with matter. Nevertheless there was some interaction between theological and philosophical views. The philosopher al-Kindī (d.c. 866), for example, says that, when the soul is purified, it is like a clear, polished mirror, and 'there is united with it a *ṣūra* from the light of the creator'. By this al-Kindī presumably means man's reason or intellect. The closeness of this passage to our Tradition is remarkable, even when allowance is made for al-Kindī's reliance on Greek sources.[155] Similarly at a later date Ibn Ṭufayl (d. 1185) can say that, as a polished surface reflects the sun's light and its *ṣūra*, so some animals, and notably man, reflect the *rūḥ* or spirit and are formed with its form (*yataṣawwarū bi-ṣūrati-hi)*; and he adds that this is what is indicated by our Tradition.[156]

Between the philosophers and the theologians stand the Sufi writers. The outstanding example of these is al-Ḥallāj (d. 922). He held that there is no radical antinomy between the creature man and his creator.[157] When Adam was presented for the adoration of the angels, it was as a divine form (*ṣūra*), and this prefigured the real affinity of men with God if they become pure.[158] It would be fascinating to consider more fully the part played by such conceptions in philosophical and sufistic thought.[159] Here, however, it must suffice to consider briefly al-Ghazālī, in whom the theological line merges with the philosophical and sufistic, and both reach a certain consummation.

Al-Ghazālī's views on most questions are complex and have many subtle nuances. Those on the interpretation of our Tradition are no exception. This sometimes gives the impression that he contradicts himself. But whether this is so, or whether there is some development in his views, are questions that may be left aside here. In general he is a supporter of the view that Adam was created in God's form, even arguing that in the story of the slave who was beaten the words 'his form' can be taken to mean God's form.[160] But he is also aware of the difficulties such a view has to face. Sometimes he is content to say that the form must be understood by the 'inner form' (*ṣūra bāṭina*) belonging to the 'supernal world' (*'ālam al-malakūt*), not the external visible form (*ṣūra ẓāhira*).[161] Elsewhere, notably in a reply to criticism of the *Iḥyā'*,[162] he deals with the question more fully and maintains that the interpretation of 'his form' as 'God's form' may be justified in two ways. Firstly, if God's form means a form in God's possession, then man may be regarded as a microcosm, a universe in little; this is a favourite conception with al-Ghazālī.[163] Secondly, if God's form means something characterizing him, then that might refer to the fact that just as God is living, knowing, willing, so man is living, knowing, willing; and the complex of these attributes might be held to constitute the 'inner form'. This would imply, however, that this inner form was a part or aspect of God's essence (*ḥāla li-l-dhāt*), and that is the mistaken view of Ibn Qutayba from which al-Ghazālī dissociates himself. He holds that when attributes are said to belong to God and also to man, the correspondence is only verbal, and similarly in saying that God has a form and man has a form the correspondence is only verbal. To suppose that God's form is external and visible would of course be anthropomorphism (*tashbīh*).

It is against this background of the philosophical and sufistic acceptance of the conception that man is in God's form or image that we must consider the strenuous efforts of the dominant trend in theology to reject it, as instanced, for example, by Fakhr-al-Dīn al-Rāzī.[164] The strength of this movement for rejection, and the degree of tension felt by al-Ghazālī between the sufistic views and those of the Ash'arite theologians, are shown by the subtleties of argument in which he is involved. The question for us to answer here is why this movement for rejection eventually won the day. Why on this point did Islam (except for the Ḥanbalites) turn away from the Judaeo-Christian tradition?

The answer cannot be simply that the body of opinion which held that God was absolutely other than man, absolutely different from him, was stronger than the opposing body of opinion. If God's absolute otherness could be reconciled with his having a hand, it could almost as easily be reconciled with his having a form. What seems to have turned the scale against acceptance of the conception of man in God's form is the way in which the word *ṣūra* and its cognates are used in the Qur'ān.

There are two main points to be noticed. Firstly, God is referred to in the Qur'ān as *muṣawwir*, 'the form-giver', 'the one who forms'; and the activity of 'forming' is closely connected with that of creating, even of creating Adam in particular.[165] Now, if creating and forming are similar or closely connected, the word 'form' would have the suggestion of something created and would therefore not be appropriate for God. Secondly, the word *ṣūra* or 'form' tends to connote something composite because the one verse of the Qur'ān where it is used runs: 'in whatever form he willed he constituted thee' (or 'set thee together').[166] Though Westerners may consider form a principle of unity, the Arabs, perhaps under the influence of this verse, seem to have thought of *ṣūra* as something complex. In this way also it was inappropriate that God should have a *ṣūra*.[167]

The study of this small point has introduced us to one of the deep tensions in Islamic thought – the tension between those who held God's absolute otherness and those who believed that there was an affinity between God and man. This study has also shown us, if the immediately preceding remarks are sound, that the steady pressure through the centuries of the Qur'ān had an important share in determining the final result.

B4. The Logical Basis of the early Kalām

Ibn Khaldūn in a well-known passage[168] explains how the later Kalām, beginning with al-Ghazālī, had a different logical basis from that of the earlier period. To understand the change brought about by al-Ghazālī it is necessary to have some idea of the earlier conceptions of knowledge and epistemology, and no better introduction can be found than the first chapter of *K. Uṣūl ad-Dīn* by al-Baghdādī (d. 1037). We have other works of a similar date, such as *K. at-Tamhīd* by al-Bāqillānī (d. 1013)[169] and *K. al-Irshād* by al-Juwayni Imām al-Ḥaramayn (d. 1085);[170] but the less subtle presentation of al-Baghdādī is more suitable for preliminary study.[171] A few simple comments are added.

Chapter I. Truth and Knowledge in General and in Particular

§ 1. Definition of Knowledge and its Real Nature

There are different views about the definition and real nature (*ḥaqīqa*) of knowledge. Some of our associates assert that knowledge is an attribute (*ṣifa*) by which a living (person) becomes 'knowing'. (This is) contrary to the view of those who allowed the existence of knowledge in the dead and in inanimate (things) as did al-Ṣāliḥī and the Karrāmiyya; (it is) also contrary to the view of the Qadariyya in claiming that God is knowing but not through knowledge, and to the view of those who hold that knowledge and all existents (*mawjūd*) are bodies (*ajsām*) and not attributes.

(Others) of our associates assert that knowledge is an attribute through which a living and competent person validly performs and accomplishes an act. The advantage of this view is that it refutes the view of the Qadariyya that many acts performed and accomplished proceed by way of secondary-causation (*tawallud*, lit. generation) from an agent who has no knowledge of them.

Among the Qadariyya there are differences about the definition of knowledge: al-Ka'bī held that it is belief in a thing (*i'tiqād al-shay'*) as it (really) is; al-Jubbā'ī held that it is belief in a thing as it (really) is, arising from necessity (of thought) or proof; his son Abū Hāshim held that it is belief in a thing as it (really) is, accompanied by a settled attitude of mind in respect of it. These three definitions are contradicted by the knowledge of the impossibility of the impossible, because the knowledge of that is not knowledge of a thing, since the impossible is not a thing; yet there is knowledge that the impossible is impossible, even when it is not a thing, (and this is) by agreement (*ittifāq*), since on their view the non-existent is a thing only when its existence is possible (*jā'iz*), like substance and accident, whereas that whose existence is impossible is not a thing – for example, the wife and children and partner of God. Another reply to them is that, if knowledge is belief of a particular kind, then everyone who is knowing would have to be believing; but God is knowing and yet not believing; and so the definition of knowledge as belief is unsatisfactory. Al-Naẓẓām held that knowledge is one of the movements of the heart, as is also volition; he has thus assimilated knowledge to volition although they differ in genus.

Comment on § I. The first Ashʿarite definition of knowledge may be that of al-Ashʿarī himself, though perhaps in al-Baghdādī's words. Elsewhere al-Ashʿarī's own definition is given as 'what necessitates its locus (or substrate) being knowing' (al-Juwaynī, *Irshād*, p. 7; al-Jurjānī, *Sharḥ Mawāqif al-Ījī,* i. 72). The context of this definition is the discussion of the attributes of God, and the question whether there is a distinct entity, his knowledge, by which, rather than by his essence, he is 'knowing' or omniscient.

The second Ashʿarite definition of knowledge as an attribute leading to the valid performance of an act (also mentioned in *Irshād*, p. 7) is concerned with the relation of knowledge to activity. A series of events can only be a man's act, according to the Ashʿarites, in so far as he foresees and deliberately wills it. What we today call natural events are due to God's volition. They therefore rejected the view of some Muʿtazilites of the 'generation' (*tawallud*) of secondary effects by inanimate objects through natural causation, and in particular denied that these were parts of a man's act.[172]

The Muʿtazilite definitions treat 'belief' (*iʿtiqād*) as the genus of which knowledge is a species. This is contrary to the common philosophical view that belief is inferior to knowledge; and al-Baghdādī implies that view in his argument that God is 'knowing' but not 'believing'. This argument is pressed further by al-Juwaynī (*Irshād*, p. 7) who, after a similar account of Muʿtazilite views, asserts a distinction between knowledge and the state of mind of the *muqallid*, the person who accepts his beliefs on the authority of others. This leads to the distinction later made by al-Ghazālī (e.g. in the *Munqidh*) between the knowledge of the scholar with its rational basis and the faith (*īmān*) of the *muqallid* or ordinary man. Al-Baghdādī does not note that his older contemporary al-Bāqillānī (followed by al-Juwaynī)[173] defined knowledge as 'cognition (*maʿrifa*) of the object-of-knowledge (*maʿlūm*) as it (really) is'. This avoids the ambiguity of 'belief' as a designation of the genus, though *maʿrifa* has also drawbacks; and while *maʿlūm* avoids calling what cannot exist a 'thing' it produces a certain circularity in the definition, as al-Ījī noted.

For the persons mentioned see *E.I.* (2), s.v. al-Ashʿari, al-Bāḳillānī, al-Djubbā'ī (where Abū Hāshim is also treated), and *E.I.* (1), s.v. al-Naẓẓām, Muʿtazila, Karrāmīya. By 'Qadariyya' al-Baghdādī usually means the Muʿtazila. For al-Kaʿbī see Montgomery Watt, *Free Will and Predestination,* pp. 80 f.; A. S. Tritton, *Muslim Theology*, pp. 157-62. For al-Ṣāliḥī see Tritton, pp. 128-31.

§ 2. THE AFFIRMATION OF KNOWLEDGE AND REALITIES.

On this point the opposing views are those of the Sceptics. Of the several sects of them one held that things have no reality, that there is no knowledge of them; these are the Pyrrhonists (*Muʿānidūn*). They must be treated with beatings, chastisement, seizure of their wealth; when they complain of the pain of the beating and demand the restoration of their wealth, they may be told, 'Neither you nor your wealth has any reality. Why do you complain of this pain? Why are you annoyed? Why do you ask for the restoration of what has no reality?' It may also be said to them, 'Has the denial of reality any reality?' If they say, 'Yes', they affirm some reality. If they say, 'No', the reply is: 'Since the denial of realities has no reality nor validity, the affirmation of them is valid.' Again they may be asked: 'Do you know that there is no knowledge?' If they say, 'Yes', they have *ipso facto* affirmed a (piece of) knowledge and a knowing (subject) and an (object) known; if they say, 'We do not know that there is no knowledge', they may be asked, 'Why do you judge that there is no knowledge, when you do not know that there is no knowledge?'

The second sect of Sceptics, (extreme) Sceptics (*Ahl al-Shakk*), assert: 'We do not know whether things and knowledge have reality or not.' If they doubt their own existence, they are in the same position as the first sect, but if they know their own existence, they have *ipso facto* affirmed one reality.

The third group assert that things have their reality as a result of beliefs, and hold that whenever a man believes a thing his object-of-belief is as he believes it to be. They ought strictly to hold that the world is both pre-eternal and originated, because some people believe in its being originated and some in its pre-eternity. Likewise they ought strictly to hold that their own view is worthless in virtue of our belief in its worthlessness, since in their view all beliefs are sound. Again, when they are questioned about the belief of the Pyrrhonists among the Sceptics, if they hold that their belief that there are no realities is a sound belief, they are similar to the Pyrrhonists, but if they declare that belief worthless, they contradict their own view of the soundness of all beliefs.

Comment on § 2. The refutation of scepticism becomes a standard part of Islamic theology, presumably because a tendency to scepticism was sometimes encountered. The three views mentioned are those of much earlier Greek philosophers, and not of any active contemporary opponents. They re-appear in numerous works of *Kalām* e.g. al-Baghdādī, *Farq*, p. 311; Ibn Ḥazm, i. 8 f.; al-Taftazānī, *Sharḥ ʿalā ʾAqāʾid al-Nasafiyya* (tr. E. E. Elder), pp. 12 f., with further references.[174] The Muʿānidūn (elsewhere called ʿInādiyya) are almost certainly the Pyrrhonists, as stated in Redhouse's *Turkish Lexicon*. The Ahl-al-Shakk (elsewhere Lāʾadriyya) are close to the Middle Academy. The third sect (elsewhere ʿIndiyya) are reminiscent of Protagoras. The whole account is doubtless taken from some late work, perhaps based on Sextus Empiricus.

§ 3. KNOWLEDGE CONSISTS OF ABSTRACT-FORMS OTHER THAN THE KNOWERS

The opposition on this point is with those of the Dahriyya who deny accidents, and with al-Aṣamm, of the Qadariyya, who agrees with these in the denial of accidents. They all deny knowledge (as a distinct entity), and affirm that it is not through knowledge that the knower is knowing, just as it is not through movement and colour (as distinct entities) that what is moving and coloured is moving and coloured.

Our refutation of this view is that in ordinary life we find the knower sometimes knowing and sometimes not knowing. He cannot be knowing through his self (*nafs*), since that exists during those states in which he is not knowing. It must therefore be that he becomes knowing only through an abstract-form other than himself. This abstract-form is what is meant by our expression 'knowledge'. Whoever affirms it and is at variance with us about its name differs from us only verbally. With this proof we affirm the other accidents also.

Comment on § 3. The word *maʿnā*, normally 'meaning', is used in a technical sense, which doubtless is derived from the Platonic *idea* or Aristotelian *eidos*. This technical use is at least as early as Maʿmar (or Muʿammar) who flourished under Hārūn al-Rashīd (786-809). Al-Ashʿarī records discussions whether *maʿānī* like 'rest' and 'movement' were attributes *(ṣifāt)* or accidents *(aʿrāḍ)* *(Maqālāt*, p. 369). Other examples of *maʿānī* are 'whiteness', 'life', 'knowledge' (ibid., pp. 372, 488; cf. pp. 168, 253; *K. al-Lumaʿ* ap. MacCarthy, *Theology of al-Ashʿarī*, p. 54; al-Khayyāṭ, *Intiṣār,* p. 55). Maʿmar also included what might perhaps be called 'relations', and became involved in infinite series. Basically the *maʿnā* was a real determination of a substance, especially one with something of a hypostatic character. In later times it was usually immaterial and not perceptible by the senses. The translation 'abstract-form' seems least misleading. The discussion in this section is linked with the Ashʿarite doctrine of God's attributes.

(For the Dahriyya see *E.I.* (2). For al-Aṣamm, a Muʿtazilite who flourished under al-Muʿtaṣim, 833-42, cf. A. S. Tritton, *Muslim Theology*, p. 126.)

§ 4. THE KINDS OF KNOWLEDGE AND THEIR NAMES

Knowledge in our view is of two kinds. One of these is God's knowledge. This is pre-eternal knowledge, neither necessary nor acquired, resulting neither from sense nor from thought and reflection. It comprehends all objects-of-knowledge in their particularity. God knows everything that has been and everything that will be; and of everything that is not, He knows how it would have been if it had been; and the knowledge by which He knows this is one, pre-eternal *(azalī)* and not originated.

The second kind of knowledge is the knowledge of men and of other living creatures; and this is again twofold: necessary and acquired. The distinction between them is that the knower has power over his *acquired* knowledge and the proving of it, but the *necessary* knowledge is present in him without his proving it or having power over it.

Necessary knowledge is of two sorts, immediate (or intuitive) (*badīhī*) and sensible (*ḥissī*). Immediate knowledge again has two subdivisions of which the first is *affirmative* immediate knowledge, such as the knowledge of the person who knows his own existence and knows what exists in himself of pain, pleasure, hunger, thirst, cold, heat, grief, joy, and the like. The second subdivision is *negative* immediate knowledge, such as the knowledge of the impossibility of impossible (things), for instance, the knowledge that a single thing is not both pre-eternal and originated, that a person is not both living and dead at one time, that he who knows a thing is not at the same time ignorant of it in the respect in which he knows it.

Sensible knowledge is what is perceived by the five senses as we shall explain below.

Reflective knowledge is also of two sorts, *rational* and *revealed (sharʿī)*, and both of these are acquired by the knower, being present in him through his proof of them. Some are clearer than others, as we shall establsh below, if God will.

Comment on § 4. God's knowledge is described in accordance with Qur'ānic conceptions. It implicitly opposes the view of the Neoplatonic philosophers that God knows only universals. Since Arabic distinguishes between what has existed for an infinite time in the past on the one hand, and what will exist for an infinite time in the future on the other hand, it is convenient to mark this distinction by the words 'pre-eternal' and 'everlasting'.

The division of human knowledge into 'necsssary' and 'acquired' has connexions with the later Ash'arite theory that human acts are created by God and only 'acquired' by man (cf. al-Bāqillānī, *Tamhīd*, ed. MacCarthy, p. 9). Too much, however, must not be made of the similarity in terminology, since al-Ash'arī speaks of the Qadarite Ghaylān holding that some knowledge is an 'acquisition' *(iktisāb) (Maqālāt,* p. 136). It is noteworthy that the senses are regarded as giving necessary knowledge – a view for which there is something to be said, though it is absolutely opposed to the Platonic outlook.

Naẓar, 'reflection' (with the adjective *naẓarī*, 'reflective'), is used in the *kalām* as a general term for intellectual activity or logical, rational argument. Whatever is not known necessarily, without effort or choice on the part of the knower, but only through intellectual effort with deliberate choice, is called 'reflective' or 'acquired' by al-Baghdādī.

The words *shar', sharī'a, shar'ī* are difficult to translate because the Arabic conceptions do not coincide with European conceptions. We are familiar with the *sharī'a* as Islamic law, but forget that for Muslims it includes prescriptions for the confession of sound credal principles and even for right belief about all religious matters. Thus *shar'* and even *sharī'a* include all that is in the Qur'ān, including anecdotes about previous prophets, and also the non-legal part of Tradition. To translate 'law' and 'legal' thus becomes misleading. In many contexts it will be found that 'revelation' and 'revealed' better express the meaning of the Arabic.

§ 5. CLASSIFICATION OF THE SENSES AND THEIR ADVANTAGES

The senses, on the view of our associates and of most rational (thinkers) are five, and by them sensible knowledge is apprehended.

The first is the sense of *sight*. By it are perceived bodies, colours, and beauty of composition in respect of forms. In our view every existent can be perceived by it, and some of the Mu'tazila, including Abū Hāshim b. al-Jubbā'ī, hold that only bodies and colours are perceived by sight; al-Jubbā'ī held that only bodies, colours, and primary-modes (*akwān*) are perceived by it, and some of the philosophers held that sight only perceives colours.

The second sense is that of *hearing*; by it are perceived speech and all sounds.

The third is the sense of *taste*, by which flavours are perceived.

The fourth is the sense of *smell*, by which scents are perceived

The fifth is the sense of *touch*; by it are perceived bodies, heat, cold, moistness, dryness, softness, and hardness. A group held that taste was one form of the sense of touch.

Al-Naẓẓām added another sense by which the pleasure of sexual intercourse is perceived. This view was similar to that of those who maintained there is a seventh sense by which is perceived the pain of a blow or a wound.

Our associates differ about the respective merits of sensible and reflective knowledge. Abū 'l-ʿAbbās al-Qalānisī considered reflective knowledge superior to sensible. Abū 'l-Ḥasan al-Ashʿarī considered sensible knowledge superior, since it is the foundation of reflective knowledge.

There are also differences about the merits of the senses of sight and hearing. The philosophers considered that hearing is superior to sight in that by hearing a man perceives from all six directions, and in both light and darkness, whereas by sight, on their view, he perceives only what is in front of him, and only by means of rays of light. Most of the Mutakallimūn asserted the superiority of sight over hearing, since by hearing a man perceives all bodies, colours, and shapes. On our view all existences may be perceived by sight. Our associates allowed visual perception from all six directions, as we shall establish below, if God will.

Comment on § 5. This section speaks for itself. The view of the Ashʿarites that all existents, and not simply all bodies, can be seen, allows for the seeing of God by the faithful on the day of resurrection. The *akwān* or 'primary-modes' are combination, separation, movement, and rest; cf. al-Juwayni, *Irshād*, p. 10 (tr. 28); etc. For al-Ashʿarī see *E.I.* (2); for al-Qalānisī see Ibn ʿAsākir, *Tabyīn Kadhib al-Muftarī*, p. 398 (contemporary of al-Ashʿarī), and Tritton, op. cit., p. 182.

§ 6. THE AFFIRMATION OF REFLECTIVE KNOWLEDGE

On this point the difference is with the Sumaniyya, who consider that nothing is known except by way of the five senses, reject reflective knowledge, and consider that all doctrines are false. According to this view they ought to reject their own doctrine since the view that all doctrine is to be rejected is itself a doctrine. We say to them, 'How do you become aware of the soundness of your doctrine?' If they say, 'By reflection and proof', they are forced to affirm reflection and proof as a way to knowledge of the validity of anything; and this is contrary to their view. If, however, they say, 'By sense', the reply is: 'Awareness of sensible knowledge is shared by all men with sound sense; so why are we not aware of the soundness of your view through our senses?' If they say, 'You are really aware by sense of the soundness of our view, but you deny what you are aware of', there is nothing to distinguish them from one who reverses this assertion and says to them, 'No, it is you who are aware by sensible necessity of the soundness of the view of your opponents and the falsity of your own, but you deny what you are aware of by sense.' Since the two views are opposed to one another, they are worthless. The correct way to knowledge of religious truth is by reflective proof alone.

Comment on § 6. The Sumaniyya or Samaniyya (cf. S. Pines, *Beiträge zur islamischen Atomenlehre*, esp. p. 122 n.) were an Indian sect with whom the Muslims seem to have had contacts at an early period; cf. Massignon, *Essai*², p. 83.

§ 7. THE AFFIRMATION OF WIDELY-TRANSMITTED STATEMENTS AS A WAY TO KNOWLEDGE

The difference on this point is twofold: firstly, with the Barāhima and Sumaniyya in that they deny that knowledge results from widely-transmitted statements *(al-akhbār al-mutawātira)*; this view is shown false by their knowledge of lands they have never visited, of nations and kings of former times, and of the appearance of claimants to prophethood; [similarly the Naẓẓāmiyya assert that the community may agree on an error, for widely-transmitted statements have no proof, since they might be false in their origin; they calumniate the Companions, and reject analogy in legal matters;] since, even if they dispute their (the prophets') truth, they know that they appeared and made their claims. And they cannot learn it except from a widely-transmitted statement upon which agreement is unsound (sc. which it is unsound to suppose men have agreed to forge).

The second difference is with a group who affirm that knowledge results from wide-transmission, but consider that the knowledge arising in this way is *acquired* and not necessary. The proof that it is necessary is that it is impossible for doubt to occur in respect of what is thus known, just as it is impossible for doubt to occur in respect of sensible or immediate knowledge.

Comment on § 7. The Barāhima ('Brahmins') like the Sumaniyya (§ 6) were an Indian or perhaps rather 'hinduizing' sect. The latter restricted knowledge to matters of sense-perception; but it is possible that the Barāhima wanted rather to restrict knowledge (in Platonic fashion) to metaphysical truth, since from al-Shahrastānī's account (Cairo, 1949/1368, iii. 342-8) it is clear they are regarded as largely rationalistic in outlook. The point most frequently mentioned in Islamic theological writing is their denial of prophethood, and that is implicit in the present context. The slightness of the Islamic references suggests that there were limited intellectual contacts at an early period but, apart from al-Bīrūnī, even fewer at a later date (cf. C. Pellat, *Le Milieu Baṣrien . . .* [Paris, 1953], p. 40; P. Kraus, *Rivista degli Studi Orientali,* xiv. 356 referring to an earlier article by H. H. Schaeder, thinks the Sumaniyya were not Indians but exponents of hellenistic scepticism).

It is important to understand the conception of *tawātur* and *al-akhbār al-mutawātira*, rendered as 'wide-transmission' and 'widely-transmitted statements'. The basic idea of the word is something like 'constant succession', and the examples show that this is applied to historical and geographical statements. If you were asked to prove that Alexander the

Great or Napoleon or Hitler existed, you could give a number of arguments, but none of these would have strict logical necessity. It is conceivable, for example, that any historical document referred to may be a forgery. Nevertheless, there are so many converging lines of argument that it is unthinkable that there should have been collusion among so many people to produce a forgery with many ramifications. The passage about the Naẓẓāmiyya elaborates this point about the absence of logical necessity. (The editor does not explain his use of square brackets; they probably indicate marginal comments.)

The difference between 'necessary' and 'acquired' knowledge was explained in § 4. Necessary knowledge is not logically necessary knowledge but knowledge which a man cannot help having, and so includes commonly accepted geographical and historical beliefs. Al-Baghdādī insists that such beliefs are necessary, because he is specially interested in the belief that Muḥammad existed and claimed to be a prophet. For his contemporaries in Iraq, even for Jews and Christians, this was knowledge they could not help having and could not doubt.

§ 8. THE CLASSIFICATION OF STATEMENTS

Statements, on our view, are of three kinds: of *tawātur*, wide-transmission, of *āḥād*, single-individuals, and those coming between the two, (or) far-spread *(mustafīḍ)*, which have a similar effect to the widely-transmitted in some respects.

Widely-transmitted statements are those which it is impossible to suppose men would agree to fabricate, and they oblige to necessary knowledge through the soundness of what is stated. Statements of single-individuals, when their *isnād* (or chain of authorities) is sound, and their contents are not rationally impossible, oblige to action in accordance with them but not to knowledge. They are analogous to the evidence of just men before the judge *(ḥākim)*; that (evidence) necessitates judgement in accordance with it in its plain meaning *(ẓāhir)*, although (the judge) does not know that the evidence (of these men) is (actually) true. The statements in the middle position between those widely-transmitted and those from single-individuals are similar to the widely-transmitted in obliging to knowledge and action, but differ from these in that the knowledge resulting from them is acquired, not (as in the case of the widely-transmitted) necessary. This class of far-spread statements in the middle position between those of wide-transmission and those of single-individuals is subdivided. Firstly, there is the statement of a person whose truthfulness is proved by miracles; e.g. the statements of the prophets. Secondly, there is the statement of a person whose truthfulness has been affirmed by a person guaranteed by miracles. Thirdly, there is the statement which is originally related by a group of reliable persons, and afterwards spread abroad through the generations until it approximates to the *tawātur* [although in the first generation the narrators were few], such as statements about the vision (of God), the intercession (of the prophet), the basin, the balance, the stone-throwing, the wiping of the soles of the feet, the punishment of the tomb, and the like. Fourthly, some statements of single-individuals [in respect of legal decisions] have been unanimously accepted by the community in every age as a basis of decision; for instance, the statements that no bequest (may be made) to an heir, that a woman is not married (to the same man as) her paternal or maternal aunt, that a thief when without means and without a safe refuge does not have (his hand) cut off. No attention is paid in these matters to the contrary views of heretics, such as the Rawāfiḍ, Qadariyya, Khawārij, Jahmiyya, Najjāriyya, since we do not indicate their contrary views on legal decisions but only in the field of theology. [All the types of far-spread (statement) oblige both to action and to acquired knowledge.]

Statements are distinguished basically into true and false. They are true when they correspond with the object of the statement (*'alā wafq makhbari-hi*), and false when they are at variance with the object. No statements are both true and false at the same time, apart from a single statement, namely when the man who never at all told a lie states that he is a liar; for this is false of him, but when the liar asserts of himself that he is a liar he is speaking truth. Thus this one statement, made by one person, is both true and false. There is here a disproof of the view of the Thanawiyya that the speaker of truth may not be a speaker of falsehood.

Comment on § 8. The conception of 'wide-transmission' has been explained. The other two classes of statements seem to be primarily Traditions in the technical sense. (The word translated 'statement', *khabar*, can also mean 'Tradition'.) The distinction between these two classes drawn by al-Baghdādī presumably reflects the contemporary stage of the science of Tradition-criticism, but it was a personal view not generally accepted. Among the *mustafīd* are many basic beliefs of the Islamic religion, and by classifying these as 'acquired' al-Baghdādī was presumably making allowance for the denial of them by non-Muslims. Yet this might be taken as admitting the possibility of doubt about them. Other theologians, following al-Bāqillānī, preferred to regard such beliefs as 'demonstrable' in that they could be justified by means of the rational arguments about the probative force of Muḥammad's miracles.

The sects mentioned are mostly early, the latest being the Rāfiḍites or Rawāfiḍ who were transformed into the Imāmites about the end of the third/ninth century. (For details see index of Tritton, *Muslim Theology*, and Watt, *Free Will and Predestination*.)

The Thanawiyya or Dualists are not the Magians or Zoroastrians but the upholders of the more philosophical forms of dualistic creed current in the age of Abū 'l-Hudhayl, though possibly insignificant later. They included Manichaeans, 'Dayṣānites', and Mazdakites (cf. R. Strothmann, art. 'Thanawīya' in *E.I.*[1]).

§ 9. THE CLASSIFICATION OF REFLECTIVE KNOWLEDGE

There are four kinds of reflective knowledge: (1) proof by reason from analogy and reflection; (2) what is known by way of experience (*tajārib*) and customs (*'ādāt*); (3) what is known by way of revelation (*shar'*); (4) what is known by way of inspiration (*ilhām*) to one person or animal and not to another.

(1) What is known by reflection and proof on the part of reason includes such knowledge as that of the contingency of the world, of the eternity and unity of its Artificer, and His attributes, His justice, wisdom, the permissibility of His imposing duties on His servants, the genuineness of the prophethood of His apostles through (His) proof of that by their miracles, and similar matters of reflective rational knowledge.

(2) Instances of what is known by experience and practice *(riyāḍāt)* are medical knowledge of remedies and treatments and the like, and knowledge of arts and crafts. In this group may be included what is apprehended by analogy in customary (or usual) fashion *('alā'l-mu'tād)*, except that its principles are taken from experience and custom.

(3) What is known by revelation is, for example, the knowledge of the permitted, the forbidden, the obligatory, the customary, and the disapproved [and the other legal categories *(aḥkām)*]. Such revelational knowledge is classified as reflective only because the soundness of the revealed-law *(sharī'a)* is based on the soundness of prophethood, and that is known by means of reflection and proof. If it were known necessarily from the senses or immediately, then there would be no dispute about it among those who have sensible and immediate knowledge and those who have different views would not maintain them stubbornly, like the Sceptics (lit. Sophists) who deny objects of sense.

(4) What is known by inspiration in special cases is, for example, the knowledge of good taste in poetry and of the metrical measures of its verses. A Bedouin urinating on his heels may know this measure, but it may be beyond the ken of a wise man who knows the rules of most of the reflective sciences. Prosodists have shown ingenuity in discovering principles by which they know the measures of poetic metres, but the poetry was composed according to the good taste of men who did not know metres nor analogy in theory. Does such a man not have a special gift for this from God? Similarly the knowledge of musical composition is not discovered by analogy, and is not apprehended by a necessity in which all rational beings share, but is from special (sources) which are known to some people and not to others.

All reflective knowledge may, on our view, be made necessary in us by God in reversal of this habit, just as He created in Adam necessary knowledge by which he was acquainted with the names (of the animals) without having received a proof of them or having read them in a book. The same may be said of all other reflective knowledge, on our view.

In the case of necessary knowledge some of our associates assert that it may all be known by reflection and proof. Others assert that what we know by the five senses may be apprehended by proof when it is absent from sense; but what we know immediately may not properly have a proof, since (items of) immediate knowledge are the premisses of proof, and undoubtedly they must be present in a man before he tries to prove anything. That is the view of our associates.

Al-Naẓẓām and his followers of the Qadariyya supposed that what is known by analogical (reasoning) and reflection may not become known by necessity, and that what is known by sense may not become known by reflection and by (hearing) a statement (about it from others). According to this view he is forced to admit that the awareness of God in the world-to-come is reflective and demonstrative, not necessary, that Paradise is the sphere of reflection and proof, that there is opportunity in it for the rejection of sin by reflective people, that they are eternally subject to duties and by the fulfilment of these duties in Paradise merit reward in some other place. The objection was made to him in respect of sensible knowledge: 'Do we not know by widely-transmitted (statements) lands we have never visited, although those who inform us about them know them by having actually seen them? Similarly every body is known by the sense of sight to the man who sees it, but the blind man knows it by touch or by the wide-transmission of statements about it.' (Al-Naẓẓām) replied to this objection that those who make statements about what they have seen are by their eyes in contact with parts of the objects-of-sense, so that it is by touch that they know the object; when they inform someone else about what they have seen, some of the parts which were in contact with their eyes and spirits are separated and come in contact with the spirits of the hearers through their statements. Thus it is by touch also that those know who hear the statements of the original observers. The same may be said of those who hear (from them).

It was further objected to him that this view forces to the admission that, when the people of Paradise hear the statements about the people of Hell and the filth and the Zaqqūm they have there, then parts of the people of Hell and their Zaqqūm and their filth separate off and come into contact with the bodies of the people of Paradise in Paradise; and that when the people of Hell hear statements about the people of Paradise and their enjoyment, parts of the people of Paradise separate off from them and come into contact with the bodies of the people of Hell; thus something of the bodies of the people of Paradise is in Hell and something of the bodies of the people of Hell is in Paradise. This is a doctrine befitting its author: he has sufficient shame thereby.

Comment on § 9. In § 4 al-Baghdādī had said that there were two kinds of reflective knowledge, rational and revelational. Here he expands these into four, apparently by distinguishing experiential and 'customary' knowledge from rational knowledge proper, and by distinguishing inspiration, such as that of the poet, from revelational knowledge proper. Muslim thinkers gradually came to pay more and more attention to these second and fourth types of reflective knowledge, since they realized the importance of the similarities and contrasts between them and revealed knowledge; cf. al-Ghazālī in his autobiographical work, *Deliverance from Error*, and in *The Niche of Lights*.

The second part of the paragraph is concerned with the attempt of al-Naẓẓām to maintain that there are essentially different classes of objects-of-knowledge, and that for these the appropriate types of knowledge are different. While there is perhaps some limited justification for this point of view, it is clear that al-Naẓẓām tried to carry it too far. Al-Baghdādī has little difficulty in finding examples – such as hearing about a distant city from others, and then visiting it – where the change of type is obvious and cannot really be explained away. He then generalizes from this and asserts that God is able to change all our reflective knowledge into necessary knowledge. This could be regarded as a change from 'faith (in what one has been told)' to 'sight'.

§ 10. THE SOURCE OF LEGAL KNOWLEDGE

Legal decisions are taken from four roots *(uṣūl)*, the Book, the Sunna, Consensus, and Analogy.

(1) The Book is the Qur'ān, which falsehood does not touch from before or behind. It contains what is general and particular, comprehensive (*mujmal*) and explanatory *(mufassir)*, absolute (*muṭlaq*) and restricted *(muqayyad)*, command and prohibition, statement and question, abrogating and abrogated, obvious and allusive *(sarīḥ, kināya)*. It also contains direct and indirect discourse *(dalīl, mafhūm)*. All this is for aspects of its demonstrations in varying degrees, though some of them are clearer than others in proving the point (to be proved). Where the way in which it gives proofs to him who is weak in reflecting is obscure the investigator who is succoured (by God) knows it, in accordance with God's word 'Those of them who investigate it would know it' (iv. 83/85).

(2) The Sunna from which legal decisions are taken is what is handed down from the Prophet, either by wide-transmission *(tawātur)* which must lead to necessary knowledge, like what is handed down about the number of prostrations, and the elements of prayer and the like, or by far-spread statement *(khabar mustafīḍ)* producing acquired knowledge, like what is handed down about the assessment for the poor tax and the essential parts of the Pilgrimage, or by narration from single-individuals

(riwāyat aḥād) obliging to action but not to knowledge. The ways in which the Sunna proves (or indicates) (legal) decisions are like the ways in which the Qur'ān proves them, namely general, particular, comprehensive, explanatory, obvious, allusive, abrogating, abrogated, direct and indirect discourse, command, prohibition, statement, and the like.

(3) The *consensus* relevant to a legal decision is restricted to the consensus of the people of a particular generation of this community with regard to a legal point. (This is effective) because (the community) will not agree on an error.

(4) *Analogy* in legal matters is (used) to gain knowledge of the decision about a thing, only where there is no explicit-statement *(naṣṣ)* or consensus about the decision. Of this type of analogy there are (several) kinds. (a) Clear analogy – that is, where the decision about the branch (or particular application) is better (supported) than that about the root (or general principle): for example, the prohibition of striking parents because of the analogy with God's prohibiting the child saying to them, 'Fie' (Qur'ān, xvii. 23–24). (b) Analogy from knowledge in every respect of the root (or general principle) which is the basis of the analogy, for example, the analogy from the male-slave to the female-slave in halving the punishment, since the two are equal in being slaves; and the analogy from the female-slave to the male-slave in respect of the estimate (?) (*taqawwum*) on one of two co-owners when he has set free his share (of the slave) and is himself in easy circumstances; and just as God forbade trade during the time of the call to the Friday (midday worship), so we treat as analogous to this the granting of protection *(ijāra)* and the conclusion of other contracts during this time. In these decisions the root is not doubtful. (c) The third kind is the analogy of a ground *('illa)* in respect of one root; for example, the ground in respect of usury, despite the difference of those drawing the analogy in respect of the ground of usury.

In this group (of topics) there are various opposing views. (1) One is that of the Barāhima who deny the laws (revealed through) the prophets; the argument against their (view) will come in the chapter on the affirmation of prophethood. (2) The second is that of the Khārijites, who deny any (validity as) proof to consensus and to legal precedents *(sunan)*. They suppose that the only (valid) proof in points of the (revealed) Law is from the Qur'ān. Consequently they reject the stoning (of those guilty of adultery) and the wiping of the shoes (instead of washing the feet before the worship) because they are not (prescribed) in the Qur'ān. They cut off (the hand of) the thief whether (he has stolen) much or little, since the command in the Qur'ān about cutting off the thief's (hand) is absolute (not specifying a lower limit), and they do not accept the Tradition about the amount (carrying liability) for cutting nor the Tradition about taking into consideration the (degree of) security (in which the thing stolen was kept). This is the view of most of (the Khārijites); but the Najadāt permit personal-interpretation *(ijtihād)* in respect of the branches of the (revealed) Law. (3) The third opposing view is that of the Rāfiḍites. They say that there is no (valid) proof today in analogy or Sunna, nor in any part of the Qur'ān, because they claim that corruption *(taḥrīf)* has taken place in it through the Companions; they suppose that the only (valid) proof is the word (*qawl*) of the imām whom they expect; and before his appearance they are uncertain and in perplexity until the imām they expect appears and delivers them, as they suppose. (4) The fourth opposing view is that of the Naẓẓāmiyya of the Qadarites in that they reject (both) legal analogy and the proof from consensus. Al-Naẓẓām supposed that the community (of Islam) from the time of its prophet until the resurrection, should it agree upon a legal decision, might in its consensus (or agreement) be wrong and erroneous. He also supposed that there is no (valid) proof from a widely-transmitted statement (or Tradition), but considered it might be false. He rejected analogy in legal decisions, and blamed those of the Companions who on (the basis of) their personal-interpretation pronounced legal-opinions about the branches (or details) of the (revealed) Law. The blamer of them (sc. al-Naẓẓām) is blameworthy in religion and ancestry. (5) the fifth opposing view is that of those Qadarites who prohibit action on (the basis of) singleton statements (or Traditions). (6) The sixth opposing view is that of some Ẓāhirites who suppose that there is no (valid) proof in the consensus of the people of any age after the Companions; only the consensus of the Companions gives (valid) proof, not that of those after them. (7) The seventh opposing view is that of those who take into consideration proof from consensus when it is linked with *(inʿaqada ʿan)* an explicit-statement or an obvious-meaning from the Book or Tradition, but do not regard consensus linked with analogy as a proof. (8) The eighth opposing view is that of those Ẓāhirites who reject legal analogy.

On these points we have refuted these opponents at some length in our books on the roots of jurisprudence.

Comment on § 10. The discussion in this section is from the standpoint of the Shāfiʿite legal rite, to which al-Baghdādī belonged. (Cf. J. Schacht, art. 'Uṣūl' in *E.I.S.*) The chief points requiring to be noted are in the discussion of the eight opposing views.

(Second). The Khārijites were restricted to the Qur'ān as the sole source of law by their principle of *lā ḥukm illā li-'llāh*. They also tended to regard most of the Companions as unsound because they had not explicitly accepted this Khārijite principle. The Najadāt had for a time ruled a large area in central Arabia, and practical necessities had forced them to modify the rigour of their principles. (Cf. 'Khārijite Thought in the Umayyad period', *Der Islam*,. xxvi. esp. pp. 219-21.) For the punishment of stoning for adultery cf. art. '*Zinā*'' in *E.I.*[1]; and for the wiping of the shoes, A. J. Wensinck, *The Muslim Creed*, pp. 158 f.

(Third). The Rāfiḍites or rather Imāmites had by al-Baghdādī's time developed their own legal system, much of it based on Traditions transmitted and authenticated by Jaʿfar al-Ṣādiq and other imāms.

(Fourth). The views of al-Naẓẓām and his followers have already been mentioned. There is some logical cogency in what they say about consensus, but al-Baghdādī really relies on the Tradition (alluded to in his remarks on consensus) to the effect that Muḥammad's community would never agree on an error.

(Sixth, eighth). For the Ẓāhirites cf. I. Goldziher, *Die Ẓāhiriten* (Leipzig, 1884); also art. 'al-Ẓāhirīya' in *E.I.*[1] They emphasized the Ẓāhir or obvious meaning of statements in the Qur'ān or Tradition.

B5. The Origin of the Islamic Doctrine of Acquisition

Considerable obscurity surrounds the introduction into Islamic thought of the orthodox doctrine that it is God who 'creates' the acts of man, whereas man merely 'acquires' them (*kasaba, iktasaba*). The doctrine is sometimes attributed to al-Ashʿarī, but in his *Maqālāt al-Islāmiyyīn* he himself frequently uses the term in his accounts of the views of other writers. This paper examines the various uses of *kasaba* and *iktasaba* in that work to see what light is thrown on the origin and development of the conception.

So far I have not come across the technical use of *kasaba* in any earlier work than the *Maqālāt*, such as the *Kitāb al-Intiṣār*. Later writers often use it in describing the views of early theologians, who, one has strong grounds for suspecting, had never heard of the conception; e.g. al-Shahrastānī (p. 97) says that the Shuʿaybiyya, a sect of the Khawārij, held that 'God is the creator of the acts of man and that man is the acquirer'; but this appears to be an application of the terms current in the time of al-Shahrastānī to what is more simply described by al-Ashʿarī as the view 'that no one is capable of doing except what God wills and that the acts of men are created by God' (*Maq*. 94). Al-Ashʿarī, on the contrary, was not inspired by the same desire as al-Shahrastānī to classify theologians as orthodox in so many respects and unorthodox in so many respects, and seems to report his sources *verbatim* mostly; but it is likely that the writers from whom he excerpted sometimes used their own terms to reproduce the views of other theologians, especially when these were opponents. With this qualification, however, the accounts given in the *Maqālāt* may be regarded as reliable.

I. ḌIRĀR B. ʿAMR

> The ground of separation of Ḍirār b. ʿAmr from the Muʿtazila was his view that the acts of men are created, and that one deed comes from two doers, one of whom creates it, namely God, while the other acquires (*iktasaba*) it, namely the man; and that God is doer of the deeds of men in reality, and that men are doers of them in reality' (*Maq*. 281).

Ḍirār also held that 'perception is an acquisition (*kasb*) of man, a creation of God' (383, 1. 10); and that what is generated in another from a man's act is the man's acquisition (*kasb*) and God's creation (408).

The latter passages smack somewhat of the repetition of a formula, but the first, and especially the expression 'two doers or agents' (*fāʿilān*), has a unique cast of phrase that argues original thinking. This uniqueness and simplicity make it probable that Ḍirār is the author of the conception of 'acquisition' as applied to human acts. He is such an obscure character, however, that before considering this doctrine, it is necessary to discover something about his general position in the development of Muslim thought.

Al-Khayyāṭ in *Kitāb al-Intiṣār* (ed. Nyberg, 133) quotes Ibn al-Rāwandī as saying: 'As for the doctrine of the essence (sc. of God – *māhiyya*) , it was held by the two sheikhs of the Muʿtazila, Ḍirār and Ḥafṣ al-Fard, and Thumāma also held it, and among others also Ḥusayn al-Najjār, Sufyān b. Sakhtān, and Burghūth.' Al-Khayyāṭ replies: 'The answer to this is: As for Ḍirār and Ḥafṣ, they do not belong to the Muʿtazila because they are Mushabbihān (anthropomorphists) through their doctrine of the essence, and their doctrine of the createdness (sc. of human acts – *bi'l-makhlūq*).' He then quotes some verses (p. 134) from a poem of Bishr b. al-Muʿtamir in which the latter, presumably speaking on behalf of the Muʿtazila, disacknowledges these two and their associates, and asserts that 'their imām is Jahm'.

Some connection of Ḍirār with the Jahmiyya is also indicated by the statement of Ibn al-Murtaḍā (*Munya*, ed. Arnold, p. 40) that, according to al-Shaḥḥām, Ḍirār denied the punishment of the tomb. The *Fiqh Akbar I*, article 10, gives this denial as a mark of the Jahmiyya (Wensinck, *Muslim Creed*, 104).

Judging from the space allotted to them in the *Maqālāt* in al-Baghdādī's *Farq*, in al-Shahrastānī's *Milal*, etc., we should imagine the Jahmiyya to be a rather minor insignificant sect, roughly equal to one of the subdivisions of the Muʿtazila. It is somewhat surprising, then to find al-Ashʿarī in the *Ibāna* placing them on the same level as the Muʿtazila and the Ḥarūriyya (or Khawārij). But there is also other evidence that in the century or so before al-Ashʿarī they had a position of considerable prominence. Many theologians are said to have opposed them or to have written books to refute their teaching, e.g. *Radd ʿala 'l-Jahmiyya* of Aḥmad b. Ḥanbal, *Ikhtilāf fī 'l-Lafẓ* of Ibn Qutayba; cf. the list given by Ibn Taymiyya, *Al-ʿAqīda al-Ḥamawiyya* (in Schreiner, *Beiträge zur Geschichte der theologischen Bewegungen im Islam*, Separatdruck, 120 ff.). It is also noteworthy that the Jahmiyya are the only sect mentioned in the earliest form of the Fiqh Akbar (as indicated above).

It may be concluded that the Jahmiyya constituted an important section of the Mutakallimūn in the time of the great Muʿtazilites, such as Abū 'l-Hudhayl and al-Naẓẓām (the reign of al-Ma'mūn, and possibly earlier). Indeed, the line of division between the two was by no means hard and fast. The *Kitāb al-Intiṣār* repudiates the suggestion that various men, such as Ḍirār (and even Jahm himself – p. 126), belonged to the Muʿtazila; but that such a suggestion could be made speaks for itself. And in *Ibāna* (p. 48, 1.10, Hyderabad) al-Ashʿarī appears to refer to Abū 'l-Hudhayl as one of the leaders of the Jahmiyya; the phrase is '*shaykh minhum*', but the only sect mentioned recently is the Jahmiyya. There are similarities between the Jahmite view that heaven and hell come to an end and that of Abū 'l-Hudhayl (as noted by Pines, *Atomenlehre*, 124 ff.); and the emphasis of the Jahmiyya on the unity of God – Jahm is called *muwaḥḥid* (unitarian) in *Intiṣār*, 126 – is in line with the Muʿtazila's preference for the designation 'People of Unity and Justice'.

It would seem, then, that there was this section of the Mutakallimūn, only vaguely distinguished from the Muʿtazila, which, like the Muʿtazila, emphasized the unity of God, but unlike them held equally firmly that He was omnipotent. It is possibly just because they approached closely to orthodoxy (and orthodoxy came close to them) that traces of them are few. Their followers would tend to merge into the orthodox Mutakallimūn. And since the Muslim is interested in the origin of beliefs mainly from the aspect of guaranteeing their authenticity, there would be little motive for studying their works, and their books, thus neglected, would soon cease to be extant. (The connection of the later Jahmiyya with Jahm b. Ṣafwān who was killed in 128 is a difficult question which need not concern us here.)

The Jahmite view of human acts is that they are analogous to the 'acts' of inanimate objects. We speak of the stone falling, the sphere revolving, the sun setting; but it is only metaphorically that these inanimate objects act. Similarly, according to the Jahmiyya, it is only metaphorically that acts are ascribed to men; it is really God who is the doer of the action (*Maq*. 279). Doubtless this theory is intended not so much to belittle human activity as to exalt the Divine omnipotence. It does not do justice to man's consciousness of 'doing something', yet it presupposes that in ordinary life men are aware of the difference (or, at any rate, distinguish) between their acts and the 'acts' of stones.

Ḍirār was in sufficiently close relationship to the Jahmiyya of his time for an opponent to say that Jahm was his imām. His theory of human acts may therefore be regarded as an attempt to remedy this weakness in the account of the Jahmiyya. Like them he does not doubt that God is omnipotent, and that the Muʿtazila are mistaken when they assert the reality of human action in such a way as to withdraw it from the sphere of Divine activity. God is the author of the existence of all that exists, and human acts are included among things that exist. Man cannot emulate God in this respect even to the very slightest extent. Yet man is not on the level of the stone or the sun. There *is* something which can be asserted of man 'in reality'; but as this was a new conception and a new distinction there was no term to express it. Ḍirār therefore selected the word *kasaba* (or its eighth form *iktasaba*), and gave it the technical meaning of 'man's share in human acts'. The word normally means 'earn' or 'acquire', and is usually translated 'acquire' in this special sense, though 'appropriate' might be better from the philosophical standpoint. The precise character of man's part in human acts is thus left vague; what Ḍirār does maintain is that it is something real, and yet is completely different from God's work of creating or bringing into existence. There is, however, sufficient analogy between the two 'parts' for activity to be predicated 'in reality' of both God and man – unless, indeed, the doctrine of the two *fāʿilān* is a slander of Ḍirār's opponents.

The selection of the word *kasaba* has its grounds in Qur'ānic use. Both the first and eighth forms occur for instance in 2. 286, which Wensinck (*Muslim Creed*, 213) translates: 'God will not burden any soul beyond its power. It shall enjoy the good which it has acquired, and shall bear the evil for the acquirement of which it laboured.'

Note. – *The Date of Ḍirār*. – The report that makes Ḍirār a contemporary of Wāṣil b. ʿAtā' is certainly mistaken. According to al-Shahrastāni (p. 63), his view that the essence of God cannot be adequately known by man is said to have been handed down from Abū Ḥanīfa (d. 150). In *Maq*. 328 we read that in respect of 'hidden things' (*kawāmin*) he held that 'there is none of the intermingling (*mudākhala*) which Ibrāhīm (sc. al-Naẓẓām) asserted'. While this statement by al-Ashʿarī does not necessarily imply that Ḍirār explicitly criticized al-Naẓẓām, it is clear from the whole passage that he was familiar with al-Naẓẓām's doctrine of Kumūn. He also criticized the view of the consequences of acts (*tawallud*) specially associated with Bishr b. al-Muʿtamir (*Maq*. 407 f.). Thus he cannot have lived before these men, though he may have been slightly older. On the other hand, there are no strong grounds for putting him later. I am therefore inclined to conclude that he flourished in the reign of al-Ma'mūn, and possibly in the earlier part.

2. HISHĀM B. AL-ḤAKAM

Hishām b. al-Ḥakam held that human acts are created by God. Jaʿfar b. Ḥarb relates that Hishām b. al-Ḥakam said that the acts of a man are his choice (*ikhtiyār lahu*) in one respect and compulsion in another (*iḍṭirār*); his choice in that he wills them (*arāda*) and acquires them (*iktasaba*), and compulsion in that they do not come from him save when there arises the cause which incites to them' (*Maq*. 40 f.).

This view is elucidated by what is said on pp. 42 f. about Hishām's account of the ability or capacity to perform an act (*istiṭāʿa*). (The account is referred to his *aṣḥāb*; but this does not mean that it was not also his:

views attributed to the 'associates of Hishām' on pp. 37 f. and 41 are attributed to Hishām himself on pp. 493 f. and 515.) The ability to perform an act presupposed (1) soundness, (2) freedom of condition, (3) adequate space of time, (4) the instrument, and (5) the cause. 'He held that the act does not come about except through the originating cause, and that whenever the cause exists and has been originated by God, the act takes place inevitably.' Thus Hishām regarded human activity as proceeding from a causal chain, determined by God, but conscious willing constituted one link in that chain.

There is no doubt about Hishām's allegiance to the view that God was omnipotent, which was held also by the Jahmiyya and Ḍirār. It may very well be that his distinction between *iḍṭirār* and *ikhtiyār* was another attempt to explain the difference between human acts and the falling of a stone which was neglected in the doctrine of the Jahmiyya. Some connection between Hishām and the Jahmiyya is indicated by the sentence in the account of Jahm (*Maq*. 279):-

> The only difference (sc. between human acts and the movement of a stone) is that in the case of man God has created a power (*quwwa*) and a will (*irāda*), through which the action takes place, and choice (*ikhtiyār*).'

Since the view is not so fully worked out here, and since the distinction between *iḍjtirār* and *ikhtiyār* is not mentioned, though it is implied, it is proper to conclude that Hishām was the first to make this distinction, and that at least the use of the word *ikhtiyār* is derived from him. The view here expressed would then be that of the Jahmiyya of about the time of Hishām or a little later.

(The Index to the *Maqālāt* is mistaken in stating that he died in 299 or 279. Hishām is probably a slightly senior contemporary of Ḍirār; he had discussions with Abū 'l-Hudhayl, which the latter reported in his books (*Maq*. 32); he knew about al-Naẓẓām's doctrine of *kumūn* (ib. 329, cf. 60); but there is no mention of any criticism by him of Bishr b. al-Muʿtamir's doctrine of *tawallud* (cf. *Maq*. 45 f. where criticisms of other Rawāfiḍ are given).)

The word *iktasaba* occurs only in the one passage quoted above out of all the numerous references by al-Ashʿarī to Hishām's views. It is used as one would use a term familiar to one's readers. A novel and original conception would require fuller explanation. The actual word may, of course, have been added to the original version by one of the reporters. If it is Hishām's own, as it might well be, it would indicate that he was aware of the conception of *iktisāb* put forward by Ḍirār, and regarded it as analogous to his own conception of *ikhtiyār* and *irāda*. (Ḍirār is called 'al-Kūfī' by Ibn Ḥazm, iv, 192; and the same writer makes much of Hishām's connection with Kūfa.)

Hishām and his associates would thus represent a line of thought parallel to that of Ḍirār and sympathetic to it, helping to disseminate the notion of *kasb*, but preferring that of *ikhtiyār*.

3. AL-SHAḤḤĀM

> One of them (sc. the Muʿtazila), al-Shaḥḥām, held: God has power over that over which He has given men power; one movement is the object of the power (*maqdūra*) of both God and man, so that if God does it, it is compulsion, and if man does it, it is acquisition (*ḍurūra, kasb*).

In respect of the question whether God has power over that over which he has given men power (*Maq.* 549 f.), al-Ashʿarī records that al-Naẓẓām, Abū 'l-Hudhayl, and others of the Muʿtazila and Qadariyya answer in the negative, and hold that it is absurd that one thing should be object of power to two 'empowered beings' (*maqdūr wāḥid li-qādirayn*). Only al-Shaḥḥām held the contrary view; the above statement is repeated, and then the report continues: 'Both of them are described as having power to perform the one act; but the Eternal is not described as having power that the movement should be the man's act as well as His, and the man is not described as having power that the movement should be the act of the Eternal as well as his own.'

Al-Shaḥḥām was one of the leaders of the Muʿtazila of Baṣra of his time, a pupil of Abū 'l-Hudhayl and teacher of al-Jubbā'ī (*Munya*, 40, etc.). His statement (ib.) that Ḍirār held a certain view indicates some contact between them; and it might be supposed that he is restating Ḍirār's conception of two agents in Muʿtazilite terms, possibly in opposition to al-Naẓẓām and Abū 'l-Hudhayl, (whose view on this question seems, in any case, to be a denial of Ḍirār's). But this cannot be so, since al-Shaḥḥām must have held the freedom of the human will. The last part of the account of his view on this question is intended to rule out any Ḍirārite or orthodox interpretation of al-Shaḥḥām's formula. He was presumably thinking of some such act as the raising of an arm which may be performed either voluntarily or involuntarily; in the one case it is 'by acquisition' and is the man's act, and in the other it is 'by compulsion' and is God's act; but the alternatives exclude one another.

The account of al-Shaḥḥām by al-Baghdādī (*Farq*, 163) notices only this point, implies that his view has been confused with that of the Ṣifātiyya (who include the orthodox), and calls attention to the difference. It is noteworthy, however, that the formula 'one object of power to two empowered beings' (*maqdūr wāḥid li-qādirayn*) is admitted as an account of the orthodox doctrine – which goes to confirm the primacy claimed for Ḍirār.

It seems probable that al-Shaḥḥām's use of *kasb* and *iktisāb* was the result of his connections with Muʿammar, either because Muʿammar himself used the terms, or because his account of human acts (on the assumption that it was accepted by al-Shaḥḥām) made some such terms desirable. That Muʿammar had influenced him to some extent is shown by al-Khayyāṭ's reference to him (*Intiṣār*, 53) as an associate of Muʿammar. Muʿammar regarded man as essentially an invisible, immaterial unity, which moderns might call 'mind' or 'consciousness'. The man is thus quite distinct from his body; he directs it, and it is his tool. Moving, resting, colour, etc., are the body's doing. The only acts of the man are willing, knowing, disapproving (willing not to do a thing), speculation, comparison; power (*qudra*) and life are also ascribed to the man (*Maq*. 405; cf. 331 f.).

This view enables one to distinguish between a man's voluntary acts and his involuntary or automatic movements, and to give some explanation of the difference. The sheer act of will is emphasized in an almost Kantian fashion. But, since the view maintains that the outward movement is the act or 'doing' of the body, it does not make clear how the will or intention comes to be realized in outward events. The movement is, in a sense, the man's act, since by it he fulfils the law; but strictly it is only the inner act which is his. For the relation between the man in his inner being and the outward act *kasb* seems an appropriate term, especially in the light of its Qur'ānic use.

The word is actually used twice by al-Ashʿarī in reporting Muʿammar's views. In a discussion of the derivation of colour from the nature of the body, there is the remark: 'it is not admissible that what results from something else should be from the body's constitution, just as it is not admissible that the acquisition (*kasb*) of a thing should be the creation (*khalq*) of something else' (*Maq*. 406). That is to say, *kasb* and *khalq* exemplify things that are mutually exclusive.

On p. 417 there is a consideration of the case where a man decides to move but in fact remains still. This 'remaining still', says Muʿammar, is not an acquired act (*fiʿl muktasab*) nor voluntary inactivity, but a 'remaining still' by structure (*binya*; presumably = *ṭabʿ* – constitution). The details of this passage are a little obscure, but this appears to give the general sense. The term 'acquired act' here stands for a voluntary act in distinction from involuntary movement or rest, as, for example, when owing to paralysis or nervous disorder the body does not obey the will.

These references are too slight for weighty conclusions to be built upon them. They may perhaps be taken at their face value, and then Muʿammar would either have invented the term for himself (and Ḍirār might have borrowed from him), or else have adapted it from Ḍirār. But it is also possible that *kasb* and *muktasab* were first introduced by the person who reported Muʿammar's views – presumably some follower of his such as al-Shaḥḥām or Muḥammad b. ʿĪsā. It does, however, seem safe to conclude that the followers of Muʿammar were prominent in the use of the conception of *kasb*, that they used it to distinguish voluntary human acts not merely from the 'acts' of inanimate things but from involuntary human 'acts', and that this was connected with Muʿammar's theory of man.

4. AL-NAJJĀR AND MUḤAMMAD B. ʿĪSĀ

There is only one passage in the *Maqālāt* where *kasb* is used in the description of the views of al-Najjār (p. 566):

> Al-Najjār said: that man is able for acquisition (*kasb*) and unable for creation (*khalq*), and that he who has been made able to acquire a thing has been made unable to create it.

Al-Najjār's views show considerable similarity with those of Ḍirār, and he shares to some extent in the mystery surrounding the latter. He is mentioned (*Maq.* 415) as the source of an account of certain views of 'a group of those who believe in the necessitating will (*al-irāda al-mūjiba*)'; and as the list, immediately above, of those who hold this doctrine consists of Abū 'l-Hudhayl, al-Naẓẓām, Muʿammar, Jaʿfar b. Ḥarb, al-Iskāfī, al-Adamī, al-Shaḥḥām, and ʿIsā al-Ṣūfī, it would appear that al-Najjār had some connection with the Muʿtazila, and, in particular, with the school of Muʿammar and al-Shaḥḥām.

According to al-Baghdādī (*Farq*, 195), al-Najjār held the orthodox view that God creates the acquired acts (*aksāb*) of men. The above passage is in accordance with this. It is probably intended to guard against the suggestion, implicit in al-Shaḥḥām's statements, that acquisition and creation were similar in kind, since they were alternatives. Al-Najjār emphasizes their difference, and the fact that man is completely incapable of anything resembling creation.

There is a long passage (*Maq.* 552-4) about Muḥammad b. ʿĪsā, mentioning *kasb*; the most important sections run:

> Muḥammad b. ʿĪsā denied that (sc. that God has power to force men to do the act which He wills from them) and said: if He compelled them to faith, they would not be believing, and likewise if He compelled them to justice, they would not be just, and likewise if He compelled them to unbelief, they would not be unbelieving, for they are commanded to have faith willingly (*ṭawʿ*) and to forsake unbelief willingly, and if they have faith against their will (*karh*) and forsake unbelief against their will, they are not believers.
>
> He said also: if God makes a knowledge, it is someone else who is knowing thereby . . . and if He makes a desire it is someone else who is desiring thereby . . . but if He makes justice it is He Himself Who is just thereby; and the Creator is not characterized as being empowered to create evil in someone else. . . . Similarly it is not permissible to say that the Creator is empowered for creating the acquisition (*kasb*) of another or to say that He creates the

acquisition of another.

This Muḥammad b. ʿĪsā is almost certainly Muḥammad b. ʿĪsā Burghūth. In general he followed al-Najjār (*Maq*. 284; *Farq*, 197). The chief special doctrine that is mentioned is that he 'held that generated effects were God's act through the necessity of their nature (*ṭabʿ*); God has impressed on the stone such a nature that it moves away when it is pushed, and on animals such a nature that they suffer pain when they are struck or cut'. This is very close to the teaching of Muʿammar that accidents proceed from the nature of the substances (though Burghūth is careful to mention the Divine supremacy). There is a strong presumption in favour of H. Ritter's suggestion (*Maq*. Index, s.v.) that he is also identical with Muḥammad b. ʿĪsā al-Sayrāfī, twice given in the *Maqālāt* as the ultimate source of a report about Muʿammar (168, 488 – the former is given wrongly in the Index).

The thought here is on the lines of that of some sections of the Muʿtazila. God cannot create man's acquisition, since acquisition, like faith, is something man must do for himself. Presumably Burghūth's idea was that voluntary acts depended on a man's nature or character, in much the same way as the colour of a body depended on its nature or constitution. But, whereas Muʿammar emphasized the relative independence of accidents, Burghūth rather pointed to their ultimate dependence on God; man's capacity for acquiring, like the body's capacity for being coloured, is God's creation.

Burghūth thus appears to have attempted to combine recognition of the reality of man's willing with the upholding of God's omnipotence. There is some indication that, in addition to the views just mentioned, he took the line that creating and acquiring are not in any way comparable or parallel. It is reported that he refused to say that the Creator is 'doing' (*fāʿil*), because in common speech 'doing' can be used as an insult (*Maq*. 540); and al-Baghdādī (*Farq*, 197) says he differed from al-Najjār in not calling the acquirer (*muktasib*) 'doing' (*fāʿil*). Such an interpretation of the statements of Burghūth would be in accordance with his relationship to Ḍirār and al-Najjār.

5. LATER DISCUSSIONS AMONG THE MUʿTAZILA

The chief reference to the conception of acquisition is in an account of some doctrines of the Baghdādiyyūn (*Maq*. 550).

> God is not characterized by power over the action of men or over anything in a class over which He has empowered men. He is not characterized by the power to create faith for men by which they shall be believers, nor unbelief . . . nor rebellion . . . nor acquisition (*kasb*) by which they shall be acquiring (*muktasib*). They permitted the characterization of Him with power to create a movement by which they shall be moving, and a will by which they shall be willing,

and a desire by which they shall be desiring. They consider that the movement which God makes (*faʿala*) is different from the movement which man makes, and that if man's making (*fiʿl*) resembled God's making, then man would be resembling God.

This has some similarities with al-Shaḥḥām (who is connected with the Baghdādiyyūn in the distinction between *ṣifat al-fiʿl* and *ṣifat al-dhāt* – *Maq*. 504 f.), and with Burghūth. An attempt is made to clear up the confusion left by al-Shaḥḥām by speaking of a class of acts. Classes which have been entrusted to man comprise faith, unbelief, rebellion, and acquisition; whether they allowed man any power over movement is not clear. The distinction between the movement God makes and the movement man makes suggests the views of Burghūth. It is curious that *irāda*, which must commonly be translated 'will' in contexts of this sort, should here stand for an act that can be created by God, and thus sharply distinguished from the voluntary acts designated by *kasb*. Perhaps it is here to be taken rather as 'desire', i.e. as something involuntary.

Only one other Muʿtazilite is mentioned by al-Ashʿarī, so far as I have noticed, as employing the conception of *kasb*, viz. al-Nāshī (*Maq*. 501, 539), and even in his case it may be used only in al-Ashʿarī's criticism of his view. He held that man does not really act or originate, but only metaphorically; God alone really and truly acts (ib., cf. 184 f.). Al-Ashʿarī himself, apparently, adds the remark that he did not go so far as to say that God originated the acquisition of men.

Al-Jubbāʿī indeed mentions the word *kasb* (*Maq*. 542), but only to complain that the technical use, which we have been considering, is improper. By this time the Muʿtazilite 'acquisitionists' had seemingly ceased to be.

6. OPPONENTS OF THE MUʿTAZILA

There are few traces of views which clearly belong to the same universe of discourse as those of Burghūth. Aḥmad b. Salma al-Kūshānī (who is called a follower of al-Najjār – *Maq*. 541) said:

> if by saying man is 'doing' (*fāʿil*) you mean 'creating', that is false, but if you mean 'acquiring' (*muktasib*), that is the case; but he would not say he was 'doing' in the sense of 'acquiring'. (*Maq*. 540.)

Yaḥyā b. Abī Kāmil (ib.) made a slight variation:

> I do not say God is 'doing' except metaphorically, and I do not say man is 'doing' except metaphorically; the truth is that man is 'acquiring' and God is 'creating'.

He is called a Mutakallim of the Khawārij (*Maq*. 120) and an account is given of his views (107 f.) which shows he was interested in problems about the reality of human activity. (These views are shared by one Muḥammad b. Ḥarb, who is probably the same as Muḥammad b. Ḥarb al-Ṣayrafī (who holds views on perception that resemble doctrines of

Burghūth, and appears to belong to the Ahl al-Ithbāt – *Maq*. 383; and it is conceivable that he is none other than Burghūth, if we assume that the latter is Muḥammad b. ʿIsa al-Sayrāfī).[175]

There are numerous references throughout the *Maqālāt* to Ahl al-Ithbāt, the 'affirmationists'. It is clear that they got their name from their affirmation of the Divine omnipotence, *ithbāt al-qadar*; cf. *Maq*. p. 93, 1. 13; p. 96, 1. 4, p. 97, 1. 2, p. 124, 1. 10. But it is not so clear who were included in them. The impression is that they comprised all opponents of the 'free will' doctrines of the Muʿtazila from Ḍirār (cf. *Maq*. 408) down to the time of al-Ashʿarī. The following passages seem to come from the time of Burghūth or later.

> Many of the 'affirmationists' said: man is really 'doing' in the sense of 'acquiring', but he is not 'originating' (*muḥdith*); I have also heard that some said man is really 'originating' in the sense of 'acquiring' (540).
>
> There were some of the 'affirmationists' who said that God really 'does' in the sense of 'creates', but man does not really 'do' but only really 'acquires' . . . if man could create some of his acquisition, then he could create all his acquisition, just as the Eternal, when He created some of His 'doing', created all of His 'doing' (541).
>
> The Men of Truth and Affirmation (Ahl al-Ḥaqq wa'l-Ithbāt) said that God is empowered for creating faith by which men shall be believing, unbelief by which they shall be unbelieving, acquisition (*kasb*) by which they shall be acquiring (*muktasibūn*), obedience by which they shall be obedient, and rebellion by which they shall be rebellious (551). (This is followed by a passage which says that most of the Ahl al-Ithbāt held the opposite view.)
>
> The 'affirmationists' said that the Creator is empowered over another's wickedness and over his evil and his faith and his acquisition (*kasb*), but He is not characterized by power to do evil or to act wickedly or to acquire (*an yaktasiba*) . They did not characterize their Lord with power over evil which men did not acquire, apart from groups of them who said that God is empowered to compel men to evil and wickedness, and that there is neither wickedness nor evil in the world of which God is not the doer (*fāʿil*) (554).

These reports give indications of theologians who stood considerably 'to the right of' Burghūth. The third passage seems to be a direct denial of views expressed by Burghūth and also by the Baghdādiyyūn of the Muʿtazila. Some of them go so far as to maintain that not merely the capacity for acquiring but specific acts of acquiring are God's creation, but this happens in such a way that the voluntary character of the act is not lost.

(For the sake of completeness it should be mentioned that *kasb* and *iktisāb* occur in accounts of the views of ʿAbdallāh b. Kullāb; in the former he says the recitation of the Qur'ān is man's acquisition (*Maq*. 602), and in the latter he says that human speech may be either by compulsion or by acquisition (605). It is hardly possible from these slight references – especially as they may come from the reporter – to indicate his connection with the general train of thought. The Zaydiyya of whom *kasb* is used (*Maq*. 72) appear to have held the common Muʿtazilite doctrine.

7. AL-ASHʿARĪ

Al-Ashʿarī doubtless shared, and may indeed have been the first to express, some of the views he describes of the Ahl al-Ithbāt. There are, however, two places where he gives a view explicitly as his own.

> The truth in my view is that the meaning of 'acquiring' (*iktisāb*) is that the thing happens through an originated power so as to be an acquisition of the person through whose power it happens (542).
>
> As for myself, I say that in the case of everything which God is characterized as having power to create as an acquisition for men, He is empowered to compel them to it; and it is permissible for God to compel them to wickedness (552).

To these may be added what appears to be the only use of the word in the *Ibāna* (p. 63, Hyderabad; 103, tr.):

> There cannot be within the sphere of God's authority any acquiring (*iktisāb*) by men which God did not will.

The word does not occur at al in al-Ashʿarī's statement of his beliefs, either at the beginning of the *Ibāna* or in the *Maqālāt* (290-7).

The position in general, seems to be that, while he admits a certain reality to man's willing (though in the passage on p. 542 he carefully avoids applying *faʿala* to man), he is primarily interested in asserting God's omnipotence.

8. CONCLUSION

This investigation shows that the conception of *kasb* had a long history before the time of al-Ashʿarī. The conception may have been introduced by Ḍirār; the Muʿtazila of the school of Muʿammar certainly played a considerable part in developing it, directly or indirectly. Al-Ashʿarī himself can have done little more than adjust the balance of the various elements in the doctrine as it had been formulated by Burghūth and others of the Ahl al-Ithbāt more or less in accordance with orthodox belief; and he seems to have attached meagre importance to the conception.

B6 Was Wāṣil a Khārijite?

In his article on the Muʿtazila in the first edition of the *Encyclopaedia of Islam* H. S. Nyberg argued for the hypothesis that 'the theology of Wāṣil and the original Muʿtazila was the official theology of the ʿAbbāsid movement'. This hypothesis has not been generally accepted. Among the points urged against it are the following: though the Muʿtazilites of Baghdad were closely associated with the caliphal government under al-Ma'mūn, they were persecuted under Hārūn al-Rashīd; the distinctive doctrine of *al-manzila bayn al-manzilatayn* ascribed to Wāṣil has no special relevance to ʿAbbāsid propaganda; the relation of Wāṣil to the later Muʿtazila is obscured, since some early sources neglect Wāṣil completely and speak of ʿAmr ibn ʿUbayd as the founder, while, as Nyberg allows, the Muʿtazilite dogmatic system was mainly the work of Abū 'l-Hudhayl (under al-Rashīd and al-Ma'mūn); there is no mention of any connection between any Muʿtazilites and the known ʿAbbāsid agents in the eastern provinces. On the other hand, one piece of evidence used by Nyberg remains puzzling, namely, the mention in an early poem of propagandist agents sent out by Wāṣil. If these were not making propaganda for the ʿAbbāsids, what were they doing?

Nyberg was aware that in the *Bayān* of al-Jāḥiẓ, in close proximity to the poem just mentioned, were four lines by Isḥaq ibn Suwayd al-ʿAdawī, of which the first was:

I keep aloof from the Khawārij – I am not of them – from al-Ghazzāl among them them and from Ibn Bāb.[176]

Al-Ghazzāl was a nickname of Wāṣil, and Ibn Bāb is ʿAmr ibn ʿUbayd ibn Bāb. Nyberg interprets this as a confusion, explicable by the fact that both the ʿAbbāsids and the Khawārij were bitterly opposed to the Umayyads. The heresiographer al-Baghdādi (d. 1037) was also aware of the verse and commented as follows:

> Wāṣil and ʿAmr agreed with the Khawārij in holding that the punishment of the grave sinner in Hell was unending, although they also held that he was a *muwaḥḥid*, not a *mushrik* nor a *kāfir*; for this reason the Muʿtazila were called the effeminates (*makhānīth)* of the Khawārij, since the Khawārij, holding that sinners are eternally in Hell, call them infidels (*kafara*) and fight them, whereas the Muʿtazila, holding that they are eternally in Hell, do not dare

> to call them infidels and do not dare to fight any sect of them, far less to fight all their opponents. For this reason Isḥāq . . . in one of his poems assigned Wāṣil and ʿAmr to the Khawārij. . .[177]

This passage of al-Baghdādī is worthy of note. While it explains how the poet came to call the two men Khārijites, it also apparently admits that there was a time when the Muʿtazila were regarded as a sect of moderate Khārijites. Since this is not in accordance with what came to be the standard views of these matters, it may be concluded that the phrase about 'the effeminates of the Khawārij' is an authentic piece of early material.

There seems to be nothing impossible in such a view of the position of Wāṣil ibn ʿAṭā'. In the period from 700 to 750 the lines of division between the sects were not clear cut. Ghaylān al-Dimashqī, who was slightly older than Wāṣil, was called both Khārijite and Muʿtazilite, and also Qadarite (as was Wāṣil) and even Murji'ite. In so far as the sect-names were nicknames, the same man might be called different names by different persons; but it is also possible that the different names were applied to him in respect of different aspects of his teaching. Thus Ghaylān was a Qadarite in respect of his doctrine of free will (and his readiness to revolt against the Umayyads) and a Murji'ite in respect of his doctrine of *īmān* or faith. It seems likely that in a similar way Wāṣil could be both Khārijite and Muʿtazilite. As this point is further investigated two questions may be kept in mind: the nature of Wāṣil's beliefs before he propounded the doctrine of the intermediate position; and the difference at this period (700-50) of Khārijite and Muʿtazilite doctrine.

The distinctive view of the early Khārijites was that the grave sinner (*ṣāḥib kabīra*) is a *kāfir*, and so goes to Hell for eternity. The most extreme upholders of this doctrine were the Azāriqa, who regarded as a grave sin the refusal to join their movement of revolt and so considered themselves justified in fighting, robbing and killing all non-Azraqite Muslims. By the early eighth century, however, there were many moderate Khārijites in Basra who were prepared to live under a non-Khārijite governor. Such persons had necessarily to modify their creed to bring it more into accord with their practice. The attempts to do this may be traced in the works of the heresiographers, especially the *Maqālāt* of al-Ashʿarī. Thus some of them held that they were living in 'the sphere of prudent fear' (*dār at-taqiyya*), that is, a situation in which some compromise with strict principle might be necessary.[178] Some, apparently from among the Ibāḍites, thought of the grave sinner as a 'hypocrite' (*munāfiq)* but not a polytheist (*mushrik*)[179] the implication was presumably that they might be treated as Muḥammad treated the hypocrites of his time. Other Ibāḍites insisted that the grave sinner could not be a *mushrik* unless he acknowledged more than one deity; if he refrained from this, he remained a 'monotheist' (*muwaḥḥid*) despite his sins, and the sphere was 'the sphere of monotheism' (*dar al-tawḥīd*)[180] This last view is precisely that ascribed by al-Baghdādī to Wāṣil and ʿAmr on this point.

A similar result is reached if we think about Wāṣil's doctrine of the *manzila*. The extreme Khārijite view was that the grave sinner was *kāfir* and *mushrik*; and the extreme Murji'ite view was that he was *mu'min*. Wāṣil's assertion was that he was in an 'intermediate position' between the two; but there were various other attempts at compromise. The basic Murji'ite view was that the judgement about him was 'postponed', but in practice he was meantime treated as a believer. Al-Ḥasan al-Baṣrī and some of the Ibāḍites preferred to call the grave sinner a 'hypocrite' and to treat him as Muḥammad treated the 'hypocrites' among his contemporaries. Thus the doctrine of the *manzila* was one of several attempts about this time to deal realistically with Khārijite exclusion of the grave sinner from the community, and might therefore be described as a modified Khārijite position.

In 1916 Carlo Nallino published a short article pointing to similarities between Muʿtazilite and Ibāḍite doctrine in North Africa.[181] He lists four items already noted by Goldziher: the createdness of the Qur'ān; the impossibility of the vision of God in the world to come; the metaphorical interpretation of the balance and the *ṣirāṭ* (on the Last Day); metaphorical interpretations of God's *istiwā'* on the throne and other anthropomorphic expressions. Then he adds other three points: grave sinners are not pardoned by God unless they repent before death; the punishment in Hell, even of the unrepentant Muslim sinner, is eternal; the attributes of God are his essence and not additional to his essence. The Ibāḍites differ only in two points: they hold that the grave sinner is a *kāfir*, and deny that there is a *manzila* between *īmān* and *kufr*; and some admit free will only in the modified form of *kasb*. Nallino then suggests explanations of this similarity, but refrains from deciding between them owing to the scarcity of material. Two of his questions, however, are almost certainly to be answered in the negative: the Ibāḍites had not adopted the Muʿtazilite views before they reached the Maghrib, since the views had probably not yet been formulated in Iraq; and it is highly unlikely that from the original common basis the two sets of views developed independently. We must agree with Nallino, on the other hand, that there is insufficient material to enable us to distinguish the channels of communication.[182]

It may be noted – though it is impossible to say how relevant it is – that a sub-sect of the Ibāḍites, the Ḥārithiyya or followers of al-Ḥārith ibn Mazyad al-Ibāḍī, adopted Muʿtazilite views on *qadar* and other points. Al-Ḥārith was himself the disciple of one Ḥamza al-Kūfī;[183] but it is unlikely that this man is to be identified with the leader of the

Ḥamziyya who were active in the eastern provinces from 795 until the reign of al-Ma'mūn, although the Ḥamziyya also had views similar to those of the Muʿtazila.[184]

Other links between Ibāḍites and Muʿtazilites are to be found in North Africa. Ibāḍite (and also Ṣufrite) preaching began in Cairouan early in the eighth century, and Tripolitania was soon dominated by the Ibāḍites. The Ibāḍite imamate there, however, was destroyed by an ʿAbbāsid army in 761, though many of the Berbers remained loyal to Ibāḍism. A westward movement made possible the establishment by the Rustamids of an Ibāḍite state in western Algeria with its centre at Tahert. At times this state flourished and extended its boundaries, but it was brought to an end by the Fāṭimids in 909. The geographer Ibn al-Faqīh al-Hamadhānī (d. 902) records the presence of Muʿtazilites at a place called Ayzarj near Tahert and another called Walīla in the region of Tangier.[185] More important still, however, there was a sect of Wāṣiliyya by the eighth century both in the territory of Tangier and in the neighbourhood of Tahert. Some of the latter were involved in fighting against the Rustamid imam who ruled from 784 to 823; and a dispute between an Ibāḍite and a Muʿtazilite over the question of free will is recorded during the reign which ended in 894.[186] Despite the fighting and the debating the distinction between the two was not as clear as might have been expected, and we find some strange phrases. According to Abū l-ʿArab al-Tammāmī (d. 945), the jurist Saḥnūn, during a reaction against the doctrine of the created Qur'ān about 848, hid *al-muʿtazila al-ibāḍiyya* in the great mosque at Cairouan,[187] while al-Bakrī (d. 1094) refers to *al-wāṣiliyya al-ibāḍiyya* in this region.[188]

From all this material two conclusions may be drawn. Firstly, it appears that in their origins the views of Wāṣil were close to those of the moderate Khārijites of Basra, such as the Ibāḍite scholar and leader Abū-ʿUbayda Muslim ibn Abī Karīma al-Tamīmī, who probably died during the reign of al-Manṣūr (754-75). Even the doctrine of the *manzila* could be regarded as a Khārijite variant. It is therefore not surprising that Wāṣil could be regarded as a Khārijite, especially before the Muʿtazilites became famous (in the reign of al-Ma'mūn) and before their link with Wāṣil was firmly established. Secondly, Wāṣil had had some influence in western Algeria. Even after in Iraq the distinction between Ibāḍites and Muʿtazilites was clear, it was not clear in the Maghrib. In the Maghrib the two sets of doctrines had ceased to be rival programmes of reform for the whole Islamic world, and Ibāḍism at least had become the mark of the separation of the Rustamid state from the ʿAbbāsid caliphate. After the rejection of Muʿtazilism by al-Mutawakkil in the years around 850 the function of Rustamid Ibāḍism was not affected by the incorporation of Muʿtazilite elements, since these were equally anti-ʿAbbāsid.

Against this background the poem by Ṣafwān al-Anṣārī, in which he speaks of Wāṣil sending out agents, is much less mysterious.[189] The poem may be rendered as follows:

O Ibn Ḥawshab, when did Ghazzāl have (in his ranks)
such a man as ʿAmr or as ʿĪsā ibn Ḥāḍir?
Was not ʿUthmān al-Ṭawīl ibn Khālid
or the chieftain Ḥafṣ (ibn Sālim) the ultimate in challengers?
Beyond the pass of China in every tract of land
all the way to farthest Sūs and beyond the Berbers, he has
Men who summon (on his behalf), whose determination is not broken
by the browbeatings of the mighty or the stratagems of the cunning.
If he says, 'March in winter', they comply;
or if in summer, unfeared is the month of heat and thirst
Despite the attendant exile, the sacrifices, the difficulties undertaken,
the extreme dangers, or the hardships of travel.
Therefore has (God) caused their endeavour to prosper, has struck their flint,
and made it spark with a victory that overwhelms opponents.
(His also are men like) God's mountains in every land,
the repositories of its authoritative decisions and of the science of debate.
They would not have been outstripped even by Saḥbān,
nor by the masters of eloquence in the two clans of Hilāl ibn ʿĀmir,
Nor by the fluent Nakhkhār (ibn Aws al-ʿUdhrī), nor by the ancient Daghfal (ibn Ḥanẓala al-Sadūsī),
when they held the staff with their right hand,
Nor by the supreme orators, the kin of Makaḥḥal (al-Minqarī)
when they pronounce themselves on peace among the tribes
Before massed meetings of both content and aggrieved,
their bedouin having marched to the rallying points.
The peerless one of his age has styled himself the Ghazzāl.
Who then is for the orphans and the outnumbered (tribe)?
Who for a Ḥarūrite or again for a Rāfiḍite
or again for a Murji'ite or for one perplexed?
(Who for) enjoining the right or forbidding the wrong,
for fortifying God's religion against all unbelievers?
In every utterance they find the crux (as unerringly)
as the butcher's knife severs the bones.
You see them (motionless) as if birds were over their heads,
with a turban-style well-known among the tribes.
Well-known are their features in their faces,

in their marching as pilgrims and (riding) on camels,
In a prayer that lasts the entire night,
and frank utterance representing (what is in) their hearts,
In their shortening of the fringe and close clipping of the moustache,
their wrapping of the turban over white hair that seems to emit light. . .
Such are the marks that round off their description –
ignorance of the group lacks the knowledge of experience.

In this poem there are three points to notice which are relevant to the present discussion. Firstly, the lines praising Wāṣil's emissaries for their skill in oratory are very much in line with the Khārijite outlook. Secondly, the Ibāḍite leader in Basra in the period up to about 765, Abū ʿUbayda al-Tamīmī, is reported to have sent out teams of emissaries to the Maghrib, the Yemen, Ḥaḍramawt, Oman and Khurasan.[190] It would not be surprising if Wāṣil had done something similar, especially in view of this poem and of the report (ascribed to Abū 'l-Hudhayl) that he sent his companions to the Maghrib, Khurasan, the Yemen, the Jazīra, Kufa and Armenia.[191] Thirdly, there is nothing in the poem to suggest that these emissaries preached an ʿAbbāsid rising. They seem rather to have proclaimed a set of religious beliefs with no immediate political connections (though these beliefs might later become a basis for a separate identity). Enjoining the right and forbidding the wrong might indeed lead to political activity, but this matter was not prominent in ʿAbbāsid propaganda, so far as we know.

The conclusion to which this brief study points is that Wāṣil came from what was predominantly a moderate Khārijite background. The doctrine of the *manzila* was insufficient in itself to mark him off clearly. He and his followers, though closely related to the Ibāḍites, seem to have been distinct from them. The probability is that the Muʿtazila were sharply distinguished from the Khārijites only after the former had accepted the nickname and given it an honourable meaning by referring it to the five principles. This happened in the early ninth century, perhaps in the time of Abū 'l-Hudhayl, and may be linked with the attempt to claim Wāṣil instead of ʿAmr as forerunner and founder.

B7. The Significance of Khārijism under the ʿAbbāsids

The aim of this paper is not to bring together the facts about the activities of the Khārijites during the ʿAbbāsid period, since this has already for the most part been done by Professor Laura Veccia Vaglieri in her article on 'Le vicende del Hārigismo in epoca abbaside'[142] The purpose here is rather to consider the general significance of the Khārijite movement durng this period and what it meant practically to its adherents, and to notice how this significance differed from that in the previous century.

Khārijism is usually held to have begun at the battle of Siffīn in 657 when a body of ʿAlī's followers forced him to accept the arbitration. One of the principles implicit in this action and in their later 'secessions' was that 'there is no decision but God's' (*lā ḥukm illā li-llāh*). A second principle implicit in the activities of these men was that the man who commits a serious sin (the *ṣāḥib kabīra* or 'grave sinner') is excluded from the community of Muslims. Before long the principles had been formulated and were being held explicitly. The second principle was in fact used to support the Khārijite view that the killers of ʿUthmān had been justified in that act, and it was also developed by the Azraqites in such a way that it became the theological basis for a course of action which was hardly distinguishable from brigandage.[193]

When one looks objectively at the polemical accounts of the Khārijites, and makes allowance for the absence of the concept of development in the Muslim writers about sects, it becomes clear that the Khārijites made an important contribution to Islamic thought and indeed to the whole formation of Islamic culture. The first of their principles was intended to be applied to the whole life of the Islamic state, and as such it was of primary importance. ʿAlī and the succeeding Umayyad caliphs must be credited with trying to follow the example of Muḥammad, but there must inevitably have been a tendency, when a new and difficult problem presented itself, to turn to pre-Islamic practice in search of a solution. Had such a tendency not been checked, there would probably never have been an Islamic empire and civilization. Thus the first Khārijite principle was in a sense eventually accepted by all Muslims, but it might well not have been so accepted if the Khārijites had not insisted on it. The later Sunnite interpretation of the principle certainly differed in one respect from the Khārijite interpretation, in that the Khārijites held that God's decision was known solely from the Qur'ān , whereas the Sunnites supplemented this with the Sunna of the Prophet; but when al-Shāfiʿī persuaded other jurists to accept Ḥadīth as one of the roots of law, he made it clear that the Sunna was divine revelation just as much as the Qur'ān , since God gave Muḥammad 'the wisdom' as well as the Book. Thus all Islamic social and political life is based on the revealed Sharīʿa; and this was essentially the ideal expressed in the first Khārijite principle.

The early Khārijite movement was almost exclusively a movement of nomads and ex-nomads. The little revolting groups can be seen as an attempt to reconstruct nomadic life, and their raiding activities are certainly reminiscent of the desert. Like nomads, too, they excelled in poetry and oratory. Unfortunately their political ideals were also those of the desert, suited to the wide spaces and rough conditions of nomadic life but not to the urban civilization of the newly conquered provinces. A desert tribe might punish one of its members by forcing him to leave the tribe, but the urban communities of Iraq could not make exclusion from the community the punishment for every crime. Thus the second Khārijite principle was in practice unworkable. This fact, however, should not make one lose sight of the underlying moral earnestness – an attitude shared by many other Muslims but no doubt strengthened in them by Khārijite assertions.

While Khārijite idealism was first manifested in little bands of men who rose in revolt against the government of the day, after about 690 there were a number of moderate Khārijites, chiefly in Basra, who were prepared to live peaceably under a non-Khārijite governor and who gradually worked out ways of modifying the more extreme formulations of Khārijite doctrine so as to justify their own present practice. Among such men the first principle seems to have been taken for granted – by this time it was probably accepted by many other thoughtful Muslims – and the discussions were mainly about the implications of the second. Such discussions must have helped to gain acceptance in wider circles for the idealistic elements in Khārijite teaching.

Khārijism entered another phase towards the end of the Umayyad period. As Julius Wellhausen has put it:

> The Khārijite movement took on a totally different character when the Umayyad Kingdom began to break up altogether: it now became part of a revolution. The difference is outwardly visible in the numbers. The small numbers of troops which usually are characteristic of the Khārijite armies, swelled to powerful masses.[194]

There are also other differences besides the increase in numbers. The Khārijite slogans were no longer principles to determine the conduct of affairs of state, but little more than a way of rousing martial ardour in men who were aware that the existing order of society was disintegrating but who had no clear idea of how to create an alternative order. These men could perhaps be described as being half way between the early Khārijite rebels and those who participated in the revolts of the ʿAbbāsid period.

After the transference of power from the Umayyad to the ʿAbbāsid dynasty in 750 Khārijite revolts occurred at intervals for nearly two centuries. The ʿAbbāsids, however, had to a greater extent than the Umayyads accepted the view that the Islamic empire and society should be based on the Sharīʿa, and this view was also accepted by most serious-minded Muslims. The significance of Khārijism in this period, therefore, must be different from what it was in the early revolts and even from what it was in the revolts of the last decade or so of Umayyad rule. Although a large number of small revolts are recorded between 750 and 930 most of these occurred in one or two regions, as has been emphasized by Professor Veccia Vaglieri.

In two regions the Khārijites succeeded in establishing their rule over extensive territories. One of these was the Maghrib (central and western North Africa) where even before 750 moderate Khārijism as taught by the Ṣufrite and Ibāḍite sub-sects had been widely adopted by the Berbers. In certain districts, notably those round Tripoli, Tahert, Tlemsen and Sijilmāsa, it became the dominant form of Islam. The most important Khārijite dynasty, the Rustamids of Tahert, fell before the Fāṭimids in 909, but many of the people continued to hold Khārijite doctrines, and one or two small pockets of Ibāḍites have continued to exist to the present day.[195] Again in Oman in south-east Arabia the Ibāḍites had some successes in a revolt about 752, but their rule was not securely established until 793. The Ibāḍites of contemporary Oman claim continuity with this distant past, but there have been times when Ibāḍism was somewhat in eclipse.

In other regions there were revolts which continued to be successful for a number of years and then disappeared. In various districts round Mosul in northern Iraq sixteen revolts have been recorded in the years from 750 to 930. Two or three of these created serious difficulties for the caliph's governors and generals, namely, that of al-Walīd ibn-Tarīf in 794, that of Musāwir from 866 until his death in 876, and the continuation of this by Hārūn ibnʿAbd-Allāh al-Bajalī from 876 until 896.[196] Another region in which there were several Khārijite revolts was Sijistan and southern Khurasan (eastern Afghanistan and neighbouring parts of Persia). The most important was that of Ḥamza ibn Adrak from 795 to 809. He is credited with being the founder of the sect of Ḥamziyya, whose views are briefly recorded by the heresiographers.[197]

After this brief account of the Khārijite revolts of the ʿAbbāsid period it is possible to call attention to several points which are relevant to a consideration of their significance. Firstly, the appeal of Khārijite doctrine and insurrectionary practice is to tribally-organized Arabs and to other peoples with a similar background such as Berbers and Kurds; there is no sign of an appeal to urban populations. It has been suggested that in the case of the Berbers Khārijism gave a focus to their anti-Arab feelings, but on the other hand Ibn al-Athīr remarks that Musāwir was supported by both Arabs and Kurds. Secondly, there was some continuity with earlier Khārijism, since old slogans and dogmas were used. In 896 Hārūn al-Bajalī kept shouting *lā ḥukm illā li-llāh* as he was being crucified. In 930 the second-last Khārijite insurgent in the neighbourhood of Mosul, one Ṣāliḥ ibn Maḥmūd al-Bajalī, proudly proclaimed two old Khārijite dogmas – 'we associate with the two shaykhs (sc. Abū Bakr and 'Umar) and dissociate ourselves from the two evil doers (sc. 'Uthmān and 'Alī)' and 'we do not allow the wiping of the sandals (as a substitute in certain cases for the washing of the feet before prayer)'.[198] Quarrels between Khārijites were also given a doctrinal basis. Ḥamza, the leader in Sijistan, had a rival in Kirman and Makran called Khalaf, and al-Shahrastānī records that they differed on the question of free will (though this had not been a point of special concern to early Khārijites). More typical was the quarrel between Musāwir and one 'Ubayda, leading to a bloody battle, over the question whether, when a sinner repented, his repentance was to be accepted.[199]

Thirdly, there is nothing to show that the doctrines asserted by the Khārijite rebels were specially relevant to the general contemporary situation. A considerable amount of historical and theological material has been preserved by the Ibāḍites, but apart from this Ibāḍite material the above few facts are practically all that has been recorded of the doctrinal views of the Khārijite rebels of the 'Abbāsid period. From this it may be concluded that they produced no new formulations of doctrine which were of interest to the theologians. The matters involved in the quarrels between Ḥamza and Khalaf and between Musāwir and 'Ubayda must have been relevant to some particular situation, but it was presumably only a local and limited situation. In any case we are given no details. Again, while one appreciates the toughness of Hārūn al-Bajalī in repeating his slogan at his execution, one wonders what the point of it was. If he took it in the most general sense, most of those present would presumably have agreed. He might have given it some more specific connotation, however; for example, he might have regarded it as a protest against the current legal system in that it made the Ḥadīth a 'root of law' on an equal footing with the Qur'ān. In this case it would be an attempt to put the clock back, since by 896 the legal rites were well established on the basis of Qur'ān and Ḥadīth. Similarly, the assertions of Ṣāliḥ in 930 about the first four caliphs were anachronistic, since by that date acceptance of the first four caliphs in their chronological order was an article of faith included in the Sunnite creeds.

There is a sharp contrast between the Khārijism of these unsuccessful rebels of the ʿAbbāsid period and that of the earliest Khārijites. The latter were acting on the basis of an ideal – the basing of the whole life of the state on the Sharīʿa – which was universally relevant and was also, within limits, capable of being acted upon. Even if some detailed suggestions were impractical, the general point remains valid. The later ʿAbbāsid insurrectionaries, on the other hand, cannot be said to have been putting forward an ideal when they spoke about a return to the past. In some circumstances this could become an ideal, but in the case of these Khārijites it seems to have been an irrational response to the unsatisfactory conditions in which they found themselves, and one which led to no practical measures to put right what was amiss. In short the Khārijite revolts of the ʿAbbāsid period must be classified as reactionary protests which did nothing to bring about any real improvements, but which gave the participants the subjective satisfaction of feeling they were achieving something. At the same time the repetition of old slogans and claims to be following past heroes seemed to remove the taint of possible innovation, which was something always hateful to the Arabs. One such hero was Ṣāliḥ ibn al-Musarriḥ, who fell fighting bravely in 695, and was so highly thought of in the region round Mosul that as late as 784 a Khārijite there claimed to be following in his footsteps.[200]

Yet another facet of the significance of Khārijism is to be seen in the successful revolts which led to the formation of a relatively permanent state, as in North Africa and Oman. Probably the original Ibāḍite and Ṣufrite revolts were little more than irrational protests against the existing political structure. With continuing success, however, it became necessary for the leaders of the movement to take decisions about the political and social structure of what was now *their* state. Such decisions were normally in accord with the basic principles of the movement, that is, in the best-attested example, with their Ibāḍite Khārijism or Ibāḍism. The final result was the transformation of a rebel band into a close-knit community with a high degree of stability. The members of the community had a strong sense of their identity as Ibāḍites, and this marked them off from the surrounding Sunnites and Shīʿites and made them feel superior to these others, while at the same time they were firmly bound to one another. Thus within the Ibāḍite state Ibāḍism came to have a function similar to that of Sunnism in the greater part of the Islamic world, but there was one important difference. The adherents of Sunnism considered it to be of universal validity not merely for the whole *dār al-Islām* but also potentially for the whole of mankind, whereas the Ibāḍites, though convinced of the superiority of their form of religion, seem to have accepted the fact that they were likely to remain a small minority within a much vaster alien society.

B8. The Reappraisal of ʿAbbāsid Shīʿism

A reappraisal of the nature of Shīʿism in the first century and a half of the ʿAbbāsid caliphate has been made possible, and indeed desirable, by a clearer awareness among scholars of the nature of the methods employed by the heresiographers, and of the different strands in the heresiographical tradition. Aspects of the subject have already been dealt with by the writer,[201] and the present article aims at carrying further the line of thought opened up elsewhere. One of the features of the early ʿAbbāsid period was that intellectual discussions on religious and political subjects took the form of arguments, about the precise character of events in the nearer or more distant past. Many of the statements about what happened from twenty-five to two hundred years earlier must have been sheer inventions – the contradictions are sufficient to assure us of this. The heresiographers, however, have taken most of these statements as if they were historical fact, and have tried to fit them into a chronological framework. They have also assumed that views first propounded long after an event were held by men who lived at the time or shortly after. Further, in a civilization where oral communications are thought more highly of than written documents, once a false assertion has been made a mere denial is ineffectual, and it has to be countered by contrary positive assertion. This naturally increases the confusion.

In dealing with material about early Shīʿism two questions are specially important: who held this view? and what did it mean to him, practically, in the particular circumstances of his life? By endeavouring to find answers to these questions – which is not always easy – doubt is thrown on several current assumptions, and an alternative conception of the nature of Shīʿism under the ʿAbbāsids is made to seem plausible. One of the main points of this alternative view is that, during their lifetime, there was little or no recognition of the twelve imams of the Imāmites as such; there was no organized party of followers and no underground revolutionary activities with the aim of making them caliphs. Insofar as this is the case, it follows that the Imāmite form of Shīʿism, and probably also the Ismāʿīlite did not receive the definite character familiar to scholars until shortly before 900. The immediate purpose of this article is to take the statements about the period subsequent to 750, found in *Firaq al-Shīʿa*, and to show that they can be interpreted and explained in a way that is compatible with the general thesis just outlined. This Imāmite work, *Firaq al-Shī'a*, has hitherto usually been ascribed to al-Ḥasan b. Mūsā al-Nawbakhtī, but is now regarded as probably by his contemporary, Sa'd b. 'Abd-Allāh al-Qummī.[202] Both men died about 912, and the book was presumably written between 900 and that date.[203]

§1. *6.14-7.6* Some members of these sects of the Murji'a belong to the early years of the 'Abbāsids: Abū Ḥanīfa (d. 767); al-Thawrī (d. 778); Sharīk (d. 793); Ibn Abī Laylā (d. 765); al-Shāfi'ī (d. 820); Mālik (d. 795). Therefore, some of the views in § 2 probably belong to this period. (For the use of the term 'Murji'ite' by Shī'ites, cf. § 8.)

§2. *7.7-8.11* Some early Murji'ite traditionists held the view – accepted by modern historians – that Muḥammad died without leaving a successor. The absence of a precedent meant that Muslims were free to advance opinions about the proper way of appointing a caliph. The view (7.13ff.) that it should be done by the exercise of judgement (*ijtihād al-ra'y*) sounds like that of Abū Ḥanīfa and his followers. Those who said it should be by reason might be members of the secretary class attracted to philosophy. The view of some later Mu'tazilites that Muḥammad designated the imam by description, that is, said what qualities he ought to have, was similar to the view of Abū 'l-Jārūd (as reported in Ash., 67). It may have been a concession to the believers in 'designation', that is, the Shī'ites, or else an argument against them. An instance of an anti-Shī'ite argument is the following view that Abū Bakr was 'designated' by being appointed to lead the worship.

The 'neglecters' (*ahl al-ihmāl*) are doubtless those who said Muḥammad made no arrangements, and the name would be given by their opponents, the 'designators' (*aṣhab al-naṣṣ*). The discussion of *fāḍil* and *mafḍūl* belongs to the circle of ideas of the Zaydis. The phrase 'imāmate of the inferior (*mafḍūl*)' is apparently not used in *Firaq al-Shī'a*. Doubtless, this is because it was a mocking way of referring to the Zaydite recognition of Abū Bakr, and one used only by opponents. Its absence in § 3 and § 7 is noteworthy.

§3. *8.15-9.5* The Butriyya (§7), a sect of the Zaydis, are trying to achieve a compromise between the Shī'ites and their opponents by saying 'Alī is best (*afḍal*), but the imāmate of Abū Bakr is not a mistake, since 'Alī 'entrusted that to the two of them' (namely, Abū Bakr and 'Umar). (Compare below 18.1-16.)

§4. *9.6-9* Sulaymān b. Jarīr, who probably flourished in the first half of the ninth century (compare *Intiṣār*. 89 and Ash., 70-73), was also a Zaydite but, according to this passage (and Ash., 68.5-7), seems to have been moving away from the usual Zaydite view.

§5. *9.10-13* Ibn al-Tammār is 'Alī (b. Ismā'īl) b. Mītham, and must have lived well into the first half of the ninth century (Friedlaender, II. 60; *Intiṣār*, 99). The puzzling thing is that he is included among the shaykhs of the Rāfiḍites (*Intiṣār*, 6; etc.), for the views expressed here are apparently Zaydite, and almost identical with those in the previous paragraph ascribed to the Zaydite Sulaymān b. Jarīr. Ibn al-Nadīm, in the *Fihrist* (175), describes him as 'the first who theologized about the doctrine of the imāmate' (*takallama fī madhhab al-imāma*). Clearly, the Shīʿite theologians of this period, as listed in *Intiṣār*, 6, were not all of one mind, for the *Fihrist* records refutations of several by Hishām b. al-Ḥakam. So Ibn al-Tammār may have belonged to the group who were working out the Rāfiḍite position, although he himself, as an early member of the group, may have held views on this point that were close to the Zaydites. It is also noteworthy that he is not said to have accepted the Zaydite principle of 'the imāmate of the inferior'. Perhaps the question to be asked is rather how Sulaymān b. Jarīr managed to combine the various views ascribed to him. Whatever the exact truth, this paragraph tends to confirm the view that, in the early ninth century, the Shīʿite position was very fluid. (Compare also Friedlaender, II. 60.)

§6. *10.10-12.9* The views here ascribed to the Muʿtazilites in general probably belong to the late eighth century and may be described as utilitarian. ʿAmr b. ʿUbayd is closer to the Shīʿites than other members of the sect, since he allows that ʿAlī had the best right to the imāmate.

§7. *12.10-16* While al-Ḥasan b. Ṣāliḥ (d. 785) seems to have been the most prominent member of the Butriyya (§3), it received its name from Kathīr al-Nawwā' al-Abtar, who was presumably earlier. Of the men named, dates are available for al-Ḥakam (d. 732) and Salma (d. 740). Thus the sect belongs partly to the Umayyad period. This is doubtless why it fully accepts the imāmate of Abū Bakr and ʿUmar, unlike, for example, Sulaymān b. Jarīr (§ 4), who thinks the recognition of these men mistaken.

§8. *15.13f.* This is a most important sentence, since it shows how Shīʿites looked on the Islamic community about the year 900. There are four sects, Shīʿites, Muʿtazilites, Murji'ites and Khārijites; and this is intended to be an exhaustive division of the community. Where then are the Sunnites? They cannot be taken for granted as 'orthodox', since the Shīʿites considered themselves the true Muslims. The Sunnites must therefore be divided between the other sects, especially the Muʿtazilites and Murji'ites. From the Shīʿite point of view, they themselves were the true community, because they followed the true imam. All others put the revealed scriptures first, and did not consider the imam inspired. The Khārijites restricted the scriptures to the Qur'ān, but the others included also Traditions, and, in varying degrees, permitted the use of reason. The three sects also varied in their attitude to ʿUthmān. The Khārijites insisted he was an unbeliever because of his sins. The Murji'ites held he should be accepted as a believer, and the judgement on his sins left to God. The Muʿtazilites said he was in an 'intermediate position. From the Shīʿite standpoint of 900, then, most contemporary Muslims must have been Murji'ites, in the sense of recognizing ʿUthmān's caliphate; this does not mean they held those Murji'ite views, on the nature of faith, later considered heretical by the main body of Sunnites. In 900, too, it must be remembered, Ashʿarism had not appeared, and all that was visible was a variety of strands in the traditionist movement.

§9. *15.15-17.16* The opening part of this section, especially 16.1f., shows how later conditions are written back into the past. The author names four men known as supporters of ʿAlī. Then he goes on to say that, on the death of the Prophet, this 'sect of the Shīʿa' split into three sects. The first is not named, but its views are basically those of the Imāmites, namely, that ʿAlī had a right to the imāmate and the position of the Prophet since he had been expressly 'designated' by name, had been preserved from sin and error, had precedence (in conversion to Islam) and was of Muḥammad's family. That the division into three sects is not historical is shown by looking at the other two. The second (18.1-16) is the Butriyya, who flourished in the later Umayyad and early ʿAbbāsid period. The third is the Jārūdiyya, who sprang from Zayd (d. 740); and the point in which they differ from the first sect is that, after the death of al-Ḥusayn, they considered there was a *shūrā* or council of the descendants of al-Ḥasan and al-Ḥusayn. Such a view could hardly have been held before the death of al-Ḥasan about 669, but was probably not propounded till much later, since the Jārūdiyya were active under the ʿAbbāsids (Ash., 67, 12-16).

§10. *19.1-7* The Jārūdiyya insisted that the rightful imam must not remain hidden, but must come forward publicly at the head of an army. The point mentioned above about the *shūrā*, and the alternative (Ash., 67, 9-11) that Muḥammad designated ʿAlī and his two sons, belong to a period before the Imāmite doctrine of a succession of imams was generally accepted. These were presumably two ways of justifying Zayd's claim to be imam. If the only designations were those by Muḥammad of ʿAlī and his two sons, this ruled out the ʿAbbāsid claim to be designated in succession from Ibn al-Ḥanafiyya. Had a series of designations to Zayd's father been generally accepted, Zayd would have based his claim on this. Silence, and the absence of counter-claims for Zayd, argue that no such claim was being made for Zayd's father ʿAlī (d. 713) or his brother Muḥammad al-Bāqir (d. 732), as late as 740.

§11. 319.8-20.9 The views ascribed to the Saba'iyya must belong to the early ʿAbbāsid period (compare Lewis, *Ismāʿīlism*, 25; etc.). Those who regarded ʿAlī as the hidden imam cannot have accepted any succession of imams after him, nor can they have accepted any of his descendants as hidden imam.

§12. *20-37* The following pages deal mainly with the Umayyad period, and need not be commented on.

§13. *37.15-41.12* This important account of the Khaṭṭābiyya has been carefully examined by Bernard Lewis in *The Origins of Ismāʿīlism*, 32-37. In the present context, the vital questions have to do with the interpretation of the material. First of all, it must be noticed that some of the reports – especially those (38.7ff., 39.14ff.) which speak of their making adultery and theft lawful – must come from opponents. It is therefore possible that some of the more heterodox statements, for example, that they considered Jaʿfar was God, are hostile deductions from less extravagant beliefs, perhaps beliefs about the inherence of light in men. Secondly, it must be noted carefully that there is nothing about a series of imams in which each was designated by his predecessor. The nearest to this is the belief (40.10ff.) that there was a series of men in whom Light inhered, each of whom 'sent' his successor. The men named are ʿAbd al-Muṭṭalib, Abū Ṭālib, Muḥammad, ʿAlī; then there is a jump to Jaʿfar and Abū 'l-Khaṭṭāb. It is strange that no one is named between ʿAlī and Jaʿfar. It would seem, either that no great importance was attached to the series as a series, or else that the names in the series were different from those later recognized by Imāmites and Ismāʿīlites. The transfer of allegiance (27.7f.) by al-Sayyid al-Ḥimyarī (d. 789) from Ibn al-Ḥanafiyya as hidden imam to Jaʿfar (d. 765) – presumably also as hidden imam – suggests that Ibn al-Ḥanafiyya may have been one of the links. Thirdly, the connection with Jaʿfar is puzzling, for Abū 'l-Khaṭṭāb probably was executed in 755 (Lewis, 33), whereas the views ascribed to him look as if they came after Jaʿfar's death. Bazīgh and the other men mentioned are doubtless a little after Abū 'l-Khaṭṭab. Whatever the explanation of the puzzle, it would seem that Jaʿfar must have had some connection with these men. Fourthly, the ideas held are 'extremist' – identification of Light with God, reincarnation, strange interpretations of the Qur'ān, etc. Some of these ideas were taken up by the later Ismāʿīlites, but it must remain doubtful if there was any organizational connection. ('Extremist' is used, in this article, to descibe all such ideas; it roughly corresponds to the Arabic 'Ghulāt' or 'Ghāliya'.)

§14. *41.13-47.9* This long section is about the ʿAbbāsiyya and Rāwandiyya, and is chiefly interesting as showing how Shīʿite ideas were applied to other than the descendants of ʿAlī and Fāṭima. The original view of the ʿAbbāsid family was that the imāmate was passed by testamentary disposition (*awṣā*) from the son of Ibn al-Ḥanafiyya to the family of al-ʿAbbās (42, 11-43 etc.). Under al-Mahdī (775-85), the ʿAbbāsid family felt this view unsatisfactory, and claimed instead that, on Muḥammad's death, the imāmate had gone to his uncle, al-ʿAbbās. The attempts to regard the general Abū Muslim as the hidden imam, and the caliph al-Manṣūr as God, may be noted, but need not be commented on.

§15. *47.10-48.2* This report of a 'sect' which recognized the imāmate of ʿAlī Zayn al-ʿĀbidīn, from his father's death in 680 until his own in 712, contains nothing which is not simply part of the assumption that there was a continuing series of imams. No contemporary names or facts are mentioned.

§16. *48.3-6* This report of a 'sect' which held that there was no imam after al-Ḥusayn (d. 680) may be taken as an admission not that there was a clearly defined sect with this view but that this was the general view even among people of Shīʿite sympathies. The view of the Jārūdiyya (§10), who flourished round about 750, that after 680 there was a *shūrā*, implies that there was no widely accepted imam between 680 and 750.

§17. *48.7-52.2* This further material about the Zaydites is mainly repetition. The most interesting part is the discussion whether the ʿAlids require to learn or have knowledge without learning (44.7-50.12). Such a discussion implies that those taking part had no thought of a recognized series of imams. The author points out that, despite the theory that all ʿAlids have perfect knowledge, Traditions are accepted from only four of them (50.1-3). (Compare §29; 74.14-76.7.)

§18. *52.6-53.8* The story of how ʿUmar b. Riyāḥ received contrary answers from al-Bāqir, and eventually attached himself to the Butriyya, reflects a series of arguments between the Butriyya (a section of the Zaydites) and their opponents. When it is argued that al-Bāqir cannot be imam because he gave contradictory answers, the reply is made that one was due to *taqiyya* (prudent concealment of one's true belief). To this it is retorted that there was no need for *taqiyya* in either case, since no one else was present. In short, it was not a properly considered reply; and a person who acts in this way, and does not come forward openly, cannot be imam. Now there is no reason to doubt that these were real arguments between the Butriyya and their opponents. What is doubtful is an actual contact between ʿUmar and al-Bāqir. For one thing, al-Bāqir died about 733 (or, perhaps, not till 737), but the Butriyya were probably not active until after 750. Again, the real conflict in the story is between ʿUmar and Muḥammad b. Qays (who appears to be otherwise unknown). Nothing is said about the precise point on which al-Bāqir's replies varied; and this suggests that it may have been a hypothetical instance, and that originally no actual imam may have been named. A later scholar, who assumed the existence of the series of imams, could have introduced al-Bāqir as the appropriate name in view of ʿUmar's date. If al-Bāqir was involved in a real argument, why does he not try to say more about the matter? These dubious points in this story mean that it does not, by itself, necessitate a recognized series of imams by 750.

§19. *53.9-55.6* 'The rest of the associates of (al-Bāqir) continued to believe in his imāmate until his death . . . then his sect divided into two sects.' One of these recognized, as imam, a descendant of al-Ḥasan b. ʿAlī, known as al-Nafs al-Zakiyya ('the pure soul'). These statements show how Imāmite views are subtly read back into the past. It is assumed that there is a large party which recognizes the imāmate of al-Bāqir, of whom a few have deserted to the Butriyya. Now, after his death, some others are found who turn to al-Nafs al-Zakiyya. One asks on what grounds the large party recognized al-Bāqir as imam. Was it by designation? If so, how did they abandon the theory of designation so easily? If not, can one say they recognized his imāmate and were not merely 'men of Shiʿite sympathies'? There is nothing here to support the view that, about 750, there was a series of recognized imams.

§20. *55.7-57.2* This section on the imāmate of Jaʿfar is, in fact, a continuation of the argument between Zaydites and their opponents, already noticed in § 18. There is here, in addition to the attack on *taqiyya* one on *badā'*, the doctrine that God changes his will for man. It is indicated that, with these two conceptions, the imams of the opponents (called 'Rāfiḍites') can never be caught out. Since Sulaymān b. Jarīr flourished in the first half of the ninth century, and Jaʿfar died in 765, the argument was taking place half a century, or more, after the events. The alleged mistake of Jaʿfar about Ismāʿīl was thus being used merely as an example. The most solid fact emerging from the story is that, by the time of Sulaymān (say 825-40), the Rāfiḍites were discussing whether Jaʿfar had 'pointed to' (*ashāra*) Ismāʿīl; it perhaps shows that this is early, since the term 'designated' (*naṣṣa*) is not used. It is possible that the Rāfiḍites were countering an Ismāʿīlite claim that Jaʿfar had appointed Ismāʿīl by asserting that Ismāʿīl died before Jaʿfar. (The doctrine of *badā'* was much discussed about the middle of the ninth century in connection with predestination; Ibn Qutayba, *Mukhtalif al-Ḥadīth*, 7; *Intiṣār*, 127-30; compare article 'Badā' in EI^2. One may also wonder whether the objections to the doctrines cf *taqiyya* and *badā'* were linked with objections to secretive and inconsistent policies of the ʿAbbāsid regime.)

§21. *57.3 15* The belief that Jaʿfar was still alive and would return can only have been held after his death. It implies that those who held it did not recognize any successor to him. They probably also did not recognize the series of designated predecessors. (Compare § 13.)

§21a. *57.16-58.8* The views here described as being of the 'pure' Ismāʿīliyya are similar to those mentioned in §20, except that the death of Ismāʿīl is denied. From what was said in the comment on §20, it would seem that these views need not have been held before 825-840.

§22. *58.9-16* This report about the Mubārakiyya presents a new argument; namely, that after al-Ḥusayn, the imamate cannot pass from brother to brother, but must pass from father to son. This means that it cannot pass from Ismāʿīl to any of his brothers. A corollary is that the imamate did not pass from al-Ḥusayn to Ibn al-Ḥanafiyya. The nerve of the argument – the practical consequence in which those who argued thus were interested – is the denial of the imāmate of Ismāʿīl's brothers.

Few were now interested in the imāmate of Ibn al-Ḥanafiyya. The ʿAbbāsids abandoned the claim through him between 775 and 785. The believers in hidden imams, who had probably regarded him as the link between al-Ḥusayn and Jaʿfar al-Sādiq, were now turning to Jaʿfar and others. So the rejection of Ibn al-Ḥanafiyya had no serious consequences. The corresponding assertion of the imāmate of ʿAlī b. al-Ḥusayn was also an academic matter – something which (on our hypothesis) had not been asserted previously, but which no one was interested in denying. While the nature and implications of the argument are thus clear, the date at which it was put forward is unfortunatley obscure. Nothing is known about Mubārak, the man who gave his name to the sect. At what time was the imāmate of Jaʿfar's sons, especially Mūsā, asserted? It has been suggested that there was some discussion, at least by the period 825-840, of the fact that Ismāʿīl had died before Jaʿfar. If this was coupled with the assertion that another son of Jaʿfar was imam, that would belong to about the same period. This suggests that, first of all, some 'pure Ismaʿilites' asserted that Ismāʿīl had succeeded Jaʿfar. Next, the Rāfiḍites replied that Ismāʿīl had died before Jaʿfar (and if there was a possibility of doubt about this point, the presumption is that it was some time after Jaʿfar's death); the Rāfiḍite reply laid them open to Zaydite attack. They probably also asserted that Jaʿfar was succeeded by his son, Mūsā al-Kāẓim. The Ismāʿīlites countered this by their theory that the imāmate could not pass from brother to brother, and thereby implicitly put forward the view that there must be a series of imams. (The argument about brothers is also relevant to the succession to al-Ḥasan al-ʿAskarī in 874; compare § 27 below.)

§23. *58.17-60.16* This is a report of the actual rising of the Khaṭṭābiyya about 755. The problem is to know why a man who died in 755 held views about what happened after Jaʿfar's death in 765.

§24. *61.1-64.14* The Qarmatians are here described as having introduced the idea of *seven* imams; but their 'extremist' ideas need not be discussed. The phrase about the denial of the imāmate of Mūsā b. Jaʿfar (d. 799), and his descendants, suggests that he is already dead.

§25. *64.15-65.7* The sect who claimed Muḥammad ibn Jaʿfar as imam is very obscure. That it should have existed, if it really did, shows that there was no general recognition of any of Jaʿfar's sons immediately after his death.

§26. *65.8-66.8* The sect who took Jaʿfar's son ʿAbd-Allāh as imam is also obscure. Their argument that the imam should be succeeded by his eldest son is a move towards recognition of the series of imams, but does not go so far as the Mubārakiyya. Some of the arguments about ʿAbd-Allāh are clearly dated after 874, since ʿAbd-Allāh b. Bukayr made them precedents for his view of the succession to al-Ḥasan al-ʿAskarī. The sect is also connected with ʿAmmār b. Mūsā (Ash., I, 28), who is found holding similar views to ʿAbd-Allāh b. Bukayr (67.3; § 27), and may be a contemporary. It is thus not impossible that little was heard of the imāmate of ʿAbd-Allāh till after 874.

§27. *66.9-67.7* The view that Mūsā was imam after his father Jaʿfar is described as being held by the leading Shīʿite scholars. Unfortunately, it is not clear at what dates these men held this view. Abān is said to have died in 758 before Jaʿfar (Index, *s.v.*), so that something must be wrong here. Jamīl is said to have died in the days of al-Riḍā, that is, probably shortly before his death in 818. The two Hishāms probably flourished from about 800 to 825. It is not improbable that the event which set most of these theories of the imāmate in motion was the caliph al-Ma'mūn's choice of ʿAlī al-Riḍā as heir-apparent in 816. Up to this point, there was possibly no generally recognized head of the ʿAlids. This event, however, forced men of Shīʿite sympathies to decide for or against ʿAlī. The list in the present section may be based on the presumption that men who approved of al-Ma'mūn's choice of ʿAlī must have accepted also his father Mūsā as imam. Actually, it seems just as likely that al-Ma'mūn's choice of ʿAlī contributed to fixing the choice of the Shīʿites on this particular line, and may also have made the opposition choose Ismāʿīl. It is noteworthy that ʿAbd-Allāh b. Bukayr, who is mentioned in the closing part of the section, is also said (p. 93 below) to have used the succession of brothers in 874. Thus the imāmate of ʿAbd-Allāh (who is said to have died in 765) was being discussed in 874; and one cannot help wondering if it had ever been discussed before that time.

§28. *67.8-72.6* The succession to Mūsā (d. 799) is chiefly interesting because it shows considerable messianic interest. Apart from the sect which accepts the imāmate of ʿAlī al-Riḍā, the sects mentioned are messianic. Most seem to be politically quietist, but one (68. 3-6) claims to have leaders in contact with the hidden imam, and this could mean revolutionary activity. It may be that Mūsā was imprisoned because he was in touch with revolutionary groups. It is possible that some of these views were held shortly after the death of Mūsā – one of the men named, Yūnus b. ʿAbd al-Raḥmān (69.2), is said to have died in 823. It is also possible, however, that some of the views continued for a longer time. The last group mentioned (70.5-71.10) are 'extremists' who held transmigration and similar views. All those who believed in Mūsā as *al-qā'im al-mahdī* must have held that the series of imams ended with him, and need not have believed in the usual series prior to Mūsā. The suggestion that his successors should be called 'caliphs' (68.15) is perhaps an attempt to show approval of the appointment of ʿAlī as heir apparent.

§29. *72.7-77.4* This section deals with the position after the death of ʿAlī al-Riḍā in 818. He left a son, Muḥammad, who was only seven. Some are said to have recognized his imāmate; but only three lines are devoted to this, so that it would seem to be merely a deduction from the conception of a series of imams. The view that ʿAlī was succeeded by his brother Aḥmad (72.11-13) seems to be part of the argument about the succession of brothers which was developed after 874 (compare § 26). Some of those who had been looking for a return of Mūsā had apparently accepted ʿAlī, but after ʿAlī's death went back to their expectation of Mūsā (72.14-16). Similarly, some Zaydites accepted ʿAlī, presumably after he became heir apparent, but went back to Zaydism after his death (73.4-7). The youth of Muḥammad became the occasion for a discussion (74.14-76.7) of how the imam came to have his infallible knowledge (compare § 17). This is probably part of an argument between Shīʿites and their opponents, where the latter were trying to show that the claim that the imams had infallible knowledge was ridiculous (compare § 18); the date of the argument may be quite late.

§30. *77.5-78.12* There is so little reported of ʿAlī al-Hādī (or al-Naqī), who is alleged to have been recognized as imam from 835 to 868, that we are justified in assuming there was little activity round him. The second part of the report describes the origin of the Nuṣayrī movement, and shows how 'extremist' ideas could be applied to an ʿAlid leader.

§31. *78.13-79.15* The next imam is reckoned to have been al-Ḥasan al-ʿAskarī (d. 874). Rivals were his brother Muḥammad, who died before his father, but was expected by some to return as the Mahdi, and Jaʿfar. Both the latter and his father were kept under surveillance by the ʿAbbāsids.

§32. *79.16-94.3* The remainder of the book may conveniently be dealt with as a single section. It describes thirteen sects which appeared after the death of al-Ḥasan al-ʿAskarī in 874. (There are said to have been fourteen, but, if there were, the description of the fourteenth has been lost; it could not have been the Ismāʿīlites, since the fourteen sects come from those who are reckoned as having accepted the imāmate of al-ʿAskarī.) This is, in some ways, the most valuable part of the book, since it is dealing with roughly contemporary material. The author's preference is for the twelfth sect which he calls 'the true Imāmite Shīʿa'. The distinctive features of the sects may be briefly indicated:

(1) Al-Ḥasan al-ʿAskarī is not dead, but absent, and is *al-qā'im al-mahdī*. They claim to differ from those who held that Mūsā was similarly absent (69.8-70.4, etc.) through the fact that al-ʿAskarī died without leaving an heir. (2) Al-ʿAskarī died but has been raised to life and is *al-qā'im al-mahdī*, because the world cannot be without a *ḥujja and qā'im*. (3) The imam, by the testament of al-ʿAskarī, is his brother Jaʿfar. The apparent hostility between them was only *ẓāhir*; the *bāṭin* was mutual amity. (4) Jaʿfar is imam in succession to his father ʿAlī al-Hādī. The claim of al-ʿAskarī is invalid, since he died without leaving an heir (an argument which suggests he had little recognition in his lifetime). (5) Since al-ʿAskarī died without an heir, and since Jaʿfar was of a

blameworthy character, the imam after ʿAlī al-Hādī, and the *qāʾim* and *mahdī*, must be their brother Muḥammad b. ʿAlī, who died before his father. (6) The imam is Muḥammad, the son of al-ʿAskarī, who was born two years before his father's death; he is in concealment. (7) The imam (in concealment) is Muḥammad, but he was born eight months after his father's death. (8) Al-ʿAskarī had no son, and arguments about a hidden son are to be rejected (some having apparently implied a pregnancy of longer than nine months). (9) Al-ʿAskarī has died and for the moment there is no imam; but the *qāʾim* will come. (10) The eleventh imam was Muḥammad b. ʿAlī (as in the fifth sect), but he made a man called Nafīs his *waṣī*, or agent, and the latter handed on the imāmate to Jaʿfar. (11) Al-ʿAskarī has died, and the position is not clear; but the earth cannot be without a *ḥujja*. (12) There is a *ḥujja* and *waṣī* who is a son of al-ʿAskarī, since the imāmate cannot pass from brother to brother after al-Ḥusayn, cannot fall to a man whose father was not imam (possibly an argument against the Ismāʿīlites) and cannot be transmitted by the *ḥujja* of one who died in his father's lifetime (against the tenth sect, or the Ismāʿīlites). This *ḥujja* is in concealment, for the world cannot exist without such a person; but it is forbidden to seek him out before he manifests himself (thus making clear that the sect is not engaged in revolutionary activity). (13) The imam is al-ʿAskarī's brother, Jaʿfar. The saying about the imāmate not falling to brothers only applies when the elder has a son.

The most important feature of this list is the all-pervasive, messianic interest and the basic belief in the necessity, to ensure the existence of the world, that there should be an imam, even if he is not manifest and is not known. The exceptions are the sects which acknowledged Jaʿfar, who must have been born after 847 and may have lived into the tenth century. Within the messianists, one may distinguish those who are concerned to leave the matter vague, especially the ninth and eleventh sects, and those who are trying to find arguments to show that a particular person is imam. Some of the arguments about the past series of imams are attempts to establish some view in the present, for example, either to assert or to deny the imāmate of Jaʿfar. Just why anyone wanted to assert the imāmate of Jaʿfar is not clear. It seems unlikely that they wanted him as an actual leader. So the probability is that they were using this assertion as a way of countering some view of their opponents that they disliked. Perhaps what they disliked was the conception of an imam in concealment. The use of *bāṭin* (82.2) makes one wonder if they were attracted to some form of Ismāʿīlism.

Concluding remarks. It remains to try to sketch, in outline, the picture of developments that is dimly glimpsed through all this mass of details. Despite the hypothetical character of many of the arguments, certain points seem to be relatively certain.

Firstly, then, there is the presence of messianism, in the sense of an expectation of a semidivine, or inspired, deliverer. This was found in the Umayyad period and was still strong when *Firaq al-Shīʿa* was written about 900. It was essentially religious, springing from a need for assurance that man's life in the world was meaningful; the assurance came from the firm belief that one day a deliverer would come and set all wrongs right. Normally, messianism was politically quietist, but occasionally a strong leader would claim that he was the imam or the imam's emissary, and would call for revolutionary action. This transition to political activism was achieved by saying that the hidden imam had come, or was about to come, out of concealment. The activism was on the whole exceptional, and seems to have been as much connected with moderate messianic views as with the 'extremist' view, later characteristic of Ismāʿīlism, which included such conceptions as those of the transmigration of souls and divine inherence in men. It should be noted that messianism, except when it becomes activist, implies that there is no active imam recognized by contemporaries. Where messianists assert that a definite person is the imam in concealment, they may justify this by speaking of a series of imams of which he is the last; but *ex hypothesi* this series cannot be continued into the historical present.

Secondly, there were pure activists, that is, actual leaders of revolts and their followers. All that was necessary was that a man should be an effective leader, and either be a member of 'the family' or make a claim to be an agent of such a person. Until the Fāṭimids, there was little mention of theological ideas, and little interest in showing that the leader came as latest in a recognized series of imams. After the failure of a revolt, there might be some resort to messianism to explain the failure and give fresh hope (as in the case of the Zaydite sect of Jārūdiyya in Ash, I, 67. 12-16).

Thirdly, there is the question whether there were moderates who were neither messianists nor activists, yet recognized a series of imams, of whom the latest was alive and not hidden. Common sense suggests that, under the ʿAbbāsids, it must have been impossible to recognize a living man as imam, unless within an underground activist movement. Apart from this, it might be possible to recognize a man as head of the ʿAlids (or the Ḥusaynid branch of the ʿAlid family), but this is far from what is usually meant by recognizing an imam. Careful examination of the statements in *Firaq al-Shīʿa* shows a complete absence of any decisive evidence for widespread recognition of the imams during their lifetime. Such recognition, then, cannot be the distinguishing mark of any moderate Shīʿites.

Yet there appear to have been a number of scholars who might be described as 'moderates'. One such was Hishām b. al-Ḥakam, who flourished about the first quarter of the ninth century. Al-Ashʿarī and others tell us many of the views he held on theological questions, and how he discussed various points with Muʿtazilites; but very little is reported about his views on the imāmate. The chief point seems to be that most of the Companions were in error in not recognizing ʿAlī in 632. Associated with this point is the view that the text of the Qur'ān had been corrupted and was not reliable (*Intiṣār,* 41, 139). Now these two points both imply attacks on the Sunnite traditionists and jurists; their views rested mainly on Qur'ān and Traditions, and if the Qur'ān was corrupt and the first transmitters of Traditions unreliable, little was left. Such a political attitude further implied acceptance of the ʿAbbāsid regime, since the chief interest was to maintain and improve one's place within the existing structure. Scholars, then, who held such views, cannot have been activist in the sense of working to overthrow the regime.

The chief remaining possibility seems to be that they were messianists, but in a vague and indefinite way, that is, not expecting the return of one particular person. The ninth and eleventh sects, in § 32, are indefinite messianists in this sense; and indeed the twelfth sect of 'true Imāmites' is less definite than the Imāmites later became, merely saying the imam must be a son of the last imam. There is thus some justification for thinking that there was a body of people who subscribed, in a vague way, to the doctrine of the coming of the Mahdī, but did not identify him with any particular person, and probably did not attach undue importance to the doctrine. These probably constituted a large part of those claimed by later Imāmites as followers of the imams during their lifetime; but this claim is, almost entirely, later propaganda.

The Zaydites began as activists and opponents of the conception of the hidden imam; but after failures, some of them, at least, accepted that conception. Their distinguishing feature, however, came to be the acceptance of the caliphates of Abū Bakr and ʿUmar; and this had the implication that the Sunnite traditions were to be accepted as sound. Perhaps most of the Zaydites continued to be activist, in the sense of supporting the ʿAbbāsid dynasty and its policy of compromise, at least until the change of policy in 849.

Another question, and a very difficult one, is that of how and when the series of imams came to be recognized. From *Firaq al-Shīʿa* it may be seen that, of the twelve imams, those to whom the messianists were most attracted were Jaʿfar (VI), Mūsā (VII), al-Ḥasan al-ʿAskarī (XI) and his son Muḥammad (XII). The reason for the attraction may have been uncertainty in the case of VII (alleged to have been killed in prison) and XII (whose very existence was questioned). In the case of XI, it was doubtless the absence of an obvious successor. Only in the case of VI (Jaʿfar) was there, perhaps, some genuine following based on personal contacts. Prior to Jaʿfar, the chief centre of messianic interest was Ibn al-Ḥanafiyya. It seems to have been in the process of justifying the belief that a particular person was the Mahdī that the series of imams gradually gained recognition. Details are uncertain. It was noted, above, that the succession of Ismāʿīl to Jaʿfar had been denied before about 840, doubtless by partisans of the Mahdī-ship of Mūsā (§ 20). Discussions before this date may also have aimed at excluding Ibn al-Ḥanafiyya and his descendants.

The need – or perhaps rather the opportunity – for further discussion came after the death of al-Ḥasan al-ʿAskarī in 874. The reports in *Firaq al-Shīʿa* show that there was still no generally accepted view on the succession to the imāmate. Most of the differences between the 'sects' described probably went back to personal reasons – various men, each wanting to improve his position by having his views accepted. It is therefore remarkable that, early in the tenth century, most of these groups of messianists and others had been brought together on the basis of a common Imāmite doctrine. By insisting that the hidden imam must not be searched for, but allowed to choose his own time for manifesting himself, they in effect declared against revolutionary activity (but it would be interesting to look into their relations with the Buwayhids during the rise to power of the latter). They were not altogether quietists, but accepted the existing regime and functioned as a party in it, and did not even gain any undue advantages under the Imāmite Buwayhids.

Finally, there are the Ismāʿīlites, about whom an Imāmite book, like *Firaq al-Shīʿa*, has relatively little information. In the early decades of the ʿAbbāsids, there were groups who combined messianism with 'extremist' views. In the light of what has been said, it is almost certain that these messianist groups, even when interested in Ismāʿīl, did not at first recognize any series of imams. It is also very doubtful whether there was any underground activism; certainly, it should not be assumed that there was any continuous organized movement. The 'extremist' ideas, of course, were propagated in various ways, but this process need not require much organizational continuity. It seems by no means impossible that most of the groups which came into the Fāṭimid and Ismāʿīlite movement were messianist and quietist until towards the end of the ninth century. It was probably this transition to activism, together with the consolidation of their rivals, the Imāmites, that made it necessary to have a definite Ismāʿīlite theory of the imāmate.

B9 Sidelights on Early Imāmite Doctrine

Túsy's List of Shy'ah Books has been known to Islamists since it was published by Alois Sprenger in the *Bibliotheca Indica* in 1854, and references to it are to be found in many of the older works; but little use seems to have been made of it recently. Interest has been directed towards the numerous works of Shaykh Ṭūsī – Abū Ja'far Muḥammad al-Ṭūsī Shaykh al-Ṭā'ifa (995/385 - 1066/458) – by the preparations for the Millenary Congress in his honour held at Meshhed in March 1970, and there have been some fresh editions and numerous articles in Persian. The present writer, on looking into the *List of Shy'ah Books*, found that its information was much fuller than that of Ibn al-Nadīm, who is frequently quoted, and that this information threw light on the development of Imāmite doctrine during the ninth/third century. This article, offered as a tribute to the memory of Joseph Schacht, has the limited aim of showing the relevance of some of the information which is to be gleaned from the *List of Shy'ah Books*.[204] It does not consider the relations of Shaykh Ṭūsī's work to that of the slightly later al-Najāshī, nor does it enter into some related questions such as the respective merits of *Firaq al-shī'a* by al-Nawbakhtī and *Kitāb al-maqālāt wa-l-firaq* by Sa'd ibn 'Abd-Allāh al-Ash'arī al-Qummī.

The general position adopted is that the doctrine of the Imāmite branch of the Shī'a did not attain definitive form until after the death or disappearance of the twelfth imam in 874. It was probably only about that date that the adherents of the doctrine began to call themselves 'Imāmites', but the name will here be applied (in accordance with Shaykh Ṭūsī's usage) to those earlier scholars whom they regarded as their predecessors. For more than a century before 874 there was some recognition for the 'Alid imams from different groups of men. Among these men there was no agreement on doctrine, but it can be asserted that the majority were not revolutionaries seeking to replace the 'Abbāsids by the 'Alids. It is probably that during the ninth century Imāmite views were the expression of a political attitude, namely, one based on the belief that the existing caliphate should be more autocratic.[205]

I. THE EARLY IMĀMITES AND THE MUʿTAZILITES

One of the points which is made clear by Shaykh Ṭūsī's *List* is that there were many contacts between Imāmites and Muʿtazilites from the time of Hārūn al-Rashīd onwards. Something of this was of course known from al-Masʿūdī's account of the assembly on the model of Plato's *Symposium* arranged by Yaḥyā al-Barmakī, where of thirteen scholars who spoke five are described as Muʿtazilites (Abū 'l-Hudhayl, al-Naẓẓām, Muʿtamir ibn Sulaymān, Bishr ibn al-Muʿtamir, Thumāma) and four as Imāmites (ʿAlī ibn Mītham, Hishām ibn al-Ḥakam, ʿAlī ibn Manṣūr, al-Shakkāk).[206]

This background of friendly contacts is relevant to the fact recorded by Shaykh Ṭūsī that Hishām ibn al-Ḥakam wrote a book on 'the imamate of the inferior' (*imāmat al-mafḍūl*) against the Muʿtazilites.[207] A work with a similar title is also attributed to a slightly earlier scholar Abū Jaʿfar al-Aḥwal (known to the opponents as Shayṭān al-Ṭāq).[208] The ascription of this doctrine to the Muʿtazilites is curious, since it is usually a distinctive mark of the Zaydites; it implies that, while the excellence or superiority of ʿAlī was admitted, yet Abū Bakr was truly caliph despite the fact that he was *mafḍūl*, 'excelled' or 'surpassed' by ʿAlī, that is, 'inferior'. There are close but obscure connections between the Zaydites and the Muʿtazilites, and this is relevant. It is also probable, however, that these two Imāmites used Muʿtazilite in a wider sense than would have been tolerated a little later by al-Khayyāṭ, a Muʿtazilite himself, who insisted that the name must be restricted to those who accepted the five principles. There is some evidence for a wide Imāmite use of Muʿtazilite in al-Nawbakhtī. Under the term he includes Ḍirār ibn ʿAmr, who was excluded by al-Khayyāṭ.[209] At another point al-Nawbakhtī makes the Muʿtazilites one of the basic sects of Islam, the other three being the Shīʿa, the Murji'a and the Khārijites.[210] This statement seems to rest on a classification of sects according to their attitude to ʿAlī. The Shīʿa are those who regarded ʿAlī as imam on the death of Muḥammad; the Khārijites are those who said he was an unbeliever and fought against him; the Murji'ites accepted and associated with both ʿAlī and his opponents; and the Muʿtazilites refused to decide between the two and dissociated themselves from both.[211] Al-Nawbakhtī does not mention the Zaydites at this point, and references elsewhere do not make clear to which of the four basic sects he would have allotted them. He probably did not regard them as Shīʿa, since they did not regard ʿAlī as rightful imam after the Prophet even though they regarded him as the 'most excellent' (*afḍal*) after him;[212] but it is not clear that he would have merged them with the Muʿtazilites. The two earlier Imāmite scholars, however, almost certainly included the Zaydites among those they called Muʿtazilites.

Hishām ibn al-Ḥakam and Shayṭān al-Ṭāq also wrote against the Muʿtazila on the question of Ṭalḥa and the other participants in the Battle of the Camel; they were presumably refuting the view ascribed to some Muʿtazilites that, while they knew ʿAlī and his opponents could not both be right, they were unable to say which side was right.[213] In yet other works they wrote on the imāmate generally and on the question of the 'testament' (*waṣiyya*). On this last topic they may have been criticizing the theory put forward by the ʿAbbāsids at least until the time of al-Mahdī (775-785), that each imam designated his successor or appointed him by 'testament' (*awṣā ilay-hi*),[214] and in particular that Abū Hāshim, the son of Ibn al-Ḥanafiyya, designated one of the ʿAbbāsid family as his successor. It is less probable that the topic was discussed in connection with the succession to the imam Jaʿfar al-Ṣādiq, though this was a matter of dispute at various times.

It was doubtless the contacts between Hishām and the Muʿtazilites which led him to write on questions they discussed, such as predestination and human free will and the originated or temporal character of things (*ḥudūth al-ashyā'*). Shaykh Ṭūsī says that Hishām went from Kufa to Baghdad in the year 199/814 and is thought to have died in the same year; but if he was familiar with Yaḥyā al-Barmakī, he must also have been in Baghdad before the latter's death in 187/803, and his contacts with the Muʿtazilites also presuppose an earlier residence there. The fact that Hishām wrote against two other Imāmites, Hishām al-Jawālīqī and Shayṭān al-Ṭāq, suggests that these men were slightly older and also shows that there were already divergences among the followers of the ʿAlid imams.

Another Imāmite scholar who frequented the Barmakid circle at least occasionally was ʿAlī ibn Mītham, also known as Ibn al-Tammār.[215] He was also from Kufa, but he settled in Basra, and it was doubtless there that he engaged in discussions with Abū 'l-Hudhayl and al-Naẓẓām. He is said to have been the first who gave a theological exposition of (*takallama fī*) Imāmite doctrine. This last statement implies either that Hishām ibn al-Ḥakam was younger or that for some reason Hishām's work was not considered a theological exposition of Imāmism. According to al-Nawbakhtī ʿAlī ibn Mītham's view was that ʿAlī was deserving (*mustaḥiqq*) of the imamate since he was the most excellent (*afḍal*) of men after the Prophet, and that those who failed to acknowledge him were mistaken though not in a sense which implied sin.

Later in the ninth century the titles of many of the polemical and apologetical works of al-Faḍl ibn Shādhān (d. 874) indicate that he moved in the same intellectual circles as the Muʿtazilites. In particular he wrote not only against the Muʿtazilites al-Iskāfī (d. 854) and al-Aṣamm (d. 850 ?), but also against various Khārijite theologians, against Ibn Karrām and Sunnite jurists, against the sects of the Murji'ites, of the Bāṭinites or Qarāmiṭa, and of the Ghulāt of the Shīʿa, and against the Philosophers and the Dualists or Thanawiyya,[216]. Such a man was clearly moving in the central currents of the intellectual life of the time, not merely in theology but also in jurisprudence.

The ninth-century books listed by Shaykh Ṭūsī include many on legal questions, but it is not necessary to suppose a distinctive Imāmite form of the Sharīʿa at this period. Some of the books are on single aspects of law or liturgical observance, such as 'divorce', 'temporary marriage' (*mutʿa)*, 'prayer', 'the pilgrimage'; and these books (except perhaps that on *mutʿa*) were presumably similar to comparable ones by scholars later claimed as Sunnite. The mention of al-Shāfiʿī (d. 820) in various titles, however, suggests that the Imāmites had begun to be concerned about the method of justifying legal presecriptions. Al-Shāfiʿī had insisted, in the case of Traditions of the Prophet, that there should be an *isnād* or chain of transmitters going back to a Companion; and the Imāmites may have come to realize that some of the generally accepted authorities were unsatisfactory from an Imāmite point of view.

Further discussion with the Muʿtazilites occurred at a still later date, conducted by the Imāmite scholars Ibn Mumlik al-Iṣfahānī and Ibn Qiba of Rayy. Ibn Mumlik had face to face discussions with al-Jubbā'ī (d. 915) on the doctrine of the imāmate, but whether at Basra or elsewhere is not stated.[217] Ibn Qiba, who had once been a Muʿtazilite, discussed the imāmate in written treatises with Abū 'l-Qāsim al-Balkhī (d. 931), often known as al-Kaʿbī.[218] The latter, though reckoned to the Muʿtazila of Baghdad, was living at Balkh during the discussions; and the treatises were carried from Balkh to Rayy and from Rayy to Balkh by al-Sūsanjirdī, a pupil of Abū Sahl al-Nawbakhtī.[219] It is perhaps worth noting in this connection that al-Ḥasan ibn Mūsā al-Nawbakhti is reported to have written a work entitled 'Answers to Ibn Qiba' and another in explanation (*sharḥ*) of his discussions with Ibn Mumlik.[220]

The frequency of these contacts between the Imāmites and the Muʿtazilites shows that they were not diametrically opposed schools, but recognized a certain affinity with one another, leading to the possibility of fruitful discussion. On various doctrinal points the Imāmites took up a position close to that of the Muʿtazilites. They spoke of God as creator of the Qur'ān, thus implying that it is his created speech; and they held that man has a power to act (*istiṭāʿa*) which is genuine and enables him to respond to God's commands in ways not predetermined by God's decree.[221] These facts show that the Imāmites were not so isolated as some Sunnīte sources suggest from the main stream of intellectual life of the caliphate from about 800 to 950; and they also lend some support to the view that the Muʿtazilites were aiming at a political compromise between Sunnism and Shīʿism.

2. THE FUṬḤIYYA OR AFṬAḤIYYA

Much can be learnt about a group of Imāmites called the Fuṭḥiyya from the reference in *Firaq al-shīʿa*,[222] but the additional information from the *Fihrist* of Shaykh Ṭūsī clarifies the picture. The name almost certainly comes from the fact that ʿAbd-Allāh, the eldest son of Jaʿfar al-Ṣādiq, was known as al-Aftaḥ because he had broad or flat feet. On the death of Jaʿfar in 765 some of his associates held that his successor as imam was ʿAbd-Allāh al-Aftaḥ; but al-Afṭah did not live very long and had no son to succeed him, so that most of the associates of Jaʿfar came to hold that the imāmate had passed to another of his sons Mūsā, known as al-Kāẓim.

At the time this divergence of view was probably not of great importance, but it involved questions of principle which at a later date were of considerable moment. The supporters of the imāmate of al-Afṭaḥ justified it in two ways. Some said that his father had made him his successor by 'testament'; but others held that Jaʿfar had asserted the principle that 'the imāmate goes to the eldest son of the imam'. These two justifications are not necessarily contradictory. After the death of al-Afṭaḥ, when the imāmate of al-Kāẓim was generally recognized by the supporters of the ʿAlids, the question arose of how this imāmate was justified. The majority held that Mūsā had succeeded his father directly. A few, however, under the leadership of ʿAbd-Allāh ibn Bukayr ibn Aʿyan[223] and ʿAmmār ibn Mūsā al-Sābāṭī,[224] held that ʿAbd-Allāh had indeed been imam and had by 'testament' made Mūsā his successor. This was the beginning of the Fuṭḥiyya.

The question of principle came to be of great importance after the death of al-Ḥasan al-ʿAskarī in 874. If one brother could succeed another (apart from the special case of al-Ḥasan and al-Ḥusayn), then the imam after al-ʿAskarī could be his brother Jaʿfar, and many maintained this. For those who wanted to maintain the standard Imāmite theory of twelve imams, there was the further difficulty that to acknowledge the imāmate of al-Aftaḥ was to make al-ʿAskarī himself the twelfth imam and his son the thirteenth; and twelve was a more significant number than thirteen.

The discussion of the Fuṭḥī standpoint, however, was by no means confined to the period after 874. Indeed it seems to have been conducted even more vigorously about half a century earlier. One of the leading protagonists was Ibn Faḍḍāl.[225] He was an associate of the imam al-Riḍā (d. 818), but apparently not of his son Abū Jaʿfar II al-Jawād (d. 835), although he is reported to have died in 838. Slightly later came another theologian, ʿAlī ibn Asbāṭ, who corresponded on the question with a fellow Imāmite, ʿAlī ibn Mahziyār; the latter referred the matter to al-Jawād, and ʿAlī ibn Asbāṭ was eventually persuaded to give up the Fuṭḥī view.[226] After the death of al-Riḍā some recognized as imam his only son al-Jawād, who was presumably young; but others preferred to acknowledge his brother Aḥmad. It must have been the latter who wanted their case strengthened by the precedent of al-Afṭaḥ.

Thus at both of these later periods – after the death of al-ʿAskarī and after the death of al-Riḍā – those who believed in the imāmate of al-Afṭaḥ were men who acknowledged a particular living imam in the present, and are not to be confused with the 'extremists', the Ghāliya or Ghulāt. Ibn Faḍḍāl wrote a refutation of the Ghāliya. Among those whom Shaykh Ṭūsī includes among the Ghāliya were Ibn Jamhūr[227] and his follower Muḥammad ibn ʿĪsā al-Yaqṭīnī,[228] both of whom wrote books expressing millennial and messianic hopes. It is perhaps significant that another scholar of the middle ninth century who attacked the Ghāliya, namely, Aḥmad ibn Muḥammad ibn ʿĪsā al-Ashʿarī,[229] is known from an *isnād* given by Shaykh Ṭūsī to have been in contact with Ibn Faḍḍāl.[230] The opposition to earlier millennial views appears to have continued even after the majority of the Imāmites had accepted the son of al-ʿAskarī as twelfth imam and Mahdī.

3. THE WĀQIFA

Another group of people occasionally mentioned by Shaykh Ṭūsī are the Wāqifa, who are said to have received their name because they were waiting for the return of al-Kāẓim.[231] The most important scholar among the Wāqifa was apparently al-Ṭāṭarī,[232] since it was his exposition of the views of the Wāqifa which was selected by Abū Sahl al-Nawbakhtī for refutation. He is said to have written thirty books, mainly on legal subjects. He had a pupil al-Ḥasan ibn Muḥammad ibn Samāʿa, who like himself lived in Kufa and who seems to have passed on his legal teaching.[233] This latter scholar died in 877, but al-Ṭāṭarī must have been a generation earlier since he had been an associate of al-Kāẓim (d. 799). Another associate of al-Kāẓim who along with his sons held the doctrine of the Wāqifa was Aḥmad ibn Muḥammad ibn ʿAlī.[234] Not much is known about him, except that, besides writing about fasting, he criticized a sect of weak persons (*ḍuʿafā'*) known as the ʿIjliyya, with views resembling those of the Zaydiyya, and collected reports about Abū 'l-Khaṭṭāb; but it is not clear what attitude he adopted towards the latter, who had acted for the imam Jaʿfar and had then been repudiated by him.[235]

The Wāqifa thus appear to have been a group of men who wanted to establish a form of Imāmite doctrine, but with seven imams instead of twelve. It would seem that their interest in law is significant, presumably indicating that in legal matters they largely shared the outlook of Sunnite scholars and jurists of the time. On the other hand, their insistence that there was no imam after al-Kāẓim implies that they rejected the imāmate of al-Riḍā and likewise his nomination in 816 as heir to al-Ma'mūn. On the assumption that they were still alive then, this means that they wanted to continue to be somewhat critical of the ʿAbbāsids, yet without engaging in any overt subversive activity. During the caliphate of al-Ma'mūn the Ismāʿīlite doctrine of the seven imams had not been made public, perhaps not even formulated. Even if it had been known to them, this was no reason why there should not be another doctrine of seven imams ending with Mūsā. It would appear, however, that al-Ṭāṭarī and the Wāqifa were not influential enough to unite all the followers of imam Jaʿfar behind this doctrine. Doubtless, too, the circumstances of the time were not so favourable as they became in the last quarter of the ninth century. Under al-Ma'mūn the ruling institution was making strenuous efforts to conciliate Imāmite opinion, whereas after the time of al-Mutawakkil it had come to rely mainly on Sunnite support and had adopted a predominantly Sunnite policy.

4. CONCLUSION

These matters lead up to a consideration of the definitive shaping of Imāmite doctrine in the years round about 900. Although there were men of Imāmite outlook from about the time of Hārūn al-Rashīd, they could not have held the definitive form of the doctrine of the twelve imams, since this was impossible until after 874 when the eleventh imam died and the twelfth disappeared. In his great book on al-Ḥallāj Louis Massignon describes the disputes about the position of *wakīl* to the eleventh imam, and also examines Shaykh Ṭūsī's list of books by Abū Sahl al-Nawbakhtī.[236] It is clear from his account that a great part was played in the organization of the Imāmite party, as it may perhaps now be called, by the Banū Nawbakht. On the intellectual side the two chief members of the family were Abū Sahl and his nephew, al-Ḥasan ibn Mūsā, named as the author of *Firaq al-shīʿa*. It was presumably these two scholars who were mainly responsible for producing the definitive form of the doctrine of the twelve imams. This intellectual achievement, however, was paralleled by the practical achievement of getting many of the divergent forms of Shīʿite opinion to unite behind this doctrine, and thus create a movement of some political significance.

The information examined above enables us to distinguish at least four bodies of divergent opinion. Firstly there are the Zaydites. Their most distinctive point of belief was that a man was only to be recognized as imam when he was actually claiming to rule. In most cases this meant that they did not recognize an imam until he had actually raised the standard of revolt; and the corollary of this is of course the non-recognition of the imams on the list of twelve, and perhaps also the recognition of the caliphates of Abū Bakr and ʿUmar. The Zaydite view might also imply recognition of the justification of the ʿAbbāsid caliphate, since the ʿAbbāsids were members of the clan of Hāshim who both claimed and occupied the caliphate.

At the other end of the spectrum were the extremists or Ghāliya, who looked for the coming of a messianic or charismatic leader who would set everything right, but who did not expect him in the foreseeable future and were therefore in effect politically quietist.

Thirdly came those who recognized the various imams during their lifetime, but apparently not as active revolutionary leaders. This last point is to be inferred from the fact that the ʿAbbāsid ruling circle did not seriously curtail the freedom of the imams, as they certainly would have done had they had any word of a serious intrigue against themselves. Some men seem to have found this position satisfactory and to have wanted to extend the list of imams beyond al-ʿAskarī. Perhaps their attitude was one of a personal loyalty to the family without any thought of exerting political pressure. The earliest Fuṭḥiyya may have been a subdivision of this group.

Fourthly, there gradually separated themselves from the third group a body of men who seem to have found it more satisfactory to have no living imam but only an agent or representative of a hidden imam. The Wāqifa, who looked for no imam after Mūsā al-Kāẓim, almost certainly held this point. Some of the Fuṭḥiyya may have had a similar outlook. In the quarter of a century or so after the death of al-ʿAskarī this standpoint was elaborated in the definitive doctrine of the twelve imams, and some unity of organisation was given to those who accepted the doctrine. Such a course had various advantages. The Imāmites could not be accused of engaging in revolutionary intrigues: and the actual administration of the 'party' could be placed in the hands of the most capable politician instead of being in the hands of an imam who might be an inexperienced boy.

What has been studied here is only one phase in the history of Imāmism, though an important one. Many further studies are required to show what were the actual practical policies in the various periods of history and how these were related to their political and theological teaching.

B10. The Significance of the Early Stages of Imāmite Shīʿism

A system of religious doctrines may serve different purposes in the life of a society. More or less the same system may in one case be the opiate of the masses and in another case the focus of emergent social forces, such as those campaigning for justice or organizing a revolution. Those who believe in the system are not necessarily fully conscious of the social ends it is achieving, though sometimes they may be. These considerations are particularly relevant to the study of the early development of Imāmite Shīʿism.

Students of the early stages of Shīʿism have a particular difficulty to face in that later Shīʿite apologists made assertions about early events which critical history cannot accept as true, though it is of course an important historical fact that such assertions were made and widely believed. In what follows I accept the general standpoint of critical history and discuss particular issues where that is relevant.[237]

In a sense the fixed point from which the investigations begin is the fact that it was only between 874 and about 920 that Imāmite Shīʿism took definite shape. It stands to reason that there could not be an Imāmite or 'Twelver' form of Shīʿism before the death of the Eleventh Imam and the disappearance of the Twelfth. To understand, however, what happened at this time – the period of the Lesser Occultation – it is necessary to look at the earlier stages of the development. These will here be brought under two headings: Proto-Shīʿism under the Umayyads; and Proto-Shīʿism under the ʿAbbāsids. Meanwhile attention may be called to certain of the dominant ideas in Shīʿite thought. First there is the idea of charisma, either personal or familial or divinely bestowed, attaching to particular leaders. The most distinctive characteristic of Shīʿism in general is indeed the cult of the charismatic leader. Secondly, there is the idea of the Mahdī. It is to be noted that this differs from Judaeo-Christian conceptions of the Messiah or Sunnite conceptions of the Mahdī, in that in these cases no one knows the identity of the Messiah or Mahdī until he actually makes the claim. For the Imāmite Shīʿites, on the other hand, the identity of the Mahdī is known but he is in concealment or occultation (*ghayba*), and it is the time of his reappearance which is not known. Third, there is the idea of the transmission of authority by designation, an idea which appears to be closely associated with the belief that the ideal form of rule is autocratic.

PROTO-SHĪʿISM UNDER THE UMAYYADS[238]

Apart from the loyalty evoked in individuals by the personal qualities of ʿAlī, the chief early manifestations of Shīʿite ideas were various revolts under charismatic leaders or under men who claimed to act on behalf of members of 'the family' or to represent their interests. The best known of these instances of activism was al-Ḥusayn's abortive bid for the caliphate in 680, which ended at Kerbela. The most successful was that of al-Mukhtār at Kufa in 685, allegedly in the interests of Muḥammad ibn al-Ḥanafiyya. In the half-century after the failure and death of al-Mukhtār in 687 there were no revolts that were in any sense Shīʿite; but the last dozen years or so of the Umayyad dynasty saw some potential and actual revolts of Shīʿite inspiration, including that which brought the ʿAbbāsid dynasty to the caliphal throne in 750. For the first few decades of the ʿAbbāsids there were also revolts against them which owed something to Shīʿite ideas.

The details of these revolts and the associated sectarian movements do not concern us here, but it is important to try to appreciate the underlying ideas and attitudes. The phenomena are brought together under the heading of Proto-Shīʿite because they do not conform exactly to later Zaydism, Imāmism or Ismāʿīlism; but they have in common some feeling for the presence in certain members of 'the family' (of Muḥammad) of special qualities of political leadership or spiritual guidance, in short, of charisma. This charisma differed, however, from that later ascribed by the Imāmites to their imams. For one thing it was not restricted to these imams, but might be found in almost any member of Muḥammad's clan of Hāshim. In the years round 750 it was claimed for ʿAlī's brother Jaʿfar and Muḥammad's uncle al-ʿAbbās. The Umayyads even seem to have tried to include themselves in 'the family' by extending it to the descendants of Hāshim's father, ʿAbd Manaf; but this was not generally accepted. Even those who took a more restricted view of the occurrence of charisma had sometimes a different account of the succession of imams and made Muḥammad ibn al-Ḥanafiyya follow al-Ḥusayn and be succeeded by his own son Abū Hāshim. The original ʿAbbāsid claim to legitimacy was that Abū Hāshim had transferred the imāmate to the grandfather of the first two ʿAbbāsid caliphs and that he had been succeeded by his descendants. All these facts show that up to 750 the Proto-Shīʿite idea of charisma was in an extremely fluid state.

The first persons to be attracted to this idea were mainly Arabs from nomadic tribes. A relatively large proportion of these came from South Arabian tribes, and this might conceivably be linked with the long tradition of kingship in South Arabia. These men were probably attracted to Proto-Shīʿism because they felt insecure as a result of the rapid transition from nomadic desert life to that of camp-cities and raiding expeditions. One of the common human reactions to insecurity is to look for a man with charisma who can lead his people to a better state of things. Since Arabs believed that the potential for noble deeds and wise counsel was transmitted through the tribal stock, it would be natural to look to some member of the clan of Hāshim for deliverance from insecurity.

Besides these activists among the Proto-Shīʿites there were also quietists, who did not contemplate revolt but consoled themselves with messianic ideas. The first man to whom such ideas were attached seems to have been Muḥammad ibn al-Ḥanafiyya (d. 700). He is mentioned by the poet Kuthayyir as being not dead but in concealment, and it is confidently expected that he will return as the Mahdī to set right all wrongs and establish justice on the earth. About the same time (early eighth century) other men held that ʿAlī was not dead but would return as the Mahdī. The attraction of this conception of the Mahdī is that it gives a measure of hope to men in circumstances which they feel to be almost intolerable, and yet does not require them to take the risks involved in trying to remedy particular abuses. Some believers in a concealed imam seem to have held that in his absence it was wrong to use force to promote justice, but that, when he appeared, it became a duty to take up the sword. This seems to indicate a strong link between belief in the Mahdī and political quietism.

PROTO-SHĪʿISM UNDER THE EARLY ʿABBĀSIDS[239]

Some, perhaps much, of the support by means of which the ʿAbbāsids were able to replace the Umayyads came from men who were Proto-Shīʿite in outlook. There has been an element of deception, however, in the propaganda of the ʿAbbāsids. Their general Abū Muslim had not said he was acting on their behalf but merely that the cause was that of 'him of the family of Muḥammad who shall be approved.' When it transpired that this was to be an ʿAbbāsid and not an ʿAlid, many were presumably disappointed, but few were prepared to take to arms in support of any ʿAlid. It is indeed possible that for the better part of a century many who supported the ʿAbbāsids did so on Proto-Shīʿite grounds. This may explain the change that was made under the caliph al-Mahdī (775–85), whose messianic regnal name is itself not without significance. ʿAbbāsid rule was now legitimized on the basis of the assertion that Muḥammad had transferred the imāmate to his uncle al-ʿAbbās, who had handed it on to his descendants, the ʿAbbāsids. Gradually, however, it would seem that men of Proto-Shīʿite sympathies came to be more and more exclusively concerned with the descendants of ʿAlī.

To bring this matter into a clearer perspective, let us consider the persons described as Rāfiḍites by Sunnite writers on sects and heresies. Rāfiḍite is a nickname, roughly meaning 'deserters', and was given to them by Sunnites because they 'deserted' Abū Bakr and ʿUmar and regarded ʿAlī as the rightful successor of Muḥammad. Because of their attitude to ʿAlī they belong to the Proto-Shīʿites. Indeed later Imāmite writers (after 900) regarded them as Imāmites, but it is doubtful if they themselves used the name, though they may have employed the term *Ahl al-Imāma*, 'people of the imāmate', or some similar phrase. One of the best known names among them is that of Hishām ibn al-Ḥakam (d. about 805). The first to give a theological exposition of the doctrine of the imāmate is said to have been ʿAlī ibn Mītham, who lived about the same time.

The fact that such men are claimed as Imāmites might suggest that they recognized the series of imams up to their own day, but there are grounds for thinking that this is impossible. Both the men named took part in a symposium on love, imitating that of Plato, held in the salon of Yaḥyā ibn Khālid al-Barmakī; and they can hardly have been friendly with the vizier if they believed that an ʿAlid was the rightful ruler of the empire. The same conclusion follows from the statement that another man defended Imāmism against Zaydism in the presence of the caliph al-Ma'mūn himself. ʿAlī ibn Mītham is said to have argued that on Muḥammad's death ʿAlī was *afḍal al-nās*, 'the most excellent of men,' as well as having been designated by Muḥammad, and that those who recognized Abū Bakr and ʿUmar were thus in error (though he did not accuse them of sin). It is to be noted, however, that there is no mention of ʿAlī designating a successor. We must also take into account the general consideration that if the ʿAbbāsids had had any suspicion of a plot against themselves, they would quickly have got rid of the rivals; but the most they did in this line was that Harūn al-Rashīd imprisoned Mūsā al-Kāẓim for a time.

If men like Hishām ibn al-Ḥakam, then, were not plotting to set up an ʿAlid as caliph, what were their political aims? Their basic principle seems to have been that authority must come from above and cannot be conferred by the votes or acclamation of ordinary people. This means that authority can only be conferred by someone who already has authority, and so the method of appointment of an imam must be designation by his predecessor, as Muḥammad had designated ʿAlī. This conception was not necessarily restricted to the series of ʿAlid imams, but seems to have been held as a general principle; for example, a friend of Hishām ibn al-Ḥakam called al-Sakkāk wrote a 'refutation of those who deny the necessity of the imāmate by designation.' Thus it would appear that the Rāfiḍites who were friendly with the viziers and caliphs were saying that the actual caliphate should be regarded as having absolute autocratic authority. In particular this would mean that the caliph ought to be a divinely inspired and guided man, capable of speaking the last word on any disputed question of God's law; the last word should not belong to the ulema.

There is admittedly an element of speculation in this account of the political attitudes of the Rāfiḍites, but there is also much evidence to support it. It has to be seen in the context of the political tensions within the caliphate from about 785 to 850. Within the heartlands of the caliphate, even, there were many diverse interest groups, and these appear to have arranged themselves – without any formal organization, of course – in two composite blocs. On the one hand there was the autocratic or absolutist block; and in this we find not only Rāfiḍites and perhaps other Proto-Shīʿites, but also the 'secretaries,' who performed the detailed work of administration under the caliph, and many Persians and Yemenite Arabs. On the other hand there was what may be called the constitutionalist bloc, which possibly reflects the tradition, found especially in northern Arab tribes, whereby decisions were taken in an assembly of all the adult male members of a tribe and ancestral practices were generally upheld. Members of northern Arab tribes tended to be found in this bloc, but the most notable group in it was the ulema, who claimed to be, and were to some extent recognized as, the authoritative exponents of the divine law as contained in the Qur'ān and the *sunna* or normal practice of the Prophet. One of the practical questions was whether the caliph and his administration could overrule the ulema, or whether, when the ulema were agreed on a point of law, the caliph was bound to accept this.

The caliph al-Ma'mūn in particular seems to have been very much aware of the tension between the two blocs, and some of the measures he adopted are apparently aimed at reducing it. His own sympathies may well have been with the absolutists, but he also knew that the ulema had strong support from the ordinary people. One of his measures, taken in 817, was to designate as heir to the caliphate ʿAlī al-Riḍā, the Eighth Imam of the series of twelve, though probably not recognized as such by many people at this time. What the outcome of this move might have been we cannot tell, for ʿAlī died in the following year. Another measure was the establishing of the so-called Inquisition (*miḥna*), by which important ulema and others were required to profess in public that they believed the Qur'ān to be the created, not the uncreated, speech of God. This was not theological hair splitting, but a political move to weaken the ulema. If the Qur'ān is God's uncreated speech, it expresses his character and so cannot be altered; but if it is created, God might have created it otherwise, and so there is not the same objection to its being altered by a divinely inspired imam.

Besides taking these particular measures al-Ma'mūn and his advisers held religio-political views designed to reduce tension. These may be described as a form of Zaydism, though they are not identical with the Zaydism of the writers on sects or later Zaydite writers. Al-Ma'mūn allowed that ʿAlī was the 'most excellent' (*afḍal*) of the Muslims after Muḥammad, but insisted that he had accepted the rule of Abū Bakr and ʿUmar. This was essentially the Zaydite principle of the 'imamate of the inferior' (*al-mafḍūl*, the one surpassed, *sc.* by others). In designating ʿAlī al-Riḍā as his heir al-Ma'mūn had in fact asserted that he was the 'most excellent' of the Muslims, and he may have had the idea that in future the caliph should be the 'most excellent' among the ʿAlids and ʿAbbāsids jointly. He presumably held that he himself was the 'most excellent' and he certainly acted as if he had personal authority. He was the first ʿAbbāsid to use the term *imām*, and he had, of course, fulfilled the Zaydite requirement of vindicating his claim to the imāmate by force of arms.

By the time of the accession of al-Mutawakkil to the caliphate in 847, the failure was clear of the attempt to reduce tension between the two blocs by some form of compromise. Within a year or two measures were taken which effectively made Sunnism the official religion of the caliphate. It was possibly because of this change that Zaydism faded away in Iraq and continued to exist only on the periphery (Daylam and the Yemen). The establishment of Sunnism was doubtless also one of the factors leading to the organization of Imāmite Shīʿism.

THE SIGNIFICANCE OF THE LESSER OCCULTATION[240]

Al-Ḥasan al-Askarī, the Eleventh Imam of the series, died on or about 1 January 874. Either at that time or a year or two afterwards his son Muḥammad mysteriously disappeared; the date is often given as 878, but the whole matter is very obscure, and even the Imāmite sources are not unanimous. Up to this time even the pro-ʿAlid wing of the Proto-Shīʿite movement had contained many different elements. One writer describes fourteen groups with varying attitudes following the death of the Eleventh Imam, and another writer names twenty groups, while the position had been almost as complex throughout the previous century. With such divisions Proto-Shīʿism could have little political influence. It is thus not altogether surprising that during the next half-century a group of skilful politicians put forward a theory – Imāmism – which was accepted by most of the pro-ʿAlid Proto-Shīʿites.

It is presumably a fact that the Eleventh Imam had a son who disappeared in mysterious circumstances. Imāmite theory, however, goes beyond the fact to an interpretation of it, namely, that the disappearance was a voluntary going into concealment or occultation, and this had the further implication that in this state the Twelfth Imam was not subject to mortality but would at an appropriate time return as the Mahdī. The idea of a Mahdī, alive but concealed, was, of course, not new. Apart from the instances under the Umayyads mentioned above, some Proto-Shīʿites had applied the conception to the Seventh Imam, Mūsā al-Kāẓim, who probably died in 799. To propound such a theory about the Twelfth Imam was clearly a deliberate political act, especially when it was also claimed that he was represented on earth by a *wakīl*, 'agent,' who was presumed to be in contact with the imam (though the evidence for this is not clear). There was in fact a succession of four agents, the last dying in 940, and the time up to that date is known as the period of the Lesser Occultation (*al-ghayba al-ṣughrā*). After 940, when there is no *wakīl* and no contact with the imam, it is the period of the Greater Occultation (*al-ghayba al-kubrā*), and this still continues.

The intellectual formulation of Imāmite theory appears to have been chiefly the work of Abū Sahl al-Nawbakhtī (d. 923), one of a powerful and wealthy family, of whom another member became second *wakīl*. The other *wakīls* seem to have been men of a similar standing. Some of their reasons for adopting and propagating Imāmism are fairly clear. It got rid of the endless bickering between rival claimants to the imāmate, of whom there had often been several, and offered the possibility of creating a united movement. It transferred the control of this movement from imams, who were often politically incompetent, into the hands of a group of men with wide knowledge of affairs and considerable political skills.

It virtually freed the movement from all suspicion of plotting against the ʿAbbāsid dynasty while enabling it to be slightly critical of ʿAbbāsid policies. It may well have followed the men a century earlier who were claimed as Imāmites in wanting the office of caliph to be thought of in autocratic or absolutist terms, but clear evidence is lacking. When one further takes into account the fact that the Imāmites thought of themselves as 'the elite' (*khāṣṣa*) and of the Sunnites as 'the common people' (*ʿamma*), it seems that the Imāmite sect constituted something like a political party whose purpose was to promote the interests of certain wealthy groups within the community.

THE SIGNIFICANCE OF THE GREATER OCCULTATION[241]

The death of the fourth *wakil* in or about 940 marked the passage from the Lesser to the Greater Occultation. Once again, this can hardly have been something which just happened, but was almost certainly a deliberate political act. The problem for the modern scholar is to discover what this change meant in actual political terms. Even if the decisive date is 940, however, it must be presumed that the new form of Imāmism was felt by its adherents to be suitable in the situation after 945 when effective rule over the central lands of the caliphate passed into the hands of the Būyid dynasty. Indeed, since there were no political changes affecting Imāmism until the time of Shah Ismāʿīl Safavī in the early sixteenth century, those who professed it must have continued to find it satisfactory, at least as a form of religious belief.

The political situation in 940 was very different from that in 874 or 878, when the Twelfth Imam had disappeared. The reign of the caliph al-Muʿtamid from 870 to 892, when control was mostly in the hands of his brother al-Muwaffaq, was a time of stability and good government; and the first sixteen years of the caliphate of al-Muqtadir (908–24) were somewhat similar. Apart from these periods, however, there had been since 862 an almost continuous struggle for power at the centre. In particular, the generals in charge of the Turkish guards on whom the caliphs relied had often shown that they had power to make and unmake caliphs. In the course of this turmoil the power and authority of the caliphs began to dwindle. Governors of distant provinces demanded that they should be succeeded by sons or other relatives, and the caliphs were forced to agree to the appointments demanded of them. Finally, in 936 the caliph al-Rāḍī found no alternative but to nominate the governor of Basra, Ibn Rā'iq, as 'chief emir' (*amīr al-umarā'*) to be in charge of the army, police, and civil administration at the centre of the caliphate. As is well known, the ʿAbbāsid caliphs continued in office in Baghdad after this until 1258 as titular heads of the caliphate, without political power but with certain ceremonial and spiritual functions, especially in respect of the legal system. Effective power was in the hands of a varying number of military commanders, each of whom was nominally appointed by the caliph as governor of a province or group of provinces.

After 936 the struggle for power continued in Baghdad, though now as a struggle for the position of 'chief emir'. In 945, however, that position, in fact if not at first in name, passed into the hands of the family or dynasty of the Būyids, already securely established as rulers of western Persia. Though they never held much more than Iraq and western Persia, they had special importance as rulers of Baghdad and the centre of the caliphate, and maintained themselves there until 1055. They are often said to have been Imāmites, but for reasons to be given presently this can hardly have been the case. They were certainly sympathetic to Shīʿism in a broad sense, however. Muʿizz al-Dawla, the first Būyid ruler in Baghdad, improved the position of the ʿAlids there. Then in 962, he gave orders for the cursing of Muʿāwiya, the first Umayyad caliph, who defeated ʿAlī, and those who had oppressed the family of the Prophet, and in the following year encouraged the celebration of the mourning for al-Ḥusayn and the feast of Ghādir Khumm, commemorating Muḥammad's designation of ʿAlī, ceremonies which later became distinctive of the Imāmites. On the other hand, it has to be noted that about twenty years later the Būyid ruler of the day suppressed these ceremonies because of the rioting occasioned by them between Sunnites and Shīʿites.

Despite these marks of sympathy for Shīʿism, a little reflection shows that the Būyids could not have been Imāmites in the strict sense. The Imāmism of the Lesser Occultation would have been quite impossible for them, since it would have meant acknowledging the superior authority of the *wakīl* of the time. Yet the Imāmism of the Greater Occultation was not much better. To profess it would have implied rejecting the nominal authority of the ʿAbbāsid caliph. This would have been politically dangerous, since for many – perhaps the majority – of their subjects the Būyids were legitimized by the fact that they held appointments from the caliph. If they were to depose the ʿAbbāsid caliph and set an ʿAlid in his place, they laid themselves open to the danger foreseen by one of their advisers, who is alleged to have said, 'no one seriously believes in an ʿAbbāsid caliph, and no one would object if you ordered his execution; but men would believe that an ʿAlid caliph was divinely inspired, and would obey *him* if he ordered *your* execution.' Another danger in such a case was that some rival might set up an ʿAbbāsid caliph in his own capital and have the advantage of legitimizing himself in this way. There was always the possibility, too, of the reappearance of the imam in occultation or someone claiming to be the imam; and this again would threaten Būyid power. Thus the Būyids, despite Shīʿite sympathies, were not Imāmites, and still less Zaydites or Ismāʿīlites. They made no effort to convert their subjects to Imāmism, and do not appear to have used Imāmite arguments in their propaganda against the Fāṭimids, the Ismāʿīlite dynasty which established itself in Egypt in 969 and claimed to be rightful rulers of the Islamic world.

In the light of this situation in the middle decades of the tenth century, what can be said about the political aims of those who proclaimed the doctrine of the Greater Occultation? Insofar as it put an end to the office of *wakīl* it may be surmised that this office had proved in practice not to have the advantages originally envisaged. This again could have come about for one of two reasons. On the one hand, it might have been the case that, even in favourable circumstances, the *wakīl* had less influence than had been expected. Moreover, there had at times been rival claimants to the office, so that the movement was no longer united. On the other hand, the office might have been affected by the fact that military commanders had replaced the caliph as effective rulers. A claimant to the office of *wakīl*, who was still alive in 945, is said to have been put in prison by the Būyids. Apart from that, some of the wealthy Imāmites were financiers involved in the money affairs of the caliphate; and financial breakdown went along with the decline of caliphal power.

Another point to be considered here is that with the assumption of power by military commanders religious doctrines lost much of their political relevance. The commanders certainly accepted Sunnism, but primarily as a legal system. They presumably did not tolerate interference by ulema in the detailed work of government, and paid little attention to religous doctrine except when the ʿAbbāsid caliphate had to be defended against Fāṭimid propaganda; but this last was more a concern of the Seljūq dynasty, which succeeded the Būyids. If the Imāmites gave up trying to influence policy by their doctrines, they would be in much the same position as the Sunnites, especially since during the first third of the tenth century they had begun to work out their own system of law, notably through al-Kulīnī (d. 939).

Leaving aside the question of the success or failure of the office of *wakīl*, it is to be noted that there was a quietist strain in Shīʿism which had been manifested during the Umayyad period in the application of messianic ideas to ʿAlī and his descendants. The doctrine of the Greater Occultation may also be regarded as a reassertion of this quietist strain. The Imāmites, while they waited for their imam, were prepared to tolerate and partially support whoever might be their ruler, but without any deep involvement in politics. It almost looks as if Imāmism had become an apolitical 'personal' religion, such as the West has had for the last two or three centuries. Certainly religious beliefs marked off the Imāmites from other Muslims as an elite community, and membership of this community was doubtless an important part of their identity.

One result of the proclamation of the Greater Occultation, probably unforeseen, was that leadership among the Imāmites passed to their ulema from the group of men from whom had come those who held the office of *wakīl*. Over the following centuries the leaders of whom we hear are scholars like Shaykh Ṣadūq and Shaykh Ṭūsī.

CONCLUSION

In the period up to the end of the tenth century Imāmite Shīʿism developed out of the earlier indefinite Proto-Shīʿism. In the course of this development we have traced a number of different stages. In some of these Shīʿism was linked with political activity, in others with an apolitical quietism. In some early activist stages revolts were led by members of 'the family' or in their name, but none of these revolts is closely related with Imāmism. Under Hārūn al-Rashīd and al-Maʿmūn, however, the forerunners of Imāmism were actively advocating a more autocratic conception of the caliphate; but about the year 850 the opponents of this policy, 'the constitutionalist bloc', were entirely successful and had Sunnism established as the religion of the caliphal empire. It was apparently in response to this establishment of Sunnism that some men who had previously belonged to the autocratic or absolutist bloc proclaimed the doctrine of the Lesser Occultation and so gave definite form to Imāmism. The mark of this stage of Imāmism was the existence of the office of *wakīl*, and it was presumably hoped that the *wakīl* would be able to influence caliphal policies in favour of the

Imāmites. These hopes were either never realized or else ceased to be realized after the loss of political power by the ʿAbbāsids. In these circumstances some of the leaders proclaimed the Greater Occultation, and in so doing seem to have depoliticized Imāmism. This was in a sense a return to the quietism manifested in the messianic Shīʿism of the first Islamic century. From the proclamation of the Greater Occultation until the fifteenth century, Imāmism seems to have been a 'personal' religion linked with a distinctive legal system.

Since its repoliticizing about the fifteenth century, Imāmism has again passed through several stages, and this study of the early period may help in the understanding of these. It suggests the existence of a tension or even a contradiction between the activist and quietist strains in Imāmism. How can an apolitical quietist doctrine become the basis of an actual state? To a state, Imāmism could certainly contribute a system of law covering most of the matters covered by law in the West: personal status (marriage, inheritance, etc.), criminal acts, commercial transactions. It could also contribute a system of philosophical theology. In these fields, then, the ulema could adequately represent the imam. There is an area, however, where the ulema had no qualifications for giving guidance, namely, the higher reaches of governmental administration. Until very recent times no Imāmites have given much thought to this area. What seems to have happened in the past usually and to be happening now is that the Imāmite tradition of autocratic, absolutist rule has taken over. Indeed, in Iran at the moment one might say that instead of there being a single *wakīl*, many people have arrogated to themselves some aspect of the office of *wakīl* and are interpreting it in an autocratic fashion. Because of this inherent contradiction (as it would seem), it is difficult to see how Imāmism can solve the problems of Iran today except in the unlikely event of a leader arising with unusual gifts of imagination and insight, a leader who could formulate policies that would be both realistic and in conformity with Islamic ideas.

B11. The Great Community and the Sects

The theme of this paper is the image created by medieval Muslim scholars of the great community of Islam and of the relation of this community to the sects. The sects are here understood in the sense given to the corresponding Arabic words by the heresiographers or writers of 'books of sects', such as al-Ashʿarī (d. 395) with his *Maqālāt al-Islāmiyyīn*, al-Baghdādī (d. 1037) in *al-Farq bayn al-firaq*, and al-Shahrastānī (d. 1153) in *al-Milal wa-l-niḥal*. A subordinate part of this same theme is the contrast between the image produced by the Muslim scholars and the image which modern European and American scholars are trying to form. The essence of the contrast is that modern scholars accept the idea of development whereas the medieval Muslim scholars found this idea abhorrent. As is well known, the Arabic word for 'heresy' is *bidʿa*, of which the primary meaning is 'innovation'. The dislike of change and novelty is deeply rooted in the Arab soul, and goes back to pre-Islamic times when the accepted ideal was to follow exactly the time-honoured practice of the tribe or clan. In accordance with this attitude medieval scholars avoided all suggestion of development in Islamic doctrine, and presented instead the image of a monolithic body of doctrine, which was accepted through the centuries by the great mass of Muslims, and from which a few sectarians at various times had deviated.

A convenient starting point for the discussion of this theme is the following curious fact. On general grounds Muslim scholars might have been expected to try to minimize the number of sects and to say as little as possible about them; but on the contrary we find heresiographers like those mentioned exaggerating the number of sects. This feature was first noticed by the great Hungarian scholar of Islam, Ignaz Goldziher, who linked it with a certain Tradition of the Prophet which had gained currency. The earliest form of the Tradition is that recorded by al-Dārimī (d. 869). According to this Muḥammad said: 'Did not the People of the Book before you divide into 72 sects (*milla*, with the variant *firqa*)? . . . and in truth this community will one day divide into 73 sects, of which 72 will go to hell, and only one to paradise.'[242] There are many other versions of the Tradition. The one most commonly quoted speaks of the Jews having seventy-one sects, the Christians seventy-two and the Muslims seventy-three.

Goldziher further argued that this Tradition had come into existence as the result of a misunderstanding of a somewhat similar Tradition, which is to be found in the collections of al-Bukhārī and Muslim. In al-Bukhārī's version Muḥammad said: '. . . faith has sixty-odd branches (*shuʿba*), and modesty is a branch of faith.'[223] There were also Traditions which spoke of Judaism having seventy-one virtues, Christianity seventy-two, and Islam seventy-three. There is some plausibility about Goldziher's suggestion that the Tradition about seventy-three sects has arisen through a misunderstanding of Traditions about seventy-three virtues. It is difficult to see why the founder of a religion should boast about the number of sects into which it is divided. If we suppose the Tradition to have been invented by later Muslims, it is just as difficult to see why they should have wanted to boast about the multiplicity of sects.

Nevertheless, when one examines the books on sects, it seems clear that the Tradition about sects had a positive value for the writers. At least from the time of al-Baghdādī onwards they were aware of the Tradition, and they so arranged their accounts of the sects that they had seventy-two heretical sects. In the introduction to the *Farq* al-Baghdādī quotes several forms of the Tradition; and it is his intention to describe seventy-two heretical sects and explain their errors, and then to expound the doctrine of the one *firqa nājiya*, 'the sect which is saved.' It is difficult to state precisely which are the seventy-two sects of his list, for there are some discrepancies between the sects he names and those he actually describes. He unnecessarily increases the number of sects by treating each of the main figures among the Muʿtazila as the founder of a sect. At other points he reduces the number of sects by asserting that several of those he describes are so heretical that they have put themselves outside the Islamic community. The procedure of al-Shahrastānī is similar.

Because the Tradition about the sects has this positive significance for the heresiographers it is unlikely that it developed through a sheer misunderstanding of the Tradition about virtues. It looks as if there had been a deliberate alteration of the latter Tradition to meet some need of the community. We may obtain some idea of what this need was if we consider another curious fact about the books on sects. This is that the men who wrote such books were going against the common practice of Muslim scholars not to describe or expound the views of those with whom they disagreed and not to treat them as a matter of intrinsic interest but to concentrate on refuting them. This was a deep-seated Arab attitude, and is well illustrated by the story of ʿUmar's decision to burn the great academic library of Alexandria; when asked what should be done with the books he replied, 'If they are in agreement with the Qur'ān they are unnecessary, and if they do not agree with it they are dangerous, so that in either case they should be destroyed.' Similarly Aḥmad ibn Ḥanbal criticized al-Muḥāsibī's book *The Refutation of the Muʿtazilites* on the ground that he began by expounding their views; Aḥmad held that this procedure was extremely unwise, since a man might read the false doctrines and be impressed by them, and might not read or appreciate the refutation. Since the general attitude was thus to pay no attention to false doctrines apart from pointing out the errors, it is remarkable that whole books should be devoted to giving an account of views regarded as erroneous. Al-Baghdādī, indeed, lists the errors of each sect and Ibn Ḥazm's book of sects consists largely of arguments against them; but al-Ashʿarī and al-Shahrastānī are content simply to expound.

Part of the reason for the interest shown by these writers in describing the sects is doubtless that in some cases it was advantageous to define true Sunnite doctrine by contrasting it with heretical views. A well-known example of this is the Ashʿarite doctrine of *kasb*, 'acquisition' or 'appropriation,' namely, that each human act is both created by God and 'acquired' or 'appropriated' by man. This doctrine can be expounded in isolation, but it is more clearly understood when it is seen to be a mean between two extremes; one extreme is the doctrine of the Qadarites according to which the man himself creates each act, while the other extreme is the doctrine of *jabr* according to which man is a mere automaton, and only 'acts' in the sense in which, when a stone falls or the wind blows, we can say they are 'acting' or 'doing something'. Heretical views, of course, are not merely useful in thus pointing out the contrast with true doctrine. Historically it was the case that the formulation of Sunnite doctrine came about in the process of correcting or rejecting heresies. The Khārijite view that the grave sinner (*ṣāḥib kabīra*) is excluded from the community was part of the stimulus which provoked much of the early theological discussion in Islam.

So much, then, for the reasons which led men to write their books of sects. Let us now try to envisage the state of affairs which confronted these writers and which they described in their own way. The phenomena of Islam as a religion up to the time, say, of al-Ashʿarī constitute a vast complex within which three groups are of special significance in a study of the development of doctrine. First, there were some clearly defined groups of rebels against the government who based their rebellion on theological principles. Among these were Khārijite groups like the Azraqites (Azāriqa), the followers of Nāfiʿ ibn Azraq, and Shīʿite groups like the supporters of Zayd ibn ʿAlī, though the latter were probably not so homogeneous theologically as the Khārijites. Secondly, there were groups and individuals whom the Umayyad rulers suspected of subversive activities, but who were executed or otherwise punished before there was any active rebellion. Ghaylān al-Dimashqī is an example of this group. About both these groups, the actual insurgents and the suspected insurgents, there is material in the historians, and this was presumably familiar to the heresiographers.

In the third place there was a large number of men interested in religion who discussed religious questions with one another. During the first century of the ʿAbbāsids some of these formed groups which might be called 'schools' because they held in common one or more heretical views. Such were some of the later nonrevolutionary Khārijite scholars and above all the Muʿtazilites. Others again are described simply as Traditionists or as jurists, constituting what Professor Schacht has called 'the ancient schools of law.' Since not all the religious-minded men were prominent in transmitting Traditions or elaborating the Sharīʿa, it is perhaps better to speak of a 'general religious movement'. In this general religious movement few men could have the label of any definite heresy attached to them, though some were known to favour certain heretical doctrines. Later Islam tended to regard all these men as more or less sound scholars who played a worthy part in the transmission of the Islamic religious heritage. Any distinctive views they held are concealed or spoken of in a way that minimizes their deviant character. Thus the impression is created that this general religious movement was monolithic.

The modern occidental scholar approaches this whole complex of religious facts with different interests. He tends to be concerned above all with the *development* of Islamic thought, which is precisely what the Muslim scholars have been trying to conceal. He must therefore be aware of the presuppositions and procedures of the heresiographers, so as not to be led astray by the assumptions implicit in their statements. He will, for example, look for divergencies of opinion within the general religious movement, and will find a certain number; and he will not take for granted that there was any generally recognized core of Sunnite doctrine during the first Islamic century or even the second. Again, he will be very suspicious of sect names, and will always consider what they meant to the person applying the name. He will not suppose that a sect existed in any significant sense merely on the ground that Muslim scholars speak of it. Views ascribed to particular named individuals he will normally consider more trustworthy material than views attributed to sects as a whole. The remainder of this paper is devoted to looking at the treatment of sect-names by the heresiographers.

The first point to be illustrated is that many sect-names were objectionable nicknames flung at opponents in the heat of theological controversy and the strength of the *odium theologicum* is notorious. A good example here is the sect of the Qadariyya or Qadarites, who, as already noted, believed that human acts are not predetermined by God but are produced by the man himself. The first Qadarites were political opponents of the Umayyads, but Qadarite views were also held by later scholarly theologians, and notably by the group known as the

Muʿtazilites. Difficulties about the meaning of the name begin to appear when it is found that ʿAmr ibn ʿUbayd, usually reckoned one of the founders of the Muʿtazilites and therefore a Qadarite, himself wrote a book entitled *Refutation of the Qadarites*. How is this to be explained? Was he originally an ordinary Sunnite who was converted to the Qadarite position, and was this book written before his conversion? Such a hypothesis is unlikely and there is no need to adopt it. ʿAmr ibn ʿUbayd was simply applying an unpleasant name to his opponents. He would presumably have argued that it was more appropriately applied to them since they were always insisting on God's Qadar or predetermination of events. ʿAmr died about 760, but more than a century later in the works of Ibn Qutayba and al-Ashʿarī there are traces of the controversy about the proper use of this name; and the two writers mentioned argue that properly speaking the Qadarites are those who maintain that they determine their own acts, and not those who uphold God's Qadar.[244]

Nowadays the use of vilificatory nicknames is perhaps more familiar in politics. In this sphere some contemporaries do not hesitate to use whatever name will blacken a man's reputation in the eyes of the public. There is no objective scientific accuracy in the choice of names. A bad name will be fixed to a man if some small trifle gives justification for it. Much the same was true in Islamic theological controversy. It follows that one cannot simply make a list of the persons to whom a nickname was applied and conclude that they formed a sect. It would be difficult to make al-Ashʿarī and ʿAmr ibn ʿUbayd members of the same sect, even if they have the same name of Qadarite. The modern scholar must always ask who applied the name. He must also remember that the Muslim heresiographers used polemical writings as sources, and sometimes took at their face value the sect-names found there. They made fewer mistakes than might have been expected, but one or two strange things happened.

Where the different applications of a name are closer to one another the danger of confusion may be greater. This may be illustrated by the Jabriyya or Mujbira, who are often said to be at the opposite pole from the Qadariyya. The Muʿtazilites and other Qadarites (in the usual sense) applied the name Mujbira to all who denied their doctrine of human acts; that is, they included under this term most Sunnites from Traditionists to Ashʿarite theologians. The Māturīdites, a school of Sunnite theologians usually reckoned parallel to the Ashʿarites, sometimes accused the latter of holding the doctrine of *jabr*, the distinctive view of the Jabriyya, though these would have considered themselves far from any such heresy. Finally the Ashʿarites, as already noted, defended themselves by maintaining that their doctrine of *kasb* was a mean between the doctrines of the Qadariyya and the Jabriyya or Mujbira. But what can the Ashʿarites have meant by this latter term? Al-Shahrastānī, an Ashʿarite heresiographer, goes so far as to adopt a classification in which pure Jabrites are distinguished from moderate Jabrites. The special view of the pure Jabriyya is that men do not act at all in reality, but only do so in a metaphorical sense. This is a strange view for anyone to hold, however; and apparently the only example of pure Jabriyya given by al-Shahrastānī is a sect called the Jahmiyya.

This alleged sect of Jahmiyya, when the early materials about it are carefully examined, proves to be entirely a fabrication of the heresiographers. There never was any sect of this name, but the heresiographers constructed one out of nicknames and out of the defence reactions of those to whom the nicknames were applied. The supposed founder of the sect, Jahm ibn Ṣafwān, certainly existed; but apart from him no persons can be named as members of the sect. It is true that in the credal work of Ibn Baṭṭa, a tenth-century Ḥanbalite writer, there is a list of those reckoned as disciples or partisans of Jahm; but the identifiable names on the list are all of men normally called Muʿtazilites. The dissemination of Jahmite doctrines, again, is attributed to Bishr al-Marīsī (d. 833), but is said to have happened after the translation of the Greek books; it is thus to be dated between 800 and 820 or later. There is no information, however, about how Bishr might be connected with Jahm, who had died in 746. Jahm is described as the secretary of al-Ḥārith ibn Surayj, who led a revolt in eastern Khorasan against the Umayyads from 734 until 746. Jahm may be regarded as the intellectual propagandist for this revolt, which professed to be aiming at a government in accordance with 'the Book of God and the Sunna of his Prophet'. This profession, it may be noted, did not prevent them frequently being in alliance with pagan Turks against other Muslims.

This is not the place to discuss such a question in great detail, but on the basis of early references given in the article on the 'Djahmiyya' in the second edition of the *Encyclopaedia of Islam* an attempt may be made to give a conjectural reconstruction of the course of events. Three steps may be distinguished.

First, under the influence of Greek ideas which were just coming to the notice of Muslim thinkers, Bishr al-Marīsī about 800 or a little later propounded certain views which in a general sense might be called Muʿtazilite. In particular he asserted that the Qur'ān was created. Because of his views he was called a Jahmī by some members of his own Ḥanafī legal rite and also by a large number of Traditionists, especially those later associated with Aḥmad ibn Ḥanbal. The name Jahmī was also applied by this latter group to all those who approved of the official adoption under al-Ma'mūn of the doctrine that the Qur'ān was the created Word of God. To call someone a Jahmī must have been objectionable, but it is not clear why this was so. Perhaps it was because Jahm had been involved in an alliance with pagans against Muslims. An early occurrence of the name Jahmiyya is found in the first and shortest form of *Al-fiqh al-akbar* ascribed to Abū Ḥanīfa, which Wensinck dated aout 750 but which may be later. In the tenth article denial of the punishment of the tomb is said to be a mark of the Jahmiyya; and a similar denial was made by certain persons commonly reckoned Muʿtazilites.

The second step may be traced in the writing of the Muʿtazilite al-Khayyāṭ in the second half of the ninth century. In his book *Kitāb al-intiṣār* he states that the name of Muʿtazilite is properly applied only to those who hold the five principles he specifies. He admits that ordinary men reckon Jahm among the Muʿtazilites because he held that the Qur'ān was created, but insists that this is only one of the five principles (namely *tawḥīd* or unity). Those who accept one or two of the five principles but reject the others are not Muʿtazilites; and he implies that Jahm, by holding the doctrine of *jabr* or 'compulsion' and denying the Muʿtazilite doctrine of Qadar, cannot be a Muʿtazilite. The same must be said of others like Ḍirār and al-Najjār who, though popularly called Muʿtazilites, affirmed God's Qadar and held a doctrine of human acts not unlike that of the later Ashʿarites.

A third step can be discerned, but there is little source material and the interpretation of it is somewhat conjectural. What we have is probably the retort of the conservative Traditionists to a suggestion implicit in the views of al-Khayyāṭ. He had hinted that Jahm held the doctrine of *jabr*, and he had also spoken of the Traditionists as Mujbira. Such a close connection with the despised Jahm was most unwelcome to the Traditionists. It would seem, however, that they avoided being explicitly called Jahmiyya. For one thing Aḥmad ibn Ḥanbal and the Ḥanbalites emphasized the connection with the doctrine of the creation of the Qur'ān, a doctrine which they vigorously rejected. Another reason was that al-Ashʿarī or some predecessor produced an account of Jahm's view of human actions in which they were assimilated to the falling of a stone. It is doubtful if anyone ever held such a view, but the mere statement of it prepared the way for the later Ashʿarite claim that their view was a mean between the extremes of the Jabriyya and the Qadariyya.

Out of this strife of names much material was produced which the heresiographers found useful in compiling their accounts of the sects. It would be anachronistic to suggest that the historical Jahm held all the views ascribed to the Jahmiyya. If the hypothesis now being developed is correct, however, it would also be the case that no other person had ever held all these views. Jahm and the Jahmiyya became a convenient peg on which to hang views one did not want attributed to one's own group. Jahm was certainly a real person, though little was known about him; but there was certainly never a sect or group of Jahmiyya in any signficant sense. The Ḥanbalites applied it to the Muʿtazilites and others who engaged in *kalām* or rational theology; and the Muʿtazilites tried to restrict it to those who disagreed with their view of human action; but in either case the connection with Jahm was tenuous in the extreme.

We may now turn to consider the Muʿtazilites, since they included many of those to whom the name Jahmiyya was applied. Goldziher once remarked that it was a mistake to speak of a Muʿtazilite *sect*[237]; but by this he meant that they were not a separate religious community like the Ibāḍites or the Imāmite Shīʿites. In fact they come nearer than many other so-called sects to being a well-defined theological school. It was only gradually, however, that they became well-defined. The following is a provisional account of the history of the term 'Muʿtazilite'.

The term 'Muʿtazila' appears to have been a nickname, but one first applied to the group, not to the individual. This presumably happened after the adoption of Greek ideas by some religious thinkers, and therefore about the same time as the term Jahmī came into vogue, though it was never so objectionable as Jahmī. It seems to have been applied to everyone who made use of Greek ideas and of Greek (or rational) methods of argument, no matter what his general doctrinal position was. This may be taken to have happened about the year 800. For a time the leading exponent in Basra of Greek-style theology was Ḍirār, who is said to have given lectures there before Abū 'l-Hudhayl, the important Muʿtazilite. Ḍirār was commonly called a Muʿtazilite, but, as has been seen, al-Khayyāṭ will not allow this since he did not hold all the five principles.

Those who employed Greek methods and ideas met with bitter criticism from some Traditionists but were shown high favour by the caliph al-Ma'mūn and his successors. Under al-Mutawakkil, about 850, government policy changed, and it was mainly the critics of Greek methods who were now in favour. It was probably in these adverse circumstances that a number of men got together and defined the five principles which made a man a Muʿtazilite. This gave cohesion to the group; and from this time onward there is a clearly defined theological school of the Muʿtazila. A little earlier – perhaps when the names Muʿtazila and Jahmiyya were first used – some men had avoided being called Jahmites by claiming that they followed one or both of two members of the general religious movement, Wāṣil ibn ʿAṭā' and ʿAmr ibn ʿUbayd (d. 748, 761). These two men may have had similar views on many points to Abū 'l-Hudhayl and other leading ninth-century Muʿtazilites, but they were not pioneers in the adoption of Greek thought. The claim that the later Muʿtazilites followed them is therefore unhistorical, and is probably to be regarded as a defence against the accusation of following Jahm. The well-known story of Wāṣil and al-Ḥasan al-Baṣrī in which the latter used *iʿtazala*, 'has gone apart,' of Wāṣil helped to remove any pejorative sense from the word Muʿtazila; and a man like al-Khayyāṭ was proud to say he belonged to this body. Thus the term Muʿtazila ceased to be a nickname and came to be the designation accepted by the members for a definite theological school. It is to be noted, however, that the school was not properly constituted until about the time of al-Khayyāṭ.

Yet other aspects of the problem of sect names are illustrated by the Murji'a or Murji'ites. One difficulty is that Abū Ḥanīfa, from whom the Ḥanafī legal rite or *madhhab* is named, is stated to have been a Murji'ite; and it is awkward to have a pillar of Sunnite Islam as member of a heretical sect. Another difficulty is that in the first century of ʿAbbāsid rule the only Murji'ites known to us, apart from Abū Ḥanīfa and some of his leading disciples, are obscure and unimportant men, whereas from the standpoint of modern scholarship the Murji'ites made important contributions to the development of Islamic thought. It is also to be noted that the heresiographers found the classification of the Murji'ites far from easy; al-Shahrastānī, for example, is driven to speaking of Murji'a of the Khawārij, Murji'a of the Qadariyya, and Murji'a of the Jabriyya. An alternative way of expressing these facts might have been to say that the doctrine of *irjā'*, the essential doctrine of the Murji'a, could be combined with other doctrines in various ways; but this, of course, is tantamount to admitting that the Murji'a are not a sect.

Even if we place the doctrine of *irjā'* in the centre of our thoughts, we find that it can be understood in various ways. The word is probably to be connected with a verse of the Qur'ān which says that 'others are postponed (*murjawna, murja'ūna*) for the command of God' (9.106/7). Again, however, the doctrine of postponement can be interpreted in various ways: it may be 'the postponement of judgement on sinners' (leaving it to God on the Last Day), or 'the postponement of ʿAlī in respect of merit' (that is, placing him after ʿUthmān), or 'the postponement of works to faith' (that is, treating them as less important when it comes to the final judgement on a man). *Irjā'* may also be taken as a causative form from *rajā* 'to hope', and will then be interpreted as 'the causing (of all) to have hope' (that is, of entering Paradise). European scholars (e.g. A. J. Wensinck)[246]) have often presented the Murji'ites as a sect which grew out of the opposition to the Khārijite doctrine of the exclusion of the grave sinner from the community; this involves taking *irjā'* in the first sense of leaving to God the decision about sinners. It may well be, however, that the earliest application of the term was in connection with ʿAlī and ʿUthmān. Of a Traditionist of Kufa called Muḥārib (d. 734) Ibn Saʿd writes: 'he belonged to the first Murji'a who used to "postpone" (the decision about) ʿAlī and ʿUthmān and not to testify to the faith or unbelief (of either)'.[247]

It is also apposite here to consider the various groups of persons who applied to others the name of Murji'a. The name was much used by al-Nawbakhtī or whoever wrote *Firaq al-shīʿa*, for he says that the fundamental sects of the Islamic community are four: Shīʿa, Muʿtazila,

Murji'a, and Khawārij. One's first impulse is to suppose that the Sunnites are not mentioned because they are not a sect but the true Islam; but reflection shows that this could not have been the intention of the author, since he was a Shīʿite and must have regarded the Shīʿa as the true Islam. It follows, then, that he has used Murji'a to cover all those men later known as Sunnites who did not in some way allow that ʿAlī was superior to ʿUthmān. A second group which used the term was the Muʿtazila, and they specially criticized the view that the grave sinner, despite his sin, remained a believer. Again the Khārijites also used the term, more specially for those who did not condemn ʿAlī, and this may have comprised the majority of later Sunnites. Even some groups of Traditionists seem to have criticized persons whom they called Murji'a because they emphasized faith and made works unimportant. The extreme statement of this view was that ascribed to Muqātil ibn Sulaymān (d. 767), namely, that where there is faith sin does no harm. This assertion was taken by many to imply a belittling of social morality; but it also contains a point which was ultimately accepted by the great majority of Sunnites, namely, that, if a man by continuing to hold the true faith remains a member of the Islamic community, he will eventually go to heaven, even though he may first have to undergo punishment for his sins.

Out of this confusion of usages the heresiographical tradition which is mainly Ashʿarite, produced a sect of Murji'a, but it is a very strange sect. Al-Ashʿarī himself, doubtless because he inherited an attitude of coolness toward the scholars of Kufa, did not hesitate to make Abū Ḥanīfa and his followers a sect of the Murji'a. A century later, however, al-Baghdādī was convinced that *irjā'* is heretical because it makes works of secondary importance compared with faith, and he denies the allegation of a Murji'ite called Ghassān that the views of Abū Ḥanīfa were similar to his own. Al-Shahrastānī also explicitly excludes Abū Ḥanīfa from the ranks of the Murji'a, but admits that he has sometimes been said to belong to the 'Murji'a of the Sunna'. The last two heresiographers are then left with a sect of Murji'a with several subdivisions. When the details are examined, however, it is found that the members of the sect are either persons usually classified with some other sect such as the Khawārij or the Qadariyya, or else are nonentities of whom all that is known is the name and a distinctive view about faith. The sect of the Murji'a, then, has not completely evaporated like the Jahmiyya; but the men who are left had little significance in the development of Islamic doctrine. The modern occidental scholar, however, as he seeks to trace the historical development of doctrine in Islam, becomes convinced that some believers in *irjā'* made a considerable contribution to this process; and he also realizes that this contribution is likely to have been the work, not of the nonentities but of men of the calibre of Abū Ḥanīfa and his leading followers.

The Jahmiyya and the Murji'a have been considered in some detail. They are extreme examples of the distortions produced by the heresiographers, but in the way in which the latter treat other sects there is much of interest. In the remainder of this paper I look briefly at the two groups of sects known as the Khārijites or Khawārij and the Shīʿites or Shīʿa.

With regard to the first of these, then, it is clear that the name of Khawārij was not employed in the earliest period of all. One name that was long in common use was Ḥarūriyya, and another may have been Muḥakkima. At first these may have had a general sense, unlike more specific names such as Azāriqa. The earliest dated example of the use of Khawārij is in correspondence, thought to be authentic, between the leader of the later Ibāḍiyya and the caliph ʿAbd al-Malik; in his letter the caliph seems to use Khawārij in the general sense of 'rebels', and does not include the peace-loving Ibāḍiyya among these rebels.[248] In the late eighth century and early ninth century there were Khārijite theologians in the cities of Iraq who had discussions with Muʿtazilites and others and who shared some of the Muʿtazilite views. My hypothesis would be that it was in the course of such discussions in the field of *kalām* or rational theology that Khawārij came to be used as a general term for a group of sects, namely, those which held that the grave sinner is an unbeliever and so excluded from the community. This was the point in which the *mutakallimūn* or rational theologians were chiefly interested, and it would be advantageous for them to have a generic term. So far as the *mutakallimūn* were concerned, however, the discussion of Khārijite views was largely an academic matter, since by the early ninth century there were few even quietist Khārijites left in Iraq.

The Shīʿa or Shīʿites differ from the other early sects in that their name was never a nickname or vituperative term. In the Umayyad period the vituperative terms used by the opponents were Kaysāniyya and Saba'iyya, both of which are obscure. With the coming of the ʿAbbāsids the usual term of opprobrium came to be Rawāfiḍ or Rāfiḍa; but some persons used it to mean moderates, others extremists. It seems likely that ʿAlī himself was in the habit of calling a group of his close associates his *shīʿa* or 'party'; and a non-technical use of *shīʿa* in the sense of 'party' is common among those who honoured ʿAlī. So far, however, the word had not the sectarian connotation with which we are now familiar. Up to the middle of the ninth century the usage seems to have been fluid, for Aḥmad ibn Ḥanbal (d. 855) is able to claim that 'the Sunnites (*ahl al-sunna wa-l-ḥadīth*) are the true *shīʿa* of ʿAlī, for they show due affection to the family of the Prophet and fully recognize the rights of ʿAlī'.[249] This shows that *shīʿa* was an honourable word which the Ḥanbalites would have liked to apply to themselves, and also that it was not yet absolutely identified with the sect.

Increasingly, however, those later called Shīʿites used the word *shīʿa* of themselves with a sectarian meaning, and forced their usage on others. In al-Khayyāṭ's *Kitāb al-intiṣār* it is noteworthy that the quotations from Ibn al-Rāwandī always have Shīʿa and never Rāfiḍa, whereas al-Khayyāṭ himself never uses Shīʿa (with one exception which can be explained) but always uses Rāfiḍa. Similarly in *Firaq al-shīʿa* the word Rāfiḍa is used only twice, and that in accounts of other men's views, whereas the writer counts himself, not without pride, one of the Shīʿa. The Sunnite Ibn Qutayba (d. 889) normally uses Rāfiḍa in the same way as al-Khayyāṭ; in *Kitāb al-maʿārif*, however, he has in addition to the sects of the Rāfiḍa a list of men whom he assigns to the Shīʿa; those on this list are respectable Traditionists who seem to have held no heretical Rāfiḍite views but who may have shown a measure of affection for ʿAlī and his house. To this extent Ibn Qutayba admitted the claim of the later Shīʿites and abandoned that of Ibn Ḥanbal. Al-Ashʿarī in the *Maqālāt* does not go so far as to use the term Shīʿa as the heading for the group of sects, but does use its plural form, *al-shiyaʿ*, 'the parties'. Al-Baghdādī retains Rāfiḍa except in one or two virtual quotations, but al-Shahrastānī is happy to use al-Shīʿa. In this way the Sunnite heresiographers and the Sunnites in general came to adopt the Shīʿites' own name for themselves.

This study of the names of sects should perhaps have been rounded off by some consideration of what occidentals call Sunnism. This is a more complex matter, however, and it is not relevant in the present context. To speak of 'Sunnites' is to regard the main body of Islam as a kind of sect, whereas the great achievement of the heresiographers was to form the image of the Islamic community as doctrinally monolithic with only a relatively small number of deviants. Their conception of the sects is not objective history but rather a constituent part of this image of the community. The impression they convey of the monolithic character of the community is enhanced by the fact that most of the sects described have completely disappeared. If an occidental scholar set out *de novo* to describe the Islamic sects, he would give a very different picture. He would omit many of those listed by the heresiographers and would only include: (a) groups of rebels with a theological basis; (b) sects which have developed separate institutions and cult forms, like the Ibāḍiyya and the Ismāʿīliyya, and (c) clearly defined schools of theologians.

If the modern occidental scholar wants to pursue his study of the development of Islamic thought, he has to learn to discount many statements of the heresiographers about the sects, since these Muslim writers wanted to show the unchanging character of that thought. Instead the modern scholar will, as far as the material allows, focus his attention on the views of particular individuals known by name. In the end he too will produce an image of the Islamic community in its relation to the sects, but for him the sects will not be mere deviants but important contributors to the growth of Islamic life and thought.[250]

B12 The Beginnings of the Islamic Theological Schools

This paper attempts, by bringing together the available scraps of information, to give some account of the early organization of theological teaching in Islam.

The first point of significance appears to be the statement in the *Tanbīh* of al-Malaṭī that before Abū 'l-Hudhayl it was Ḍirār who had the *majlis* and the *kalām* in Basra.[251] This implies that there was some organized teaching, with at least one teacher, and also that this organization was distinct both from the teaching and discussion of legal matters and also from the Christian schools where Greek philosophy and science were taught. Although Ḍirār is said to have been a qadi, the presumption is that the participants in this *majlis* were Muslims who were interested in Greek thought both for its own sake and for its relevance to Islamic theological concerns. Since Ḍirār was often called a Muʿtazilite by his contemporaries and immediate successors, and since he is said to have been succeeded by Abū 'l-Hudhayl, it would follow that the *majlis* of Ḍirār was in some respects a forerunner of the Muʿtazilite school of Basra. This was not the only teaching of these subjects. Hishām b. al-Ḥakam, for example, taught in Kufa and probably also in Baghdad, and in Baghdad there were discussions on similar questions in the salon of the Barmakids; but the *majlis* in Basra seems to have been more fully organized and more purely academic.

The second significant point was the adoption by a number of Muʿtazilites of a strict definition of who belonged to the Muʿtazila and who was excluded. The earliest reference to this appears to be in al-Khayyāṭ where he asserts: 'none of them (*sc.* people who share some views with his friends) deserves the name of *iʿtizāl* unless he holds all the five principles, namely, *tawḥīd, ʿadl, al-waʿd wa-l-waʿīd, al-manzila bayn al-manzilatayn, al-amr bi-l-maʿrūf wa-l-nahī ʿan al-munkar*'.[252] The date of this work is about 300/912, but it is probable that the five principles had been formulated nearly a century earlier. The Zaydite imam al-Qāsim b. Ibrāhīm al-Rassī, who died in 860, arranges his teaching under five heads which are similar to those of the Muʿtazila, although he differs from them in some fundamental ways.[253] Again al-Ashʿarī, in the first part of his book of sects, *Maqālāt al-islāmiyyīn,* arranges his account of the different views of the various Muʿtazilites under the five principles, but the first two principles fill one hundred and eleven pages whereas the remaining three occupy only twelve. This suggests that the five principles had become distinctive of the Muʿtazila long before the growth of interest in the philosophical subtleties discussed under the first two heads. On the other hand, in the verses in which Bishr b. al-Muʿtamir repudiates Ḍirār and his party the reason he gives is that their imam is Jahm whereas his is ʿAmr b. ʿUbayd;[254] but too much should not be made of this, since even if the five principles had been formulated, Bishr might have thought the reference to the imam more effective with an external audience.

The acceptance (at whatever date) of the five principles as a definition of Muʿtazilism, together with such evidence as the verses of Bishr just referred to, implies that there was a body of men who had some awareness of a corporate identity (but not a legal one). The growth of this awareness of identity doubtless went along with increasing opposition to the practice of Kalām or rational theology. Hārūn al-Rashīd (786-809) is said to have persecuted some of the Mutakallimūn or students of Kalām, but it was probably on account of the political implications of their views and not merely because they practised Kalām. There was a great change, however, after the return of al-Ma'mūn to Baghdad in 204/819, since some of the more important offices of state were occupied by Muʿtazilites, and the caliph's policy of the Miḥna or Inquisition in respect of the Qur'ān was based on Muʿtazilite teaching. The need to define Muʿtazilism seems, then, to have arisen from two matters: (1) it was difficult to defend Muʿtazilism if the term Muʿtazilite had the wide sense hitherto current; (2) the close association of some Muʿtazilites with the caliph's government presumably led to a distinction between those who approved of their policies and those who did not. On the other hand, Bishr al-Marīsī, who has been described as the leading juristic authority in Baghdad and as providing the intellectual basis for the policy of the Miḥna,[255] though sometimes called a Muʿtazilite, did not accept the second of the five principles (*ʿadl*, justice, implying human free will), and is not, for example, included in the *Ṭabaqāt al-Muʿtazila* (or *Munya*) of Ibn al-Murtaḍā. Bishr al-Marīsī died about the same time as al-Ma'mūn, 218/833, or perhaps a year or two later, but certainly before the ending of the Miḥna by al-Mutawakkil, about 236/850. Since there is an element of defensiveness in insisting on a strict definition of Muʿtazilism, perhaps the most likely period for the acceptance of the definition was when the political importance of the Muʿtazila declined after the end of the Miḥna.

The Muʿtazila had not merely an awareness of corporate identity, but apparently also some organization for teaching their intellectual methods and their distinctive doctrines.[256] This was probably the case in Basra, and there their *majlis* was almost certainly a continuation of that of Ḍirār. References occur, though admittedly in late texts, to the *ri'āsa* or headship of the school. The line of succession was from Abū 'l-Hudhayl to al-Shaḥḥām to al-Jubbā'ī to Abū Hāshim. It is reported of al-Ashʿarī that he sometimes substituted for al-Jubbā'ī, and that, had he remained a Muʿtazilite, he would have succeeded him – presumably in this *ri'āsa*. At Baghdad the position is not so clear. Bishr b. al-Muʿtamir was the founder and first head, but in the following generation no one stood out above the others. The dates of al-Khayyāṭ are not certain, but it is possible that from about the end of the reign of al-Mutawakkil he was head of the school of Baghdad, and that he was succeeded by his disciple al-Kaʿbī (who is also known as Abū 'l-Qāsim al-Balkhī); the latter is reckoned as belonging to the Muʿtazilites of Baghdad, though he eventually settled in Khurasan. It is perhaps worth noting that in Baghdad Bishr al-Marīsī had his own *majlis*, but this may have been chiefly concerned with *fiqh*.

In the third place, there are several relevant points with regard to the relation between the legal *madhāhib* and the study of Kalām or more generally theology. In the case of Aḥmad b. Ḥanbal and his followers there was no Kalām in the strict sense, but theological doctrines were discussed and creeds were produced. The point of importance here is that the same persons studied and presumably lectured in both jurisprudence and theology. From the 5th/11th century onwards most Ashʿarite theologians seem to have been Shāfiʿites in jurisprudence, but a discussion of the later relationships of the two disciplines is beyond the scope of the present paper. Up to the 5th/11th century the two disciplines must have been distinct, since it is not certain that al-Ashʿarī himself was a Shāfiʿite,[257] and al-Bāqillānī was certainly a Mālikite. Despite al-Bāqillānī, and perhaps one or two others, there was no close association of the Mālikites with any particular theological school; but some Mālikite jurists discussed theological doctrines and produced creeds after the fashion of Aḥmad b. Ḥanbal.

It is in the Ḥanafite *madhhab* that there is most evidence of an interest in theology, including Kalām. It is to be borne in mind that for many decades after the death of Abū Ḥanīfa the Ḥanafites were not a unified school of jurisprudence, but a widespread movement which included several teachers lecturing in different centres. Among the Ḥanafites there were some who were strongly opposed to the whole method of Kalām, and there is evidence for this by the reign of Hārūn al-Rashīd and perhaps a little earlier. One such was Abū Yūsuf (d. 182/798), who played an important part in the creation of the *madhhab*; he accused Ḍirār of *zandaqa*, presumably because of his practice of Kalām, and was furious when his pupil Bishr al-Marīsī became an expert in Kalām. Two Ḥanafites who died ten or twenty years before Abū Yūsuf are reported to have made attacks on the sect of the Jahmiyya (Ibrāhīm b. Ṭahmān of Khurasan, and Nūḥ b. Abī Maryam al-Jāmiʿ who was qadi of Merv), but it is difficult to know what is meant by Jahmite views by these men at that time.[258] The first form of *Al-fiqh al-akbar,* which Wensinck thought might go back to Abū Ḥanīfa himself, denounces the denial of the punishment of the tomb by the Jahmiyya. It is not clear why this point receives special attention, but the most likely view is that it was somehow connected with a discussion of the ultimate fate of sinners who were believers; and, if so, it would be linked with the Muʿtazilite principle of *al-waʿd wa-l-waʿīd*.

Bishr al-Marīsī is said to have been the first person to teach that the Qur'ān was created. According to a Ḥanbalite source he was also the first to spread a 'Jahmi doctrine' (*maqāla jahmiyya*); but this is probably the same point, since for the Ḥanbalites the term 'Jahmi' meant primarily acceptance of the doctrine that the Qur'ān was created. The deep division of the Ḥanafis over the question of Kalām reappears at the time of the Miḥna. As is not surprising in the case of people who called themselves *Ahl al-Ra'y*, there were among the judges who administered the Miḥna at least seven Ḥanafites, including Aḥmad b. Abī Du'ād, the chief qadi. A grandson of Abū Ḥanīfa, who was also a qadi, Ismāʿīl b. Ḥammād, is said to have accepted the doctrine of the createdness of the Qur'ān when the matter was first raised by al-Ma'mūn, but died shortly afterwards (about 212/827). On the other hand, there were Ḥanafites who rigorously opposed official doctrine, notably Bishr b. al-Walīd al-Kindī who refused to make the required declaration and in consequence suffered somewhat.[259]

Unfortunately, despite all this information about the Ḥanafites, it is impossible to discover much about the teaching of rational theology or Kalām by those who approved of it. The creed of al-Ṭaḥāwī (who died about the same time as al-Ashʿarī but as a very old man) appears to represent the views of those who disapproved of Kalām.[260] The creeds which take more account of the rational discussion of theological doctrines, the *Waṣiyya* and the second form of *Al-fiqh al-akbar*,[261] are anonymous; and the biographical dictionaries, though they have many names, have little information about teacher-pupil affiliation. In this absence of information it might perhaps be concluded that the Ḥanafite form of Kalām was taught along with Ḥanafite jurisprudence. Something of this sort appears to be the case in Samarqand where the theological school of al-Māturīdī developed, but even here there is little information.

Although little is known about the organization of Ḥanafite theological teaching, it is clear that it took place in several different cities and that there was some communication between these. A number of Ḥanafite creeds are extant and these bear a family likeness to one another which marks them off from Ḥanbalite and Ashʿarite creeds.[262] One of the test points is whether faith is indivisible (as Abū Ḥanīfa had said), or whether it increases and decreases. Much remains mysterious, however, about the Ḥanafite study of Kalām, perhaps because of the habit of the members of the *madhhab* of seeking anonymity – for example by ascribing later creeds to Abū Ḥanīfa himself. This last matter could conceivably have been a result of the divisions arising from the question of the permissibility of Kalām. Certainly all the Ḥanafite Mutakallimūn whose names are known (after the 4th/10th century) seem to belong to the school of al-Māturīdī in Samarqand.[263] On the other hand, Ḥanafite Kalām in general and individual writers are not mentioned by Ashʿarites until the 8th/14th century. It was only at this late date that the idea gained currency of al-Ashʿarī and al-Māturīdī as two parallel leaders of Sunnite Kalām. This neglect of the Ḥanafites, however, might be due to the contempt of metropolitans for provincials, since the Māturīdites mention the Ashʿarites about half a century after al-Ashʿarī's death (in *Sharḥ al-fiqh al-akbar* ascribed to al-Māturīdī).

The close relationship between the Ḥanafites and the Muʿtazilites is seen in the case of Bishr al-Marīsī; but there are some pieces of evidence which show that the relationship continued for at least about a century. The important Muʿtazilite of Baghdad, al-Kaʿbī, was reckoned a Ḥanafite in *fiqh*. There is also the curious fact that al-Ashʿarī is claimed by the Ḥanafites as well as by the Shāfiʿites. There is nothing surprising, however, in a student of Kalām under al-Jubbāʾī also attending lectures in *fiqh* by a Ḥanafite. It is also not impossible that at some period he attended lectures by a Shāfiʿite. The matter is obscure, however; his Ḥanafite teacher is not named, while the Shāfiʿite named by al-Subkī receives no notice in al-Subkī's own *Ṭabaqāt al-Shāfiʿiyya*. In so far as any conclusion can be drawn here, it is that the Muʿtazilite teaching of Kalām was not closely linked with any teaching of *fiqh*.

Finally, something may be said about the development of the Ashʿarite school of Kalām. When al-Ashʿarī left the Muʿtazila he presumably did not go into the wilderness, as it were. Nor is it likely that, although he was attracted to Ḥanbalite views, he became attached to any Ḥanbalite school. It appears, however, that Kalām was being cultivated by a group of followers of Ibn Kullāb, of whom the most prominent may have been al-Qalānisī, and it is likely that al-Ashʿarī became associated with this group. It appears that he did some lecturing in Kalām, since three men of the next generation are named as having studied under him, and these three were in turn the teachers of three notable Ashʿarites, al-Bāqillānī, Ibn Fūrak and al-Isfarāʾinī. Despite this teaching it seems likely that he was in some respects subordinate to al-Qalānisī. The heresiographer al-Baghdādī, who reckons himself an Ashʿarite, can nevertheless speak of al-Qalānisī as 'our shaykh', and at one point seems to make him the leader of a sub-group of the Ashʿariyya by using the phrase 'al-Qalānisī and those of our associates who followed him'. In a matter where there is much obscurity it seems clear that al-Qalānisī and al-Ashʿarī must both have been lecturing on Kalām about the same time. It is not impossible

– though there is no real evidence for it – that al-Qalānisī was mainly in Baghdad, while al-Ashʿarī was in Basra. If for a time there were two distinct groups, they must soon have been merged into one, since the geographer al-Maqdisī, writing in 985, says that the Kullābiyya have been absorbed into the Ashʿariyya. Ibn Fūrak, who died in 406/1015, and whose *Ṭabaqāt al-mutakallimīn* is the primary historical source for the early history of Ashʿarism, also wrote a book comparing al-Ashʿarī with al-Qalānisī; and it may be surmised that this book led to general acknowledgement of the superiority of al-Ashʿarī and the neglect of al-Qalānisī.[264]

From the various points that have been made here it would seem to be possible to draw the following conclusions. In the schools of the legal *madhāhib,* notably those of the Ḥanbalites and Mālikites, and probably also those of the conservative Ḥanafites, there was no discussion of Kalām or philosophical theology. A possible exception is the Māturīdite school of Kalām at Samarqand which was closely associated with the school of Ḥanafite jurisprudence; but there is little information about this. For the most part Kalām seems to have been cultivated in separate institutions, at least until the middle of the 5th/11th century. The schools of the Muʿtazilites are a clear example of this, and probably also those of the Ashʿarites.

Original Sources of Publication of the Articles

PART A

1 *Muslim World*, xlii (1952). 160-71.
2 *La Vie du Prophète Mahomet* (Colloque de Strasbourg, 1980), Strasbourg, 1983, 31-43.
3 *Journal of the Royal Asiatic Society*, 1957, 46-56.
4 *Journal of the American Academy of Religion*, xlvii (1979). 721-31.
5 *Muslim World*, xliii (1953). 110-17.
6 *Ex orbe religionum*, ed. C. J. Bleeker, vol. ii, Leiden, Brill, 1972, 155-8.
7 *The Muslim East: Studies in Honour of Julius Germanus*, ed. Gy. Kaldy-Nagy, Budapest, 1974, 31-4.
8 *Iran and Islam*, ed. C. E. Bosworth, Edinburgh U.P., 1971, 565-74.
9 *Malik Ram Felicitation Volume*, New Delhi, 1972, 155-7.
10 *Muslim World*, lvii (1967), 197-201.
11 *Journal of Semitic Studies*, ii (1957), 360-5.

PART B

1 *Transactions of the Glasgow University Oriental Society*, xvi (1957), 50-62.
2 *Transactions of the G.U.O.S.*, xiii (1951), 1-10.
3 *Transactions of the G.U.O.S.*, xviii (1962), 38-49.
4 *Islamic Quarterly*, viii (1961), 3-10; ix (1962), 31-9.
5 *Journal of the Royal Asiatic Society*, 1943, 234-47.
6 *Islamwissenschaftliche Abhandlungen*, ed. R. Gramlich, Wiesbaden, 1974, 306-11.
7 *Recherches d'Islamologie*, Louvain, Peeters, 1978, 381-7.
8 *Arabic and Islamic Studies in Honor of Hamilton A. R. Gibb*, ed. G. Makdisi, Leiden, Brill, 1965, 638-54.
9 *Studia Islamica* xxxi (1970). 287-98.
10 *Religion and Politics in Iran*, ed. Nikki R. Keddie, New Haven, 1983, 21-32.
11 *Theology and Law in Islam*, ed. G. E. von Grunebaum, Wiesbaden, 1971, 25-36.
12 *Revue des Etudes Islamiques*, xliv (1976). 15-21.

Permission to reproduce the articles from the above sources is gratefully acknowledged.

Transliterations, etc, have been standardized to conform with the present practice of Edinburgh University Press, but a few discrepancies remain.

Notes

1 Cf., Schacht, *Origins of Muḥammadan Jurisprudence,* 40f. This present article is in part an attempt to consider how his methods and conclusions affect the study of historical traditions.

2 *Ib.*, 57, etc.

3 Cf., Goldziher, *Muhammedanische Studien,* II, 112, etc.

4 *Ib.*, II, 140 quoting from al-Tirmidhī, I, 44, 8 and II, 333.

5 *Ṭabaqāt*, V, 226.

6 There is some doubt whether two other alleged grandsons of Sa'd b. Mu'ādh, Wāqid b. 'Abd al-Raḥmān and Wāqid b. 'Amr. are distinct persons (*Tahdhīb,* XI. nos. 183, 184); so there may be a mistake in the name here.

7 Ibn Ḥajar, *Tahdhīb*, VII, no. 488; cp. Ibn Athīr, *Usd,* IV, 15.

8 *Op. cit.*, 170.

9 In *Historians of the Middle East,* ed. B. Lewis and P. M. Holt, London, 1962, 23-34.

10 Patricia Crone and Michael Cook, *Hagarism, The Making of the Islamic World*, Cambridge, 1977; John Wansbrough, *Quranic Studies, Sources and Methods of Scriptural Interpretation,* London, 1977.

11 'Materials', 23, quoting from Becker, *Islamstudien*, Leipzig, 1924, i. 520 f. (reprinted from *Der Islam*, iv (1913), 263 ff.).

12 *Le problème de Mahomet*, Paris, 1952.

13 *Geschichte des arabischen Schrifttums,* i. 275-287.

14 Ed. Wüstenfeld, 973-999.

15 Cf. 'Materials', 32.

16 *Muhammedanische Studien,* Halle, 1889, i. 89-93 (also in Eng. tr.).

17 Watt, *Muhammad at Medina*, Oxford, 1956, 202, with reff.

18 *Sīra*, ed. Wüstenfeld, 573 f.

19 Cf. report from Yāqūt, *Irshād*, i. 36, in *EI*^{2}, art. Abān.

20 Edinburgh University Press, 1953.

21 Cf. *Introduction to the Qur'ān,* 115 f.

22 *Translation,* 635; *Introduction*, 131.

23 *Introduction,* 130.

24 A. Guthrie and E. F. F. Bishop, 'The Paraclete, Almunhamanna and Aḥmad', *Muslim World*, xli (1951), 251-6 esp. 255.

25 *Usd al-Ghāba*, iv, 310, s.v. Muḥammad b. Uḥayḥa.

26 Ibn Sa'd, v. 50; cf. iii. 1.66f.; 'Umar is also said to have asked those called after prophets to change their names, ib., v. 2.2.

27 *Die Person Muhammeds*, Uppsala, 1917, 273.

28 Ibn Sa'd, i. 1.64.

29 150 (ed. Wüstenfeld).

30 Ibn Sa'd, i. 1.64; cf. ib., i. 2.89, where 'Utayba occurs instead.

31 Ibn Sa'd, i. 2.89.

32 119.

33 *Woodbrooke Studies*, ii. 33ff.

34 Quoted from M. J. Lagrange, *Évangile selon S. Marc,* Paris, 1911, on 10.25.
35 Goldziher, *Muhammedanische Studien*, Halle, 1890, ii. 385, n. 1. Cf. Lane, *Lexicon*.
36 The interpretation 'rope' without reading or *isnād* is found in the *Tafsīr* of Sufyān al-Thawrī (d. 788), published at Rampur in 1965.
37 See Goldziher, *Koranauslegung,* 107-10.
38 Art. 'Ikrima in *EI*².
39 Cf. Lane, *Arabic-English Lexicon*, s.v.
40 Glaser, *Corpus Inscriptionum Himyariticarum*, no. 618, dated 543 A.D. (quoted from R. Blachère, *Le Coran*, Paris, 1949, II, 241n.).
41 Cf. Nöldeke-Schwally-Bergsträsser, *Geschichte des Qorans*, III, 148n.1; 210n.6; Ibn Mujāhid had 84 assistants to whom the term *khalīfa* was applied. In Ottoman Turkish the word was applied to quite humble persons; cf. J. W. Redhouse, *Turkish-English Lexicon,* s,v,
42 See p. 63 below.
43 I am indebted for this material to a post-graduate student, Dr Awn al-Sharīf Qāsim of Khartoum. The editions referred to are: Jarīr, *Dīwān*, Beirut, 1960; al-Farazdaq, *Dīwān*, Beirut 1960, two vols. These are indicated by 'J.' and 'F.' respectively.
44 F. I, 70, 144.
45 F. I, 264; cf. 262.
46 F. II, 282; I, 124.
47 F. I, 25.
48 F. I, 285.
49 F. II, 309. Banū 'Abd-Manāf are regarded as responsible for the blood of Muḥammad in Ibn Hishām, 325.
50 F. I, 62.
51 F. II, 210.
52 In the passage from the *Musnad* mentioned in note 17, Abū Bakr, 'Umar and 'Uthmān appear to have held a *khilāfat nubuwwa*, which was then followed by *mulk*. One wonders if this is derived from Umayyad propaganda which denied that 'Alī had ever been caliph.
53 J, 380
54 F. I, 22.
55 Cf. Goldziher, *Muhammedanische Studien*, II, 31; also Aḥmad b. Ḥanbal, *Musnad*, V, 44, 50f., etc.
56 F. I, 348.
57 F. I, 24.
58 J, 380.
59 F. II, 76, addressing Sulaymān; the mountains are described as *awtād* in the Qur'ān.
60 J, 278.
61 J, 21.
62 Wellhausen, *Arab Kingdom*, 238; Ibn Ḥajar, *Tahdhīb,* II, 210f.
63 J, 355.
64 F. I, 22; F. I, 47; F. II, 312; J, 195; etc. The opponents considered themselves *mu'minīn* (Ṭabarī, II, 1066).
65 Cf. J. 195, 210 f., 303; there are also phrases like *amīn Allāh* and *rā'ī Allāh*. Also Ḥassān b. Thābit, *Dīwān*, 98.15 (in elegy on 'Uthmān) or ed. H. Hirschfeld, XX, 9; *Aghānī,* XV, 6 (of 'Abd-al-Malik), XVIII, 71 (*banī khulafā' Allāh* used of Umayyads in presence of Mu'āwiya I); al-Ṭabarī, II, 78.10 (used of Mu'āwiya I by the poet Ḥāritha b. Badr); al-Mas'ūdī, *Murūj*, V, 105 (of Mu'āwiya), 152 (of Yazīd I), 330 (of 'Abd-al-Malik).
66 I. Goldziher, 'Du sens propre des expressions Ombre de Dieu, Khalife

de Dieu pour désigner les chefs dans l'Islam', *Revue de l'Histoire des Religions*, XXXV (1879) 331-8, esp. 337.

67 *Muhammedanische Studien*, II, 61.

68 *Aghānī* III, 95.5; IX, 44.4; XXI, 28.5. Al-ʿIqd, III, 30.3 (from foot), 32.14. Al-Ṭabarī, III, 2177.9, in an edict of al-Muʿtaḍid (regn. 892-902) the ʿAbbāsids are called *khulafā' Allāh wa-a'immat al-hudā*. (The references here and in note 65, apart from J, are from *Muhammedanische Studien,* II, 61, but not all have been verified.) There are some instances of the use of the phrase for Ottoman and Indian rulers in T. W. Arnold, *The Caliphate*, Oxford, 1924, 117, 157, 158. Khalīfa b. Khayyāṭ (d. 241/855) quotes the Khārijite, al-Yashkurī, as taunting the caliph al-Mahdī with claiming to be 'caliph of God'. (*Ta'rīkh*, fol. 310, quoted from a London thesis by Farouk Omar; not in *G.A.L.*)

69 *Al-ʿIqd*, V, 332 f.

70 Al-Māwardī, *Statuts Gouvernementaux*, tr. Fagnan, 29 f.; cf. Ibn Khaldūn, *Muqaddima*, tr. Rosenthal, I, 388 f.

71 I, 10.

72 Al-Dhahabī, *Tadhkirat al-Ḥuffāẓ* (Hyderabad 1955) I, 101.

73 In this question the word 'orthodox' is to be taken in a general sense, and not as referring specifically to the Holy Eastern Orthodox Church. It should even be provisionally extended to include Nestorians and Monophysites, since the question should be left open whether Islam is closer to, say, Nestorianism, than to any other Christian doctrine.

74 Cf. Watt, 'The Early Development of the Muslim Attitude to the Bible', *Transactions of the Glasgow University Oriental Society*, xvi (1957). 50-62, esp. 50-53 (reproduced below).

75 Cf. 3.51/44; 5.117.

76 Philippians, 2.7; cf. Parrinder, 34-37, with fuller references.

77 4.153/2 – 159/7, esp. 157/6.

78 Originally read as a paper to the Association of British Orientalists, Cambridge, September 1956.

79 The ostensible date of the *Risāla* is the caliphate of al-Maʿmūn (813-33), but some of the technical theological terms used suggest that it was written in the early tenth century; cf. G. Graf, *Geschichte der christlichen arabischen Literatur*, II, 135-45

80 Cf. the summary of discussions by A. Jeffery, *The Foreign Vocabulary of the Qur'ān*, Baroda, 1938, 114.

81 Théodore Abū Qurra, *Traité Inédit sur l'Existence de Dieu*. . . (ed. L. Cheikho, Beirut, 1912), p. 12. Abū Ṣāliḥ (thirteenth century), *The Churches and Monasteries of Egypt,* ed. and tr. B. T. A. Evetts, 230f. Cf. *Kitāb al-Burhān*, ascribed to Eutychius (Saʿīd ibn Biṭrīq) – Graf, *op. cit.* II, 35-8 – ad init. (to be published in *Corpus Scriptorum Christianorum Orientalium)*. Other occurrences have been reported to the writer but the references are not available.

82 Cf. R. Bell, *The Origin of Islam in its Christian Environment*, London, 1926, 88; Jeffery, *op. cit.* 139. *Rūgzā* apparently occurs four times in the Syriac N.T. (Matt. iii. 7; Luke iii. 7, xxi. 23; John iii. 36), in each case with an eschatological connotation.

83 So also did Ibn Masʿūd (A. Jeffery, *Materials for the History of the Text of the Qur'ān*, Leiden, 1937, 105); this is curious because *rujz* is said to be a Hudhalī form (al-Suyūṭī, *Itqān*, Cairo, 1935/1354, I. 134; cf. Jeffery, *Foreign Vocabulary,* 139), and yet Ibn Masʿūd was a Hudhalī!

84 E.g. *Lisān al-ʿArab*; cf. Lane.

85 Al-Ṭabarī (XXIX. 80 on 74. 5) seems to assert that al-Kisā'ī distinguished *rijz* as 'punishment' or 'conduct leading to punishment' from *rujz* as 'idols'; but he regards this view as mistaken.

86 Ibn Hishām, ed. Wüstenfeld, 477.
87 *Rijs* may mean 'punishment'; cf. Lane, *s.v.*, and Fakhr al-Dīn al-Rāzī, *Mafātīḥ al-Ghayb*, Istanbul, 1307, I. 537 (on 2. 59/56).
88 So the standard Egyptian text. Flügel vocalizes to read 'punishment of a painful *rijz*'.
89 Cf. al-Bayḍāwī on 45. 11/10 and 34. 5.
90 I. 234 (on 2. 59/56).
91 IX. 26 (on 7. 134/131); for *wa-lammā waqa'a 'alay-him al-rujz* he gives the paraphrase *wa-lammā nazala bi-him 'adhāb Allāh wa-ḥalla bi-him sukhṭu-hu.*
92 Cf. Abū 'l-Faḍl al-Mālikī (sixteenth century), *Disputatio pro Religione Mohammedanorum adversus Christianos* ed. F. J. van den Ham, Leiden, 1877-90, 10, l. 4, where the Muslim author uses the word *r-jz* in quoting Eph. v. 6.
93 2.42/39, 140/134, 146/141, 159/154, 174/169, 3.71/64; 5.15/18; 6.91; 2.76/71.
94 E.g. 11.18/21; cf. concordances.
95 Cf. 3.78/72; 10.59/60; 16.116/117.
96 Cf. Richard Bell, *Translation of Qur'ān*, note to 2.93/87.
97 Cf. A. Jeffery, *The Foreign Vocabulary of the Qur'ān*, s.v.
98 3.78/72; cf. 79/73
99 Cf. 2.79/73.
100 Ibn Sa'd, *Ṭabaqāt*, i/2.89.14-25.
101 *Ib.*, i/1.104.5-10.
102 Ibn Hishām, ed. Wüstenfeld, 395; Ibn Isḥāq gives this on the authority of Sāliḥ b. Kaysān, who died after 757/140 and was a pupil of al-Zuhrī (d. *c.* 741/124), the authority for the main account of the incident.
103 *Ib.*, 135.
104 *Ib.*, 286 f.; cf. 134, 373 f.
105 Ibn Sa'd, i/1.105.23-106.8; 108.22-109.1; 107.12-15.
106 *Ib.*, 111.18-21, etc.
107 *Ib.*, i/1.104.17-20; i/2.87.21-88.14; Ibn Hishām, 135 f., 353, 354.
108 Ibn Hishām, 354, 393 f.; Ibn Sa'd, i/1.104.10-20; 107-25-108.11.
109 *Ib.*, i/1, 103.17-104.5.
110 Ibn Hishām, 115-17; Ibn Sa'd, i/1.99-101; cf. the story of Muḥammad's recognition by two unnamed monks, ib. 98.27-99.11.
111 Ibn Hishām, 136-42.
112 Ibn Sa'd, i/1.108.11-22.
113 *Ib.*, 104.21-105.11; cf. Ibn Hishām, 135 f.
114 Cf. J. Schacht, art. 'Zinā'' in EI(S).
115 Ibn Hishām, 393-95.
116 E.g. Ibn Qutayba, *Ta'wīl Mukhtalif al-Ḥadīth,* Cairo, 1908/1326, 356-62. Cf. Goldziher, *Koranauslegung,* 58-61.
117 E.g. al-Ṭabarī, i, 278 (on 2.75/70); v. 70 f. (on 4.46/48).
118 Ibn Sa'd, i/2.88.14-24; al Ṭabarī, *Tafsīr*, ix.53 (on 7.156); al-Bukhārī, *Ṣaḥīḥ*, 65 (on 48.8). Cf. also Ibn Sa'd, i/2.87.2-6, 6-10, 10-13, 13-21; 89.2-5, 11-14.
119 Ibn Hishām, 150.
120 A. Guthrie and E. F. F. Bishop, 'The Paraclete, Almunhammana and Aḥmad', *Muslim World*, xli (1951), 251-56.
121 'His Name is Aḥmad', *Muslim World*, xliii (1953), 110-17 (reproduced above).
122 A. Mingana, *Woodbrooke Studies,* ii.33-38; cf. L. Cheikho and E. Batarekh, *Trois Traités Anciens. . . ,* Beirut, 1923, 11-14.
123 E. Fritsch, *Islam und Christentum im Mittelalter,* Breslau, 1930, 77, quoting from C. Brockelmann, *Beiträge zur Assyriologie*, iii.48-54 and

ZATW, xv (1895), 138-42.

124 *K. al-Dīn wa-'l-Dawlah,* ed. A. Mingana, Manchester, 1923; cf. Fritsch, l.c.

125 *ZATW*, xiii (1893), 315-22, 'Über Bibelcitate in muhammedanischen Schriften'; the statement that Ibn Qutayba asserted that in the Torah ivory was said to swim in vinegar and to act as a charm against pregnancy is mistaken – some words were omitted from the text used by Goldziher; cf. Ibn Qutayba, *op. cit.* 294.

126 *Jāmiʻ Bayān al-ʻIlm*, Cairo, n.d., ii. 40-43.

127 *Ib.*, 41.4-18, 20-24 – various versions; there are also similar traditions in al-Bukhārī.

128 Ibn ʻAbd al-Barr, 42.3-5, given as an addition to a previous tradition which forbids questioning.

129 *Ib.*, 41.1-3.

130 *Ib.*, 42.5-7.

131 *Ib.*, 40.18-22; 42.1-3.

132 *Ib.*, 42.8-17; cf. 41.18-20; 42.23-25.

133 *Ib.*, 42.17-23.

134 Cf. C. Becker, *Islamstudien,* i.435.

135 For later developments of the attitude cf. Fritsch, *op. cit.*; J. W. Sweetman, *Islam and Christian Theology*, ii/1.178-308; I. di Matteo in *Bessarione*, xxxviii (1922), and xxxix (1923); I. Goldziher in *ZDMG*, xxxii (1878), 341-87. Christian precedents of the idea of corrupting the scriptures are discussed by E. F. F. Bishop, 'Al-Tahrif', *Bulletin of the Henry Martyn School of Islamic Studies,* April-June, 1956, 9-15, esp. 2 Cor. ii. 17, iv. 2; Gal. i. 7; 2 Pet. iii.16.

136 I. Goldziher, *Muhammedanische Studien,* ii. 386; Mark 9.50 appears as a verse of poetry in *Iḥyā'*, Cairo, 1316, i, 53.

137 Ibn Qutayba, *Ta'wīl Mukhtalif al-Ḥadīth,* Cairo, 1908/1326, 277, ascribes this treatment of the (presumed) first form of the Tradition to Aṣḥāb al-Kalām. Cf. al-Qasṭallānī (ix. 144) on al-Bukhārī, *Isti'dhān* (79), 1; also al-Nawawī on Muslim, *Birr* (45), 115.

138 Cf. al-Baghdādī, *Uṣūl al-Dīn*, 74-6; he emphasizes that Adam was created as a mature being and did not develop from sperm.

139 Fakhr-al-Dīn al-Rāzī, *As'as al-Taqdīs*, Cairo, 1935/1354, 84-6.

140 This date is inferred from the *isnāds* of the Traditions, by making various assumptions along the lines of the theory of Joseph Schacht. In the case of the Traditions given by Ibn Khuzayma, *Tawḥid*, Cairo, 1935/1354, 26-9, the effective name appears to be Muḥammad ibn ʻAjlān of Medina, who died in 765/148 (and others of about this date), though it is also possible that the preceding persons in the *isnāds* (i.e. who died between 735 and 750, such as Saʻīd ibn Abī-Saʻīd, Qatāda, Abū Zinad) may have known the Tradition in something like its later form. It is noteworthy, however, that Ibn Khuzayma says (p. 26 last two lines; add *ʻan* between Yaḥyā and Ibn ʻAjlān) that the mention of the creation of Adam was absent from Ibn ʻAjlān's Tradition; this might lead one to think that a later generation was responsible for the addition, but that seems to be excluded by the different lines of transmission from Ibn ʻAjlān,

141 Ibn Khuzayma, *loc. cit.* Muslim, *Birr* (45), 115.

142 Fakhr-al-Dīn al-Rāzī, 83 f.

143 Ibn Qutayba, *op. cit.*, 277 f.; al-Ghazālī, *Imlā'* (on margin of al-Zabīdī, *It ḥāf al-Sāda*, i), 219 (also in F. Jabre, *Notion de la Maʻrifa chez Ghazali,* Beirut, 1958, 204).

144 Cf. note 139 above.

145 Al-Bukhārī, *Ist'idhān* (79), 1; Ibn Ḥanbal, *Musnad*, ii, 315. It is to be noted that al-Bukhārī received from a different informant what is

essentially the same Tradition, but with the words 'in his form' omitted. A very similar Tradition is found in Ibn Ḥanbal, ii. 323 and Ibn Khuzayma, 29. 1-2; but a note at the end of Ibn Ḥanbal's version suggests that the words 'his height being sixty ells' may be an addition.

146 J. W. Sweetman, *Islam and Christian Theology*, London, 1945, i/I. 32n. refers to Epiphanius, *Haeresibus,* xix. 4, where ideas about the Heavenly Man or Adam are applied to Christ, conceived of as an angel of huge size.

147 Ibn Qutayba, 278.

148 Ibn Khuzayma, 27. Cf. al-Ghazālī, *Mishkāt al-Anwār,* Cairo, 1904/1322, 24, 34 (translation by W. H. T. Gairdner, 65, 75 f.); Fakhr-al-Dīn al-Rāzī, 87. These versions are usually ascribed to Ibn 'Umar.

149 H. Laoust, *La Profession de Foi d'Ibn Baṭṭa,* Damascus, 1958, 57 (tr. 104). The beginning of the sentence is an abbreviated reference to the Tradition as it is usually given.

150 *Op. cit.*, 279 f. The Ḥanbalites, to whom Ibn Qutayba was close, seem generally to have adopted the same view; cf. Laoust, *op. cit.*, 104, n. 4.

151 'Ubayd ibn Mihrān al-Mukattib al-Kūfī, in al-Shahrastānī, *Milal*, Cairo, 1948/1368, i. 224. Cf. al-Ash'arī, *Maqālāt*, i. 153.

152 *Maqālāt*, i. 34, 152 f.; al-Baghdādī, *Al-Farq bayn al-Firaq*, 216; *Uṣūl al-Dīn*, 74-6; al-Nawbakhtī, 61. The view seems to have been begun by Muqātil ibn Sulaymān (d. 767), who was followed a little later by Hishām ibn Sālim al-Jāwālīqī and his pupil Dāwūd al-Jawāribī. Both Muqātil and 'Ubayd were pupils of Mujāhid (d. 722).

153 95, 4, 'we have created man in the finest form (*taqwīm*)'. The Tradition is given in *Uṣūl al-Dīn*, *loc. cit.* as *'alā ṣūrati-hi.*

154 Aḥmad ibn Ḥā'it (d. 841-6). Cf. al-Baghdādī, *Farq*, 260 (tr. Halkin, 99, with further references); al-Khayyāṭ, *K. al-Intiṣār*, ed. Nyberg, 223 f. Other sectaries who spoke of God in the *ṣūra* of man are al-Muqanna' (d.c. 779) and Abū Ḥulmān (d. 951); cf. *Farq*, 243-6, etc.

155 *Rasā'il al-Kindī al-Falsafiyya,* Cairo, 1950/1369, 276. Al-Kindī has just been referring to a Greek author whom the editor identifies as Pythagoras. On p. 273 he said of the soul that 'its *jawhar* is a divine, spiritual *jawhar*'. This would appear to be reason, and it is conceived as having in itself, when purified, the forms of all other things – just as a polished mirror has the forms of all visible objects.

156 *Ḥayy ibn Yaqẓān*, ed. Jamil Saliba and Kamil 'Ayyad, Damascus, 1939/1358, 83 f.; cf. 116 ff.

157 Louis Massignon, *Passion d'al-Ḥallāj,* 527, with references to several verses of the Qur'ān used by al-Ḥallāj.

158 *Ib.,* 485; cf. 599, predetermination of Adam's *ṣūra*. In 482n. Massignon refers to the discussion between Imāmite theologians and the philosophers; the Imāmites understood *ṣūra* as 'corporeal appearance', whereas for the philosophers it was 'spiritual form'.

159 E.g. according to al-Ghazālī (*Imlā'*, i. 172) al-Shiblī (d. 945) held that the Tradition meant that Adam was created according to God's names and attributes, not according to his essence; this may indicate an attempt to move closer to the theologians.

160 *Imlā'*, i. 219 ff. (the whole passage is in Jabre, *Ma'rifa,* 204-6). In *Iḥyā'*, iv. 251 f. (Jabre, *Ma'rifa,* 192 f.) al-Ghazālī speaks of an affinity and resemblance (*munāsaba, mushākala*) between man and God, and of man's duty to imitate God and to be characterized by the characters of God (*takhalluq bi-akhlāq Allāh*); cf. *Al-Maqṣad al-Asnā, passim* (Jabre, *Ma'rifa*, 196-203).

161 *Iḥyā'*, iv. 205 (Jabre, 189 f.).

162 *Imlā'*, i. 219-22; the continuation of the passage is on pp. 171-4.

163 Cf. *Mishkāt al-Anwār*, 34 (tr. 75), where al-Ghazālī claims that the

proper version of the Tradition when thus interpreted is 'in the form of the Merciful'; but on p. 7 of the same work he had quoted the version 'in his form', so that he cannot have rejected it completely.

164 Cf. n. 139 above. Al-Juwaynī (al-Ghazālī's teacher) in *Irshād*, 93 (tr. 155), argues against the Ḥashwiyya that the pronominal suffix refers either to the man beaten or to Adam. At an earlier period the Muʿtazila had been vigorous opponents of *tashbīh* and of the naive conception of *ṣura* (al-Khayyāṭ, *Intiṣār*, 5, 7, 144-8).

165 7.10; 40.66 (64.3); 59. 24; 3.4. Al-Bayḍāwī on the first of these passages notes that God's creation and *taṣwīr* precede the command to the angels to worship Adam.

166 82.8.

167 Al-Taftazānī, *Commentary on the Creed of Islam* (tr. E. E. Elder), 43; God is not *muṣawwar*, because this involves quantities and qualities.

168 *Muqaddima* (ed. E. Quatremère, iii. 41, tr. F. Rosenthal, iii. 52).

169 Quoted from the edition by R. J. McCarthy, Beirut, 1957.

170 Quoted from the edition, with translation, of J. D. Luciani, Paris, 1938.

171 The translation is made from the Istanbul edition of 1928/1346.

172 Cf. Montgomery Watt, *Free Will and Predestination in Early Islam*, 74, etc.

173 *Tamhīd*, p. 6; *Irshād*, p. 7; criticized by al-Ījī, ap. al-Jurjānī, op. cit. i. 71.

174 Cf. also Wensinck, *Muslim Creed*, 251 f.; M. Horten, *Spekulative and Positive Philosophie des Islam*, 213, 331f.

175 The correct forms appear to be: M. b. Ḥarb al-Ṣayrafī and M. b. ʿĪsā al-Sīrafī; this makes it very unlikely that the two men are identical. (added 1989).

176 Al-Jāḥiẓ, *Al-bayān wa-tabyīn*,Cairo, 1926, i. 36. The first transmitter, al-Muʿtamir b. Salāmān, is described as a Muʿtazilite by al-Masʿūdī, *Murūj*, vi. 372 f. For the author, see al-Masʿūdī, ii. 142 (he held both Nizār and the Persians descendants of Isaac); Ibn-Saʿd, vii/2. II (died 131/748). Al-Yaʿqūbī, *Taʾrīkh*, Baghdad, 1960, ii. 363 says (wrongly) he was a *faqīh* in the time of al-Maʾmūn.

177 Al-Baghdādī, K. *al-farq bayn al-firaq*, Cairo, 1910, 98 f.

178 *Maqālāt*, i. 104, 110; for the matters discussed in this paragraph cf. *Der Islam*, xxxvi [1961]. 223-6.

179 *Maqālāt*, i. 105; cf. al-Khayyāṭ, *Intiṣār* (ed. Nyberg), 164-8.

180 *Maqālāt* i. 104 f.

181 *RSO*, vii 455-60.

182 The most plausible suggestion is that of Vanna Cremonesi, in 'Un antico documento ibāḍita sul Corano creato', *Studi Magrebini* (Naples), i. (1966). 133-78, esp. 159 f.; the essential suggestion is that the Ibāḍites of the Maghrib continued to be in close contact with the Ibāḍites of Basra.

183 *Maqālāt*, i. 104; *Farq*, 84; al-Shahrastānī, *Milal*, 101. For Ḥamza al-Kūfī see art. 'Ibāḍiyya' in *EI*², iii. 651.

184 *Farq*, 76-80; cf. *Maqālāt*, i. 93 f.; al-Masʿūdī, *Murūj*, viii. 42; al-Shahrastānī, 96.

185 Ed. de Goeje, 80.5; 84.8 (quoted from Nallino in *RSO*, vii. 453).

186 Details in *RSO*, vii. 454.

187 Quoted from Vanna Cremonesi in *Studi Magrebini*, i. 159.

188 *Description de l'Afrique septentrionale*, ed. De Slane, Algiers, 1910, 72 (Arabic text).

189 From al-Jāḥiẓ, *Bayān*, i. 37 f. (in other editions pp. 14f., 25 f.) I am indebted to my colleague Dr. Pierre Cachia for the translation (in line 2 he reads *mukhāṭir*; in the last line *ʿilm*). The second last line yields no reasonable meaning as it stands, and has been omitted. Various difficulties require discussion, but they are not directly relevant to the

points made in this article.
190 *EI*[2], art. 'Ibāḍiyya', 650B.
191 Ibn-al-Murtaḍā, *Ṭabaqāt al-Mu'tazila*, ed. S. Diwald-Wilzer, Wiesbaden, 1961, 32.
192 *Rivista degli studi orientali*, XXIV (1949). 31-44.
193 Details of the Khārijites during the Umayyad period will be found in Watt, *The Formative Period of Islamic Thought*, Edinburgh, 1973, ch. 1.
194 *The Religio-Political Factions in Early Islam*, Engl. trad. Amsterdam, 1975. 80.
195 Veccia Vaglieri, *op. cit.*, 32f.: T. Lewicki. art. 'al-Ibāḍiyya', in *EI*[2], iii.
196 Veccia Vaglieri, *op. cit.*, 39f.; cf. Ibn al-Athīr, years 178, 252, 254, 255, 256, 263, 267, 272, 273, 279, 282, 283.
197 Ibn al-Athīr, years 179, 180, 185, 192; Al-Shahrastānī, *Milal* (ed. Cureton), 96f.; Al-Ash'arī, *Maqālāt*, 93f.; Al-Baghdādī, *Farq.*, 76-80.
198 Ibn-al-Athir, Cairo, 1353 A. H., vi. 210 (year 318).
199 *Op. cit.*, v. 355 (year 256).
200 *Op. cit.*, v. 70 (year 168).
201 'Shi'ism under the Umayyads', *Journal of the Royal Asiatic Society* (1960), 158-172; 'Political Attitudes of the Mu'tazilah', *ibid.* (1963); 'The Rāfiḍites', *Oriens*, XV (1962); *Islamic Philosophy and Theology* (Edinburgh, 1962), especially chap. 6; *Muslim Intellectual* (Edinburgh, 1963), especially chap. 4; 'The Muslim Yearning for a Saviour', *E. O. James Presentation Volume* (1963).
202 Cf. *GAL, suppl.* I, 319 f.; *Oriens,* VII, 204; *Der Islam*, XXXVII (1961), 43n.
203 Abbreviations used: Ash. = Al-Ash'arī, *Maqālāt al-islāmiyyīn*, ed. H. Ritter, Istanbul, 1929. Friedlaender = I. Friedlaender, 'The Heterodoxies of the Shī'ites. . .' *Journal of the American Oriental Society*, XXVIII (1907), 1-80; XXIX (1909), 1-183 (referred to respectively as I and II). *Intiṣār* = Al-Khayyāṭ, *K. al-Intiṣār*, ed. H. S. Nyberg, Cairo, 1925. Lewis, *Ismā'īlism* = Bernard Lewis, *The Origins of Ismā'īlism*, Cambridge, 1940.
204 A paper on a similar topic was read by the writer at the Meshhed Congress. The following abbreviations are used below:
List: *Tusy's List of Shy'ah Books* (cf. GAL[2], i. 512). I-Nadīm: Ibn al-Nadīm, *Fihrist*, ed. G. Flügel, Leipzig. 1871. Nawb: al-Ḥasan ibn Mūsā al-Nawbakhtī, *Firaq al-shī'a*, ed. H. Ritter, (Bibliotheca Islamica, 4), Leipzig, 1931.
205 For a further discussion of these matters cf. Watt, 'The Rāfiḍites', *Oriens*, xvi (1963), 110-21; *Islamic Political Thought, the Basic Concepts*, Edinburgh, 1968, 82-9.
206 *Murūj al-dhahab*, vi.368-76; Mītham is corrected from Haytham, and al-Sakkāk from al-Sakkāl (Shakkāl in I-Nadīm, 176 and al-Shahrastānī, *Milal*, ed. Cureton, 145), the latter in accordance with the clear note in *List*, 292, no. 634.
207 *List*, 355, no. 771; I-Nadīm, 175f.
208 *List*, 323, no. 698; I-Nadīm, 176.9-13.
209 Nawb:, 11.16; cf. *Intiṣār*, ed. Nyberg, 133.
210 Nawb., 15.
211 Nawb., 2.13; 6.3; 6.11f; 12.1-9. There are some variations in the Mu'tazilite attitude to 'Alī.
212 Nawb., 12.18; 19.1; 49.3.
213 Nawb., 13.14.
214 Cf. Nawb., 42.11.
215 *List*, 212, no. 458; I-Nadīm, 175.19-21; Nawb., 9.10-13.
216 *List*, 254f., no. 559; I-Nadīm, 231.20-3.

217 *List*,369, no. 810; I-Nadīm, 177.26-8.
218 *List*, 297f., no. 648; I-Nadīm, 176.17-19.
219 *List*, 371f., notes of ʿAlam al-Hudā.
220 Cf. H. Ritter, Introduction to *Firaq al-Shīʿa*, nos. 14 and 35 (quoting from al-Najāshī).
221 Cf. A. A. A. Fyzee, *A Shīʿite Creed*, London, 1942, chs. 32, 9, 7.
222 Nawb., 65f.; 72.13; 82.5; 93.5; 94.1. Cf. al-Shahrastānī, *Milal*, 126 (i.274), al-Aftaḥiyya.
223 *List*, 188 (no. 405); cf. Nawb., 67.3; 93.6.
224 *List*, 235 (no. 509).
225 *List*, 93f. (no. 191); I-Nadīm, 223, 5-8. He was Abū ʿAlī al-Ḥasan b. ʿAlī b. Faḍḍāl al-Taymulī.
226 *List*, 211 (no. 456); 231f. (no. 498).
227 *List*, 284 (no. 617); I-Nadīm, 223.9-12.
228 *List*, 311 (no. 675); I-Nadīm, 223.13-18. Cf. *List*, 211 (no. 455), another *ghālī*, perhaps a relative.
229 *List*, 46f. (no. 82); cf. 164, notice of Sahl al-Ādamī.
230 *List*, 188 (no. 405).
231 Nawb., 68.11-13; etc.
232 *List*, 216f. (no. 470); I-Nadīm, 177.22f.
233 *List*, 97f. (no. 205); I-Nadīm, 222.18-20.
234 *List*, 45f. (no. 81).
235 Cf. art. 'Abū 'l-Khaṭṭāb' (B. Lewis), *EI*².
236 *Passion*, Paris, 1922, i.144-50.
237 Since this study is a piece of interpretation rather than of primary research, detailed footnotes are out of place. For the period up to about 925 full references to the sources will be found in my book *The Formative Period of Islamic Thought* (Edinburgh: Edinburgh University Press, 1973).
238 *Formative Period*, chap. 2, 38-59.
239 *Ib.*, 157-62; also 162-66 (Zaydites); 186-89 (Hishām ibn al-Ḥakam).
240 *Ib.*, 274-78.
241 Louis Massignon, *La Passion d'al-Hallaj*², Paris: Gallimard, 1975; cf. my *The Majesty that was Islam*, London: Sidgwick & Jackson, 1974, 212-14.
242 I. Goldziher, 'Le dénombrement des sectes musulmanes', *Revue de l'Histoire des Religions,* XXVI (1892) 129 ff.; cf. *Vorlesungen über den Islam*, 2nd ed.; Heidelberg, 1925, 188 f.
243 Cf. A. J. Wensinck, *A Handbook of Early Muhammadan Tradition*, Leiden, 1927, s.v. 'Modesty'.
244 Cf. G. Lecomte, *Le traité des divergences du ḥadīt d'Ibn Qutayba*, Damascus, 1962, 91; R. J. McCarthy, *The Theology of al-Ashʿarī*, Beirut, 1953, 74 f. For ʿAmr cf. Ibn Khallikān, *Biographical Dictionary*, trans. Wm. MacGuckin de Slane, London, 1961, II, 395.
245 *Vorlesungen*, 189.
246 *The Muslim Creed*, Cambridge, 1932, 38.
247 *Ṭabaqāt*, vi.214, ed. E. Sachau *et al.*, London, 1905-1940.
248 Laura Veccia Vaglieri, 'Sulla denominazione Ḥawāriğ', *Rivista degli studi orientali,* xxvi (1951), 46.
249 Cf. H. Laoust, *La profession de foi d'Ibn Baṭṭa*, Damascus, 1958, 44n.
250 An earlier form of this paper was given in French at the Sorbonne in March 1968, and an abbreviated version at the Congress of Arabic Studies at Coimbra in September 1968.
251 *Tanbīh*, 30; for Ḍirār see J. van Ess, *Ḍirār b. ʿAmr und die 'Cahmīya'* in *Der Islam*, XLIII, 1967, 241-79; XLIV, 1968, 1-70, 318-20; also Watt, *Formative Period of Islamic Thought,* Edinburgh, 1973, 189-95.

252 *K. al-Intiṣār*, ed. H. S. Nyberg, Cairo, 1925, 126.
253 W. Madelung, *Der Imām al-Qāsim ibn Ibrāhīm*, Berlin, 1965.
254 Al-Khayyaṭ, *Intiṣār*, 134.
255 J. van Ess in *ZDMG*, CXXVI, 1976, 63; other references to Bishr al-Marīsī in *Formative Period*, 196-9.
256 References in *Formative Period,* 217-50.
257 Cf. *Formative Period*, 288, 304, n. 112.
258 Cf. *ib.*, 143-8.
259 Cf. *ib.*, 178 f., 280-6, etc.
260 Cf. *ib.*, 132, etc.
261 A. J. Wensinck, *The Muslim Creed*, Cambridge, 1932, 125-247.
262 Cf. *Formative Period*, 131-6.
263 Cf. *ib.*, 312 f.
264 Cf. *ib.*, 288, 311 f.

Bibliography

(Fuller bibliographical details are given here for references in the notes which were incomplete. In the alphabetical ordering the Arabic article al- is disregarded.)

Abū Ṣāliḥ, *The Churches and Monasteries of Egypt,* ed. and tr. B. T. A. Evetts, Oxford, 1894, 1895.

Aghānī: Abū 'l-Faraj al-Isfahānī, *Kitāb al-Aghānī*, twenty vols., Bulac 1285/1868.

Aḥmad ibn Ḥanbal, *Musnad*, six vols., Cairo 1313/1895.

Andrae, Tor, *Die person Muhammeds in lehre und glauben seiner gemeinde*, Uppsala 1917.

al-Ash'arī, *Maqālāt al-islāmiyyīn*, ed. H. Ritter, two vols., Istanbul 1929, 1930.

al-Baghdādī, *Al-Farq bayn al-firaq*, ed. M. Badr, Istanbul 1328/1910.

—, *Uṣūl al-dīn*, Istanbul 1928.

al-Bayḍāwī, *Anwār al-tanzīl* (commentary on the Qur'ān), two vols., Leipzig 1846, 1848; many other editions (reference is by sura and verse).

Becker, Carl Heinrich, *Islamstudien*, two vols., Leipzig 1924, 1932.

Bell, Richard, *Introduction to the Qur'ān*, Edinburgh University Press, 1953.

—, *The Origin of Islam in its Christian Environment*, London, Macmillan 1926.

—, *The Qur'ān*, translated with a critical rearrangement of the Surahs, two vols., Edinburgh, Clark, 1937, 1939.

al-Bukhārī, *Ṣaḥīḥ* (collection of Ḥadīth); various editions (reference is by 'book' and number within 'book').

EI²: *Encyclopaedia of Islam*, new edition, Leiden and London, 1954 continuing.

EI(S): *Shorter Encyclopaedia of Islam*, Leiden and London, 1953 (articles from the first edition).

Flügel, G.: *Qur'ān*, various editions, Leipzig (standard European edition).

Gairdner: see al-Ghazālī.

GAL: C. Brockelmann, *Geschichte der arabischen Literatur*, second edition, two vols., Leiden 1943, 1949.

—, *Suppl.*: *Supplementbände* to first edition, three vols., Leiden 1937-42.

al-Ghazālī, *Iḥyā' 'ulūm al-dīn*, four vols., Cairo 1316/1898; and other editions.

—, *Imlā': Al-Imlā' 'alā kashf al-Iḥyā'* (defence of *Iḥyā'*), see note 143.

—, *Mishkāt al-anwār*, Cairo n.d.; tr. by W. H. T. Gairdner as *The Niche for Lights*, London, Royal Asiatic Society, 1924.

Goldziher, Ignaz, *Koranauslegung: Die Richtungen der islamischen Koranauslegung*, Leiden 1920, 1952.

—, *Muhammedanische Studien*, two vols, Halle 1889, 1890; tr. S. M. Stern and C. R. Barber as *Muslim Studies*, two vols, London 1967, 1971.

Graf, Georg, *Geschichte der christlichen arabischen Literatur*, five vols., Vatican City, 1944-53.

Ḥassān ibn Thābit, *Dīwān*, ed. H. Hirschfeld, Leiden/London 1910; also ed. W. Arafat, London 1975.
Ibn ʿAbd al-Barr, *Jāmiʿ bayān al-ʿilm*, Cairo n.d.
Ibn al-Athīr, *Al-Kāmil fī'l-ta'rīkh*, nine vols., Cairo 1348/1929; and other editions.
—, *Usd al-ghāba*, five vols., Cairo 1286/1859.
Ibn Ḥajar, *Tahdhīb al-tahdhīb*, twelve vols., Hyderabad 1325-8/1907-10.
Ibn Ḥanbal: see Aḥmad ibn Ḥanbal.
Ibn Hishām, *Sīra*, ed. F. Wüstenfeld, two vols., Göttingen 1858, 1860 (a recension of the *Sīra* or biography of Muḥammad by Ibn Isḥāq); Eng. tr. by A. Guillaume, *The Life of Muhammad* . . . , London 1955 (with Wüstenfeld's paging in the margin).
Ibn Khaldūn, *The Muqaddimah, an Introduction to History*, tr. Franz Rosenthal, three vols., London, Routledge 1958.
Ibn Saʿd, *Ṭabaqāt*, ed. E. Sachau et al., nine vols., Leiden 1904-40.
Iḥyā': see al-Ghazālī.
ʿIqd: Ibn ʿAbd Rabbi-hi, *Al-ʿIqd al-farīd*, three vols., Bulac 1293/1876.
Jabre, Farid, *La Notion de la Maʿrifa chez Ghazali*, Beirut 1958.
James Presentation Volume: The Saviour God, ed. S. G. F. Brandon, Manchester 1963.
al-Juwaynī, *Al-Irshād (El-Irchad)*, ed. and tr. J. D. Luciani, Paris 1938.
al-Khayyāṭ, *Kitāb al-Intiṣār*, ed. H. S. Nyberg, Cairo 1925.
Lane, E. W., *An Arabic-English Lexicon*, London 1863-93.
Lisān al-ʿArab: by Ibn Mukarram, twenty vols., Cairo 1308/1890.
Massignon, Louis, *La Passion d'al-Hosayn-ibn-Mansour al-Hallāj*, two vols., Paris 1922; second edition, four vols., Paris 1975; Eng. tr. by Herbert Mason, four vols., Princeton, N. J., 1982.
al-Masʿūdī, *Murūj al-dhahab (Les Prairies d'or)*, ed. and tr. by Barbier de Meynard and Pavet de Courteille, nine vols., Paris 1861-77.
al-Māwardī, *Les Statuts gouvernementaux*, tr. E. Fagnan, Algiers 1915.
Mingana, A., *Woodbrooke Studies*, vol. ii, Cambridge 1928.
Muslim, *Ṣaḥīḥ* (collection of Ḥadīth), various editions (reference is by 'book' and by number within 'book').
al-Nawawī, *Minhāj al-muḥaddithīn* (commentary on Muslim), various editions.
al-Nawbakhtī, *Kitāb Firaq al-shīʿa,* ed. H. Ritter, Leipzig 1931.
Nöldeke, Theodor, *Geschichte des Qorāns*, second edition (with F. Schwally, G. Bergsträsser, O. Pretzl), three parts in one, reprinted Hildesheim 1961.
Parrinder, Geoffrey, *Jesus in the Qur*'ān, London, Faber, 1965.
al-Qasṭallānī, *Al-Mawāhib al-laduniyya*, Cairo 1281/1864; etc.
Redhouse, J. W., *A Turkish and English Lexicon*, reprinted, Constantinople 1921.
RSO: Rivista degli studi orientali (Rome).
Schacht, J., *The Origins of Muhammadan Jurisprudence*, Oxford 1950.
Sezgin, Fuat, *GAS: Geschichte des arabischen Schrifttums*, vol. 1, Leiden 1967.
al-Shahrastānī, *Kitāb al-Milal wa-l-niḥal*, ed. W. Cureton, London 1846; also three vols., Cairo 1368/1948.
al-Ṭabarī, *Ta'rīkh* (history), ed. M. J. de Goeje et al., Leiden 1879-1901.
—, *Tafsīr: Jāmiʿ al-bayān*, thirty vols in ten, Cairo, 1321/1903.
al-Taftazānī, *A Commentary on the Creed of Islam*, tr. E. E. Elder, New York 1950 (the creed is that of al-Nasafī).

Watt, W. M., 'Materials': 'The Materials used by Ibn Isḥāq' in *Historians of the Middle East*, ed. B. Lewis and P. M. Holt, London 1962, 23-34.
Wellhausen, Julius, *The Arab Kingdom and its Fall*, tr. Margaret G. Weir, Calcutta 1927.
Woodbrooke Studies, ii: see Mingana.
al-Ya'qūbī, *Ta'rīkh*, two vols., Beirut 1960.
Yāqūt, *Irshād al-arīb*, ed. D. S. Margoliouth, seven vols., London 1908-27.
al-Zabīdī, *Itḥāf al-sāda*, ten vols., Cairo 1311/1893.
ZATW: Zeitschrift für alttestamentliche Wissenschaft.
ZDMG: Zeitschrift der deutschen morgenländischen Gesellschaft.

Index

(In the alphabetical ordering the Arabic article al- is disregarded. Only the more significant names are included.)